THE
P·O·R·T
COMPANION
A Connoisseur's Guide

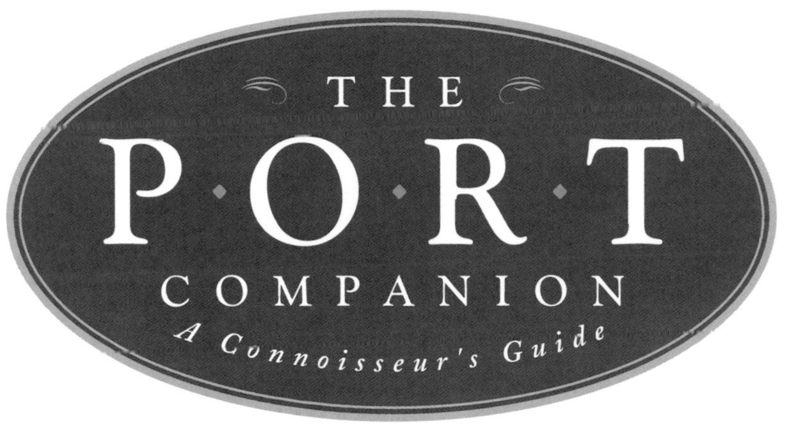

GODFREY SPENCE

APPLE

Dedication
To Catherine and Rosalind

A QUINTET BOOK

Published by the Apple Press
Sheridan House
112-116A Western Road
Hove
East Sussex BN3 1DD

ISBN 1-84092-374-1

Reprinted in 2002

Creative Director: Richard Dewing
Art Director: Clare Reynolds
Designer: Ian Hunt
Project Editor: Clare Hubbard
Editor: Janet Charatan
Photographer: Paul Forrester
Illustrators: Richard Chasemore and Fred Van Deelan.

Typeset in Great Britain by
Central Southern Typesetters, Eastbourne
Manufactured in Singapore by
Bright Arts Pte Ltd.
Printed in China by
Midas Printing Limited

Acknowledgments

Particular thanks are due to an enormous number of people who have helped with the research for this book. Many in the marketing and public relations departments will, unfortunately, have to remain anonymous. It would, however, be wrong not to mention some people by name. The following have all helped with my general research into port, or specifically with the research for this book: Dr Bianchi de Agiuar of the IVP, Carlos de Almeida and George Sandeman of Sandeman, Fernando Alves of ADVID, Adrian Bridge of Taylor, Fladgate and Yeatman, Jeremy Bull formerly of A.A. Cálem and Filho, Dr John Burnett of Croft, Peter Cobb and Vasco Maghlães of Cockburn Smithes, Bruce Guimaraens of Fonseca Guimaraens Limited, Dirk Niepoort of Niepoort Ports, João Nicolau de Almeida and Jorge Rosas of Ramos Pinto, and Christian Seely of Quinta do Noval.

My thanks are also due to an understanding family, who had to put up with an invasion of bottles and a disturbed domestic routine; to Clare Hubbard, for all her efforts as an efficient go-between and whose chivvying kept the project moving; and to Gareth, John, and the others who selflessly helped with the tastings.

Contents

PART ONE

The Story of Port

PART TWO

The Port Directory

FOREWORD

I feel very privileged to have been asked to write the foreword to Godfrey Spence's *The Port Companion*. The timing for such a book is right. It is a book that is written as much for the interested consumer as for the professional, and it comes on the market at a time when there is a tremendous interest in all aspects of port, particularly in the United States.

On a recent visit to the United States I was asked by a wine retailer to name the definitive book on port. Over the last 20 to 30 years there have been a number of excellent books published on port, although the majority of these books were written with an emphasis on one particular facet of the trade. For example, James Suckling's expert treatise, entitled *Vintage Port*, is the definitive work on that subject. The classic book on port published by the Port Wine Institute is exceptionally good on the technical side of the business, while Sarah Bradford's book *The Story of Port* is not only beautifully written, but also has the most comprehensive section on the history of the port trade than any other book I have on the subject.

I have read Godfrey Spence's book with a lot of care and I do not hesitate in calling this the definitive book on port, as it is such a mine of information. It is interesting to note that a lot of care has been taken on the order in which the chapters occur. Whereas most books start with the historical section, Godfrey's first chapter immerses one immediately into the atmosphere of the Douro district in Northern Portugal, with its rugged beauty and hostile climate. The first chapter sets the tone for the rest of the book, which is written with imagination and in a style that keeps the reader, whether layman or professional, completely absorbed. By far the largest part of the book is dedicated to the history and current activities of the various shipping firms and the larger farmers involved in the commercialization of their ports. This is followed by tasting notes which are very professional and accurate, if the notes on the Fonseca Guimaraens ports are anything to go by! In addition, I was very pleased to see single quinta ports mentioned in such detail.

There is an ever-increasing interest today in the viticultural side of the business, which Godfrey fully delves into. The viticulturalist is as much in demand for giving presentations, tastings, and lectures as is the winemaker. Forty years ago, the composition of grape varieties in a vineyard did not have the importance that it does

VIEW OF THE DOURO RIVER FROM QUINTA DO SEIXO.

today. When evaluating a farmer's vineyard for grape purchasing, the shipper would always make sure that the top five varieties were prevalent in his tour of the vineyard, but there was never any separation of varieties during the fermentation as there is today. This separation now gives the shipper and winemaker much greater scope in deciding when to pick and ferment, as well as when blending. Does this mean that we will be able to make even better ports in the future than we have in the past?

We must always strive to improve quality, and while I have no doubt that we shall, it will never be easy to attain the exquisite perfection of a 1927, a 1948, a 1963, or, hopefully, a 1985! Having said that, much more research needs to be done on grape varieties in the Douro district. It is indeed an exciting time for viticulture!

In closing, I should like to felicitate Godfrey Spence for his excellent work. I firmly believe that quality port has a bright future and it is with the help of a book such as this that sparks interest in what is, undoubtedly, one of the world's greatest wines.

BRUCE GUIMARAENS
Oporto
April 19, 1997.

PART ONE

THE STORY OF PORT

WHAT MAKES PORT UNIQUE?

Port is a fortified wine made from select grapes in northeast Portugal's Douro Valley. Its uniqueness comes as much from natural factors – soil, climate, and aspect (position of growing surfaces) – as it does from the way the wine is made. The key to port's production is fortification: adding a high-strength grape spirit, or brandy, to the fermented grape must (grape juice) to arrest fermentation, increase the alcohol content, and preserve some sweetness.

There is a saying in the port trade that goes: "All wine would be port ... if it could." Like so many prestige products, port has its imitators. Winemakers in locations as diverse as California and Australia use the same fortification process to produce a sweet after-dinner wine. Few of these, however, reach the quality of even middle-ranking port, much less the fine old vintage and tawny ports highlighted in this book.

Port takes its name from the city of Porto, "Oporto" in English, located where the Rio Douro, which means the river of gold, flows into the Atlantic. The river's name stems from the color of the fast-flowing water before it was tamed by dams; it is hardly an appropriate metaphor for the port region, which has been for centuries one of the poorest and most isolated in western Europe. Port wine was, and mostly still is, shipped from Oporto, but the vineyards surrounding the city do not, in fact cannot, supply grapes for port. The local wine is the fresh, young *vinho verde*; it is crisp, dry, and light in alcohol, the very antithesis of the heavy sweet wines meant for long aging that carry the city's name. The difference between the two wines is a combination of both human and natural factors.

THE RUGGED DOURO

The Douro region encompasses the upper reaches of the Douro River, where it forms the frontier with Spain, to Barqueiros, some 44 miles upstream from Oporto and the coast. Although the river flows past other vines after leaving the port region (and indeed flows through the city of Oporto itself), to port shippers and wine lovers alike "the Douro" is synonymous with port wine vineyards.

CITY OF OPORTO.

This is rugged country, a land of hills so steep that it is impossible for mules, let alone normal tractors, to work the vineyards. The soil is only a thin covering for a bedrock of hard slate over even harder granite. The soil is so low in organic matter that only rough scrubby weeds, the olive, and, of course, the vine can survive. Add to this a mountain range that separates the region from the rest of the world and a climate of extremes, both hot and cold, and it becomes a mystery why growers have persevered in planting vines here. The answer lies in every bottle of port.

RUGGED, SUN-BAKED VINEYARDS.

PATAMAR TERRACES, QUINTA DE VARGELLAS.

Portugal's climate, particularly in the north, is dominated by the Atlantic, making it humid with fairly moderate temperatures. But the Douro is protected by the Serra Marão, a range of hills to the northwest of the region that puts the Douro in a rain shadow, much as Alsace in France and the Pfalz in southern Germany are kept dry by the influences of the Vosges and the Haart. As a result the climate is one of extremes. Snow is not unknown in the winter; historical pictures depict pruners wearing coats of straw and thatch to protect them from icy winds. Yet in the summer the vineyards are baked by almost constant sun, with temperatures reaching 110°F.

The landscape in the Douro is one of the most dramatic of any vineyard region. The Douro River and its tributaries have, over the millennia, cut deep, steep-sided valleys so that flat land is rare. Nine-tenths of the region is on a gradient steeper than one in three. To make the vineyards workable at all, the growers had to cut terraces like giant staircases out of the rock. Each terrace was originally supported by a wall to retain the "soil" created by the excavations. Vines grown on these terraces, many of which still exist, must be tended entirely by hand.

The very narrow terraces gradually developed into wider ones with more rows and fewer walls, but it was not until the early 1970s that serious consideration was given to rebuilding them to allow for the use of machinery. Since then new terraces, called *patamares*, which omit the supporting walls in favor of earth banks, have gained widespread acceptance. Without the walls, small tractors can get into the vineyards in an unprecedented way, dramatically improving efficiency. Patamares were originally introduced at Taylor's Quinta da Vargellas in 1973, and rapidly became the standard way of replanting. The fortress-like dry-stone walls of the old terraces have been systematically – and largely – replaced by rocky slopes of earth, changing the shape of the viticultural Douro forever.

However, some growers prefer the German pattern of planting, following the slope of the land. If the slope is not too steep (and opinions differ as to the maximum gradient) this system, called *vinha ao alto*, has many advantages, particularly for mechanization. Pioneered by the port firm Ramos Pinto shortly after the introduction of patamares, vinha ao alto plots can be seen in many places, but none is as impressive as Ramos Pinto's Quinta da Ervamoira in the Douro Superior.

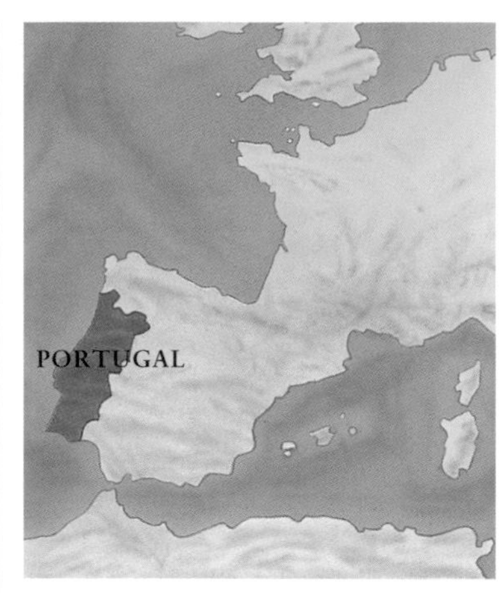

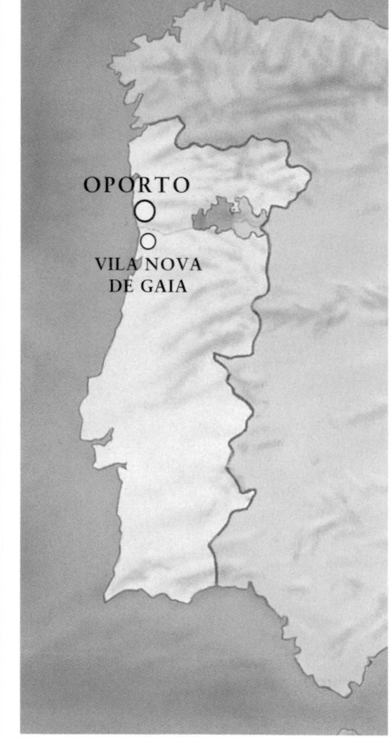

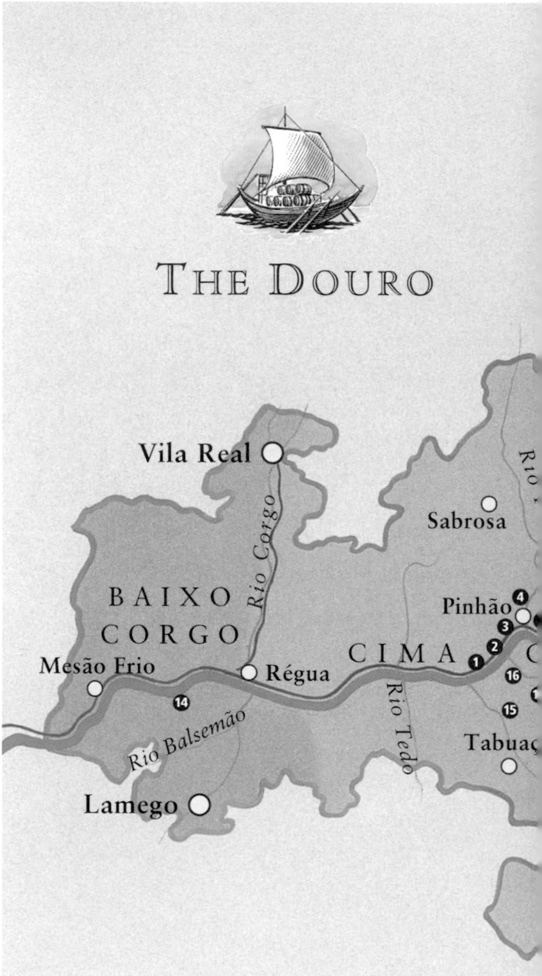

THE DOURO

Vila Real
Rio Corgo
Sabrosa
BAIXO
CORGO
Pinhão
Mesão Frio
Régua
CIMA
Rio Tedo
Rio Balsemão
Tabuaç
Lamego

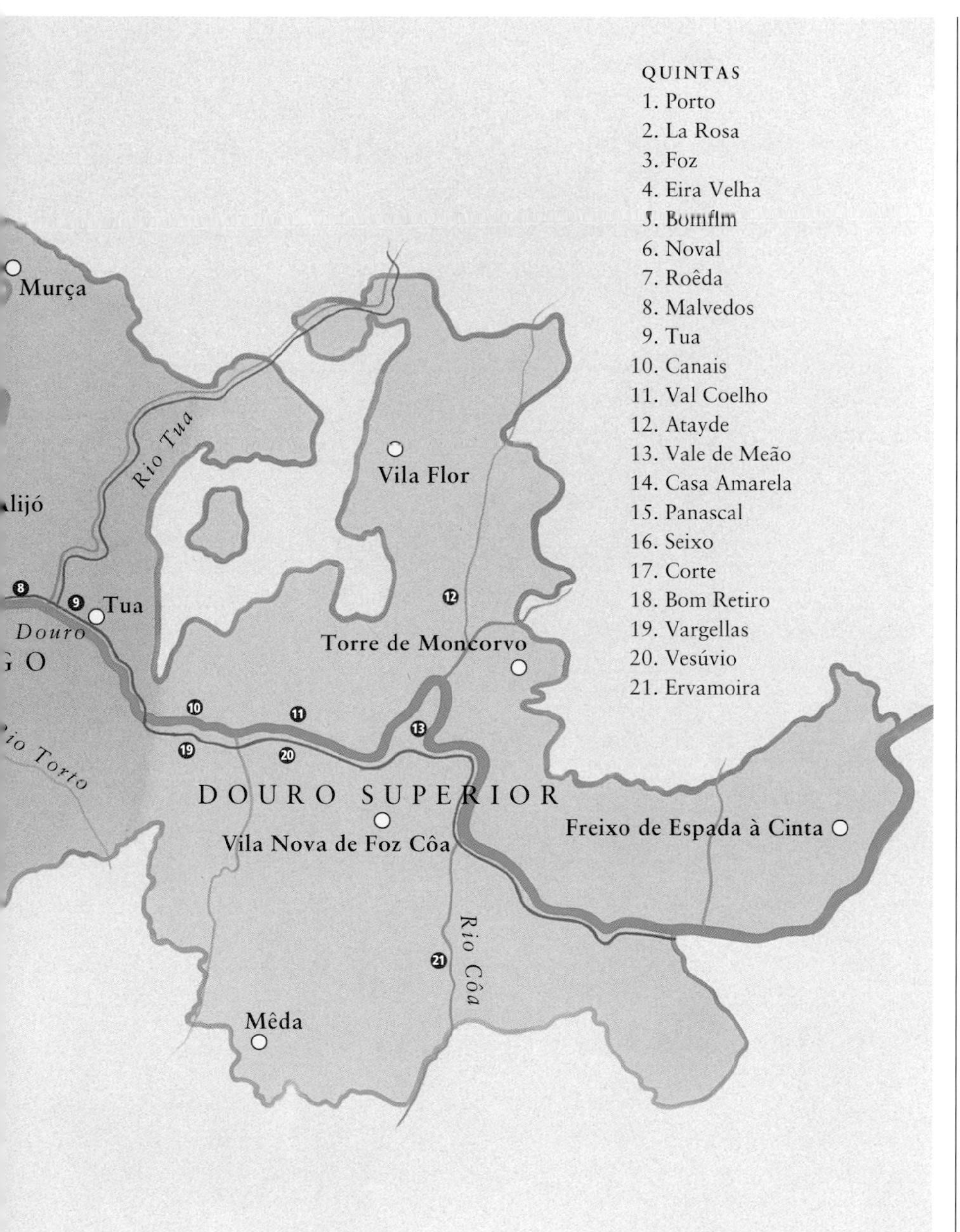
QUINTAS
1. Porto
2. La Rosa
3. Foz
4. Eira Velha
5. Bomflm
6. Noval
7. Roêda
8. Malvedos
9. Tua
10. Canais
11. Val Coelho
12. Atayde
13. Vale de Meão
14. Casa Amarela
15. Panascal
16. Seixo
17. Corte
18. Bom Retiro
19. Vargellas
20. Vesúvio
21. Ervamoira
Murça
Rio Tua
Vila Flor
Tua
Douro
Torre de Moncorvo
DOURO SUPERIOR
Vila Nova de Foz Côa
Freixo de Espada à Cinta
Rio Côa
Mêda

PLANTING IN THIS ROCKY LANDSCAPE IS HARD WORK.

Because of the terrain, the topsoil is rarely more than four inches thick. Beneath the bedrock is a slate-like sedimentary rock called schist. This must be broken up with hand tools or dynamite to enable vines to be planted. Schist allows the vine roots to penetrate a great distance, important when the growing season is so dry.

Officially the Douro region is divided into three districts: the Baixo Corgo, Cima Corgo, and Douro Superior. The three sub-regions are really only of academic interest to the consumer; they rarely appear on labels, certainly not in the way the districts of, for example, the Médoc (red wine-producing area in Bordeaux) do. However, each has its own basic character, although other factors such as the annual weather conditions and vineyard management, have their role to play. The Baixo Corgo tends to be the wettest region; here the grapes are less ripe, so the wines are less concentrated than those produced in the Cima Corgo. The Cima Corgo offers the best balance of heat and rainfall, producing fully ripe grapes with a concentrated flavor. The Douro Superior produces equally high-quality grapes, but there are relatively fewer vineyards here due to its isolated location.

AROUND THE PORT DISTRICTS

The Baixo, or Lower, Corgo extends from the region's western boundary to the confluence of the River Corgo near Régua, the region's capital. The Baixo Corgo accounts for only 28 percent of the area, yet encompasses more than half of the total vineyard territory, so densely is it cultivated. This district has the least extreme climate, with higher rainfall than further inland and lower maximum temperatures. With less stress, the vines can produce more fruit so despite its size, the Baixo Corgo turns out the majority of the region's wine.

STA. MARTA IN THE BAIXO CORGO.

Large estates are rare in the Baixo Corgo; most of the vineyards are small and run on a part-time basis. There are a few outstanding quintas that make excellent premium wines, but this is predominantly an area for the young wines – ruby, tawny, and white – that make up 85 percent of the port market.

Beyond the River Corgo is the Cima Corgo, the heartland of quality port production and home to most of the top quintas. Surrounding the little town of Pinhão, this area has the greatest concentration of the finest and most famous estates. Pinhão itself sits on the confluence of the Douro and Pinhão Rivers, overlooked by Quinta do Noval and Quinta da Eira Velha, while quintas Bomfim, Foz, and Roêda look onto the Douro from the outskirts of town. Other tributaries in the area are home to yet more famous names, including Bom Retiro and Côrte in the Torto valley, and Fonseca's Panascal in the Távora. Wherever one looks, the names of top quintas can be seen in bold letters on the white walls of the wineries or painted onto their red-tiled roofs – easily visible because of the steep terrain.

STEEP VINEYARDS IN THE CIMA CORGO.

Just a few miles from Régua, the Cima Corgo has a much drier climate than that of the Baixo Corgo, which claims, on average, 50 percent higher rainfall. Due to the very hot, dry weather, the vines have to work harder to increase the flavor concentration in the grapes, and therefore the final quality of the wine.

Further up the river, the valley narrows to a gorge at Valeira. Now dammed, the river here was once unnavigable because of rocks. Without the use of the Douro River, the lifeline of the port industry, and with access to the land beyond the gorge cut off, planters avoided growing port vines there. The river was finally opened up in 1793, and for the first time the Douro Superior became viable for port production. The historical isolation means that even today, less than 5 percent of the area is planted with vines, but the few quintas that do exist here are generally large. Many are at the forefront of viticultural innovation; the larger areas and wider valleys permit increased mechanization with hardly a terrace to be found. Successful experiments have already influenced quintas further down river. Some Douro Superior estates date back as far as the sixteenth century, with viticulture becoming important in the early nineteenth. Others, like the Ervamoira and Atayde estates, were established as recently as the 1970s.

QUINTA DE ERVAMOIRA IN THE DOURO SUPERIOR.

THE ROLE OF THE QUINTA

The quinta, Portuguese for "farm" or "estate," is the heart of the Douro wine country. It is, however, a rather nebulous term and definitions vary widely. To the rich in Lisbon, a quinta is a country mansion, usually in Sintra or Estoril, a far cry from a Douro vineyard. Certainly not all quintas have grand houses akin to the châteaux of Bordeaux; many offer little more than the most basic accommodation. By the same token not all vineyards in the Douro are quintas. Most are small plots of land, often less than an acre in size, worked on little more than a subsistence basis.

Since there is no formal definition of the word, it is impossible to state how many quintas are in the Douro region, but estimates range from 1,500 to 2,000 out of a total of 80,000 registered vineyards.

In the past, almost all port was blended from a number of vineyards to increase complexity and ensure a continuity of style. Thus the individual quinta was rarely mentioned. In recent years, however, numerous ports have come on the market from a single quinta. As a result, the concept of a quinta has become more widely understood in the trade and by port connoisseurs.

MALVEDOS, A TYPICAL LARGE QUINTA.

VINEYARD CLASSIFICATION

There is no Grand Cru system in the Douro as there is in France, but every vineyard in the area is classified on a system called the Cadastro Grading. The grading runs from A to F, with A being the best, and is based on a points system. Up to 70 percent of the points are awarded for the following four variables:

Altitude (the lower the better)	21%
Yield (the lower the better)	21%
Soil	14%
Locality	13%

The remaining points are given for factors such as aspect, vine variety, vine age (the older the better), vineyard upkeep, and slope of the land. Positive and negative points are awarded; for example, a low altitude vineyard will gain points, but if it is planted on granite, points will be subtracted.

Approximately 20 percent of vineyards are classified as A or B, 75 percent of vineyards are classified as C or D, and 5 percent of vineyards are classified as E or F. A and B vineyards are mainly found in the Cima Corgo and Douro Superior, while most of the lower-graded vineyards are found in the Baixo Corgo and in the higher parts of the other sub-regions.

Class A quintas around Pinhão.

Port's Rich History

Port is a wine that was developed through adversity; had England and France not been at odds throughout the last 500 years, port might never have been invented. For 300 years, since the French Eleanor of Aquitaine married Henri d'Anjou (Henry II of England) in 1152, the English taste had been for claret imported from France. When supplies dried up in 1667 as a result of England's continuing conflict with France, the wine merchants of London and Bristol had to look elsewhere for their stock, eventually finding an alternative in Portugal in the mid-1600s.

Long before the early wine trade settlers arrived in the seventeenth century, there is evidence that the Romans cultivated the vine in the region during their occupation 200 years before Christ. Later, the Visigoths (the tribe that ruled the area until early in the eighth century), encouraged viticulture, but when the Moorish armies advanced north, local vine-growing came to a standstill. Vine cultivation resumed in the Douro Valley in the eleventh century just before Portugal became a nation state.

At that time wine consumption must have been strictly local. Communication and transport within the valley and to the outside world are difficult enough today, even with reasonable roads, and were surely almost impossible then. Only with the arrival of English and Scottish traders in the seventeenth century did the region open up and become as famous as it is today.

Marquis of Pombal.

Initially, the merchants bought "red Portugal" from the vineyards around Viana do Castelo, a verdant and populous region north of Oporto. At the time, the vines were trained up trees, thus limiting the ripening of the grapes and producing wines that resembled the red vinho verde made here today – tannic, acidic, and often slightly effervescent. Since the British preferred a heavier, sweeter wine, the more adventurous traders started looking further inland.

Port as we now know it can trace its history to 1678, when two events fortuitously coincided. The British government placed an embargo on trade with France, creating a demand for a substitute to French wine. Then two Englishmen, visiting a monastery at Lamego, were introduced by the abbot to a wine from Pinhão that was richer and smoother than most red Portugal. The abbot eventually admitted that local brandy had been added during fermentation, a practice used today in all port production. It was to be another 50 years before all port was fortified, but the scene had been set.

The continued embargo on French wines encouraged port wine trade throughout the latter part of the seventeenth century, but the real resurgence in trade occurred at the beginning of the eighteenth century. The signing in 1703 of the Methuen trade treaty promised favorable duty rates for Portuguese wines in exchange for a similar treatment of English textiles imported into Portugal. This gave the industry an enormous lift and resulted in very rapid development of the Douro. With this growth came the establishment of many of today's wine firms. Moreover, existing companies whose trade previously involved textiles or fish began concentrating on wine. But growth also brought about fraud and wine adulteration to the detriment of the peasant farmers on whom the trade relied. The poor wines were not selling but supplies were increasing. By 1754 trade was so bad that the shippers bought no wine from the growers.

The solution came in the form of Sebastião José de Carvalho e Melo, later to become famous as the Marquis of Pombal. Given almost dictatorial powers by King José I following his handling of the aftermath of a major earthquake in Lisbon, Pombal took firm control of the port trade. He established the Companhia Geral da Agricultura das Vinhas do Alto Douro as a monopoly on setting port prices; it was also empowered to rewrite the rules governing port production. In 1756 company officials began mapping the Douro Valley and rating the wines, a task completed in 1761. The best wines went for international export, the middle-ranking wines were destined for Brazil, and the lesser wines were reserved for local consumption. Although Tuscans and Hungarians disagree, this is often cited as the earliest demarcation in the wine world, predating the French Appellation Contrôlée by 180 years.

GOOD TIMES, BAD TIMES

With Pombal behind it, the company was all-powerful. Prices for wine in Oporto taverns increased, resulting in civic unrest – which was rapidly quelled by hanging the agitators. Adulteration with elderberry juice was rife. To end this, the company had all the elderberry trees within the region uprooted; when that tactic failed, all elderberry trees in northern Portugal were destroyed.

NINETEENTH CENTURY OPORTO.

The value of the company to the port trade is clear. The quality and origins of the wine were assured, and during its reign the Valeira Gorge was made navigable, opening the Douro Superior for the first time. Also, at the turn of the nineteenth century, many of today's shippers established themselves in Oporto. However, the company gradually lost much of its power. The combination of a new monarch and wars with both France and Spain left Portugal in dire straits and mortally wounded the company. It was abolished in 1834, only to be resurrected temporarily four years later.

By this time port was very much the fortified wine we know today. The practice of adding brandy to the fermenting must was well established, and the long bottle had been introduced in the late eighteenth century, enabling wines to be laid down in cellars for the first time. Not surprisingly, many shippers disagreed on the definition of port. Joseph James Forrester, later Baron Forrester, otherwise a far-sighted man, published a pamphlet severely criticizing his colleagues for producing fortified wines. Had the trade taken any notice, port would have been relegated to the relative obscurity of so many light wines.

Less than ten years after Forrester's criticism, the Douro was to suffer two invasions far worse than any human attack. Oidium and phylloxera were the twin scourges of all

THE STRAIGHT BOTTLE MADE VINTAGE PORT POSSIBLE.

Baron Forrester.

European vineyards in the middle to latter part of the nineteenth century. Oidium, a fungus from America, arrived in 1852 and spread rapidly, devastating vineyards. The cure, dusting the vines with sulfur, was an expense many growers could not afford, and many became bankrupt. No sooner had production returned to normal when phylloxera, a vine louse also from America, arrived to cause further damage and loss of production. The effects of phylloxera are visible even today in abandoned vineyards. These *mortórios* were never replanted with vines; olives or scrub grow on terraces still supported by stone walls built more than 100 years ago.

These were bleak times for farmers, with costs rising and production plummeting. Paradoxically, what was bad for the growers proved to be good for the shippers and the general future of the trade. Since phylloxera had devastated French vineyards earlier in the nineteenth century, there was a ready market for port in the thirsty countries to the north. A whole new class of port firms opened for business; names like Wiese and Krohn, Cálem, and Ramos Pinto all date from this period. At the same time, established shippers began to

The Ramos Pinto lodge on the waterfront at Vila Nova de Gaia.

Quality guarantee from the Instituto do Vinho do Porto.

invest in vineyards. For the first time the line between grower and shipper, long seen as a source of conflict, was crossed.

Looking back on the last few decades, it might appear that the twentieth century has been good for port. However, many crises in the first 50 years made the future seem uncertain. Trade before World War I was very depressed. Wines selling at less than cost went unsold as world demand fell, and imitations from other countries undercut sales of real port. The only positive event at this time for the port industry was the protection of the name "Port" as a result of trade treaties with Great Britain in 1914 and 1916. Henceforth only Portuguese port could be sold as "Port" in the United Kingdom. Subsequent actions have protected the Portuguese term "Porto" in the United States although similar wines – proudly labeled "Port" on their domestic markets –

Porto, Port, and Vinho do Porto are all protected names in different countries.

continue to be made as far apart as California and Australia. Only in Portugal itself is it always referred to as *vinho do porto*, or port wine, emphasizing its true nature.

After 1918 trade improved, but accusations of malpractice throughout the port industry again became widespread, while the Douro farmers continued to live in extreme poverty. Only in 1932, when the government of Antonio de Oliveira Salazar imposed new controlling bodies, were supply and demand brought into balance. When World War II made shipping port almost impossible, economic crisis was averted. Since the 1960s, multinational corporations have moved in. Allied Domecq, IDV, and Seagram all own shippers, and the trend continues. Concurrently, larger groups have developed in Oporto. Barros, Almeida and Royal Oporto incorporate smaller firms, and the Symington family, who first arrived in 1882, has built an empire of port firms.

PORT TODAY

Tradition and history are synonymous with the port industry; the wine, the region, and its people are all steeped in a long common past. Names of port firms like Sandeman, Delaforce, and Graham still appear on labels as they have for generations. Grapes are still trodden by foot and British shippers still meet for lunch at the Factory House each Wednesday (see page 25); they still pass the decanter to the left as they always have. But even with this rich tradition, port has a contemporary image.

In a world where the trend is toward more bland flavors, vodka sales are increasing at the expense of whiskey and brandy, and where health concerns are limiting the consumption of high-strength drinks, port has continued to be a favorite. Among the other fortified wines, sherry sales are depressed and Marsala is used more for cooking than as part of a barman's repertoire. Port alone has thrived. Sales internationally have increased, with a healthy trend toward the premium types.

France is the biggest export market and has been for more than 30 years. Here, port is a preprandial drink, so sales reflect the lighter, younger types – ruby, young tawny, and white. Yet France is also the largest export customer for aged tawnies. The best premium markets are the United Kingdom and the United States, where sales of late bottled vintage

SALES OF 1991 VINTAGE PORTS FLOURISHED.

(LBV) and vintage ports increase each year. Britain has long been the main vintage port market, but the United States has recently developed a taste for this excellent wine. The 1991 vintage will be remembered as the one where for the first time sales to America were greater than those to Britain.

The United States has not only taken to vintage port in a big way, but sales of premium tawny wines are also rising faster than even the most optimistic marketing manager in Oporto might have hoped. Sales of colheitas to the United States (see Port Styles page 38), have shown a tenfold increase in the last three years alone, and the United States is now second only to France in consumption of the indicated age tawnies

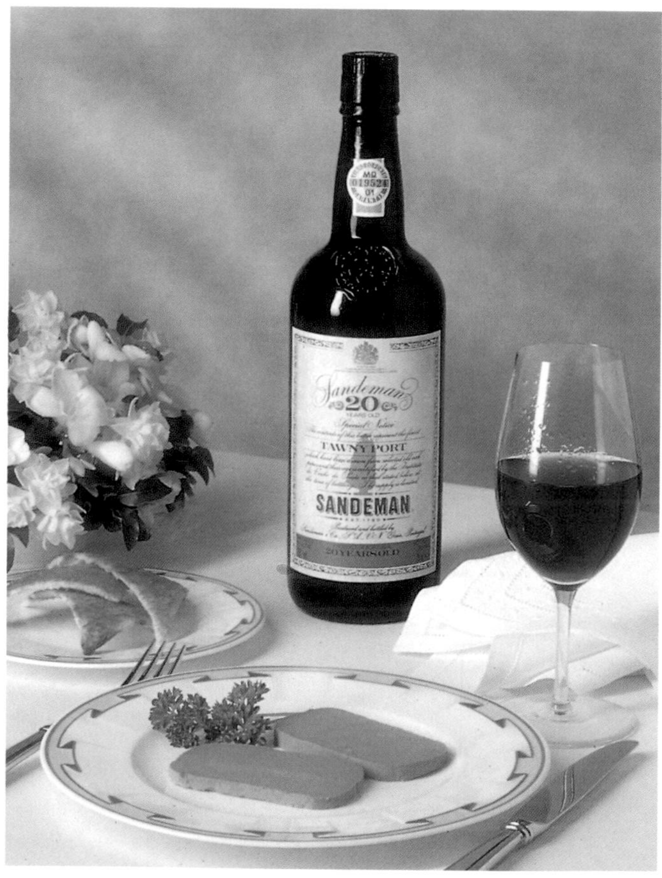

PORT IS A PERFECT DINNER PARTY BEVERAGE.

(10-, 20-, 30-, and over 40-year-old wines). Sales to France have dropped slightly, but with sales to other countries either stable or rising, it cannot be long before the prices of these exceptional wines increase as producers begin to run short of stock.

SOMETHING FOR EVERYONE

Port is a "hierarchical" drink, with clear rankings from ruby to vintage character, then to LBV, and finally to fine vintage and aged tawnies. Choosing the right wine for the occasion is made easy by the hierarchy. The wine is increasingly enjoyed by all age groups, but the 30- to 40-something group is the biggest consumer. It is purchased by the dinner party generation for entertaining friends at home; it has become one of the trappings of success. And of course, port is no longer a male preserve – it is far removed from the days when women retired while the men drank port and smoked cigars.

Trends in wine drinking are constantly changing, and today few people are prepared to wait for their wines to mature. The success of wines from Australia and California is partly due to their accessibility when young, and many new converts to vintage port also enjoy drinking them young. Sweetness and fruitiness come through in young vintage port; indeed the fashion in the United States is for very young port. To enjoy the energy of port's youth, however, is to forego the complexities and subtleties that these wines take on with age. Very young vintage port is deep, dark, and powerfully fruity. After a few years the wine closes up: the nose becomes dumb showing very little fruit and the tannins become harsh and astringent. Only after very long cellaring – 10, 15, or 20 years – does the wine reopen into one of the greatest drinks made. Aficionados will continue to enjoy their young port, while keeping some bottles aside for the future.

THE FACTORY HOUSE

The Factory House stands in the Rua do Infante Henrique in Oporto, a granite monument to the permanence of the British influence on the port industry. Completed in 1790, the Factory House was built by the British Association, a group of English and Scottish traders working out of Oporto, selling all manner of goods. It is an elegant mansion in the old part of the city, surrounded by narrow cobbled streets and conveniently close to the bridge across the Douro River to Vila Nova de Gaia.

On one level, the Factory House is little more than a very exclusive club – membership is restricted to the British port firms. On another it is equivalent to a chamber of commerce in that it is a place where the shippers discuss common problems and, without giving away too many trade secrets, decide on ways to address them. The

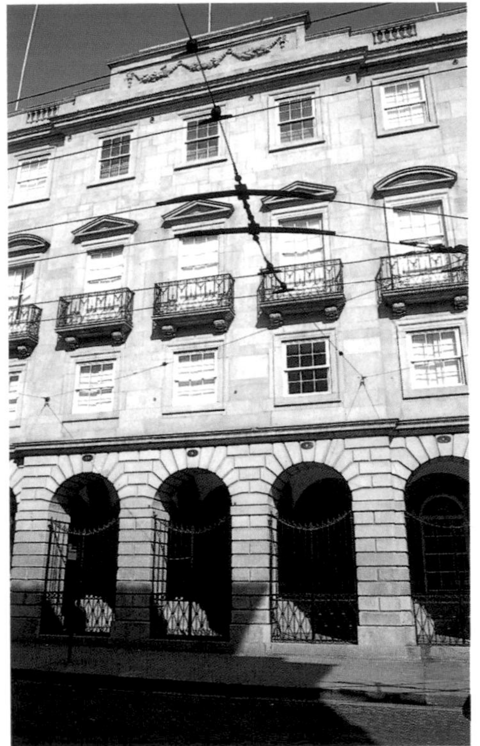

THE FACTORY HOUSE IN OPORTO.

Factory House maintains the rigid etiquette of the British abroad. It is certainly a powerful weapon in the public relations battle and an ideal place to entertain trade guests. In any of its roles, the Factory House has become as much a part of the heritage of the trade as terraces and *barcos rabelos*, the historic wooden boats that once brought every drop of wine down river from the vineyards to the lodges.

The granite from which the Factory House is built ensures constant temperatures so that even in the height of summer, gentlemen are expected to wear jackets at the Wednesday lunch. This is one of the rituals of Oporto life for the British shippers. Each week senior managers from the member companies assemble, along with invited guests, for luncheon. This is a strictly male affair; women, however important in the wine trade, lunch elsewhere. The meal, a fairly informal buffet, is preceded by a glass of sherry or white port, accompanied by the unfortified wine of the Douro, and followed by both tawny and vintage ports. The tawny serves as a palate cleanser so that due attention can be given to the vintage, which is always served blind (masked). Great discussion follows with the weekly game of identifying the wine and its vintage year.

Dinners are served in the same dining room, but are far more formal. Once the food is eaten, one, and only one, glass of venerable tawny is served. Before anyone has a chance to finish it, and certainly before anyone notices the lack of circulating decanters, the doors to an identical adjoining room swing open. To the astonishment of any guest who has not done his homework, everyone rises and, taking their white starched napkins with them, moves through the doors and into the same seat at the table in the second room. Here, by the delicate light of candles, the vintage port is served, away from the distracting smells of food.

The Grapes and the Harvest

In a world where chardonnay and cabernet sauvignon are grown everywhere (and pinot noir and merlot wines all compete for the consumer's hard-earned cash), the lack of grape varietal labeling on port comes as a refreshing change. Port is, by nature, a blended wine, although the attitude of some growers toward the subject might seem cavalier to wine makers in other countries. As one producer was heard to remark, "Who cares what the grape varieties are; they are grapes and they go into port." Often, in the older terraces, each vine in a row will be different. There are, however, some rules. About four dozen grape varieties, black and white, are permitted, and 20 or so are officially approved. Despite these guidelines, research has identified over 10 dozen varieties actually in use.

The old stone-walled vineyards are usually planted in the haphazard manner of the past, but most new vineyards are planted with the top five grape varieties, divided into blocks so that each variety is grown in a different area of the vineyard. Different grape varieties develop at different rates, so with block planting the grower is able to treat each variety at the right time, pick at optimum ripeness, and separate vinification. Originally identified from research carried out by the Ramos Pinto and Ferreira port firms, the following five varieties have been universally adopted as being the best – so much so that when the World Bank started a scheme to invest in the Douro, only these varieties attracted grant money.

Touriga Nacional – the best port grape.

Touriga Nacional is now almost universally viewed as *the* port grape, producing very deeply colored and tannic wines with black currant notes to the nose and an intense fruit character. There is, of course, a down side: it is low-yielding, giving only about 2.6 pounds of grape per vine. The structure of its wines is much sought after by blenders, as it gives grip to the wine.

Tinta Roriz, better known as Rioja's Tempranillo, is grown widely throughout Spain and Portugal. It does not produce deeply colored wines, but has very powerful tannins and an herbaceous, spicy flavor. Roriz does best in richer soils and average temperatures.

Touriga Francesa is often grown on the exposed south-facing slopes since it has good heat resistance and, indeed, flourishes in these conditions. For the same reason, it also does well in dry years. Its wines are lighter in style than the Barroca or Roriz, with floral, rose petal notes.

Tinta Barroca gives highly colored wines with firm structure and body, a very high sugar content, and a cherry or mulberry character. Barroca ripens early and is suited to the less hot, north-facing slopes. As such, it is a prime candidate for block planting.

Tinta Cão, or the "red dog" grape, very nearly became extinct in the Douro. Its yields are tiny (Jancis Robinson quotes less than 10.5 ounces per vine in her book, *Vines, Grapes and Wines*), although better clonal selection is improving the count. It is now extremely popular with quality producers since it is particularly good for wines destined for long aging.

Since the designation of the original five varieties, a few other grapes have gained approval with certain producers. Tinta Amarela has acquired many fans, and Sousão has one or two admirers like Quinta do Noval, although others adamantly avoid it. Other favored grapes include Malvasia Preta, Tinta Francisca (different from the Touriga Francesa), Mourisco Tinto, and Tinta da Barca. White port is made from Malvasia Fina, Malvasia Rei, Rabigato, Codega, and Viosinho, among others.

WORKING THE VINEYARDS

Isolated as it is, the Douro is generally a quiet area. The quintas employ very few full-time staff, so for most of the year there are not many people around. Harvest time, however, animates the region in late September when itinerant workers and villagers from the surrounding area arrive to pick grapes and make the wine. While much routine vineyard work has been eased by the introduction of tractors, one function that still must be done by hand is the harvest. No machine picker has yet been designed to work in territory like this. In the larger quintas the pickers stay in special dormitory blocks; in smaller vineyards the owner's family and friends are called on to do the work. As dawn

HARVESTING ON A VINHA AO ALTO PLOT.

breaks the sound of pickers, the *rogas*, going to work can be heard echoing across the valleys. Facing a day of backbreaking labor in baking heat, they sing to the accompaniment of an accordion and drum as they walk the rocky paths.

Women, children, and older men pick the grapes, collecting their harvest in buckets that are emptied into large baskets called *gigos*, or into the more modern steel grape bins. Gigos, which weigh up to 130 pounds when full, are hoisted shoulder high by the younger men, balanced on a crude headdress of hessian, a coarse cloth, and a bundle of twigs, and carried to the quinta. The grape bins take the less prosaic route to the winery via tractor and trailer.

In more modern quintas with up-to-date winemaking facilities, work stops when evening comes; an efficient winery needs remarkably few operators. In many quintas, however, nightfall brings only a pause in the day's work. After a meal and glass or two of wine, the treading starts. Even today, the majority of top-quality port is made with the aid of the human foot.

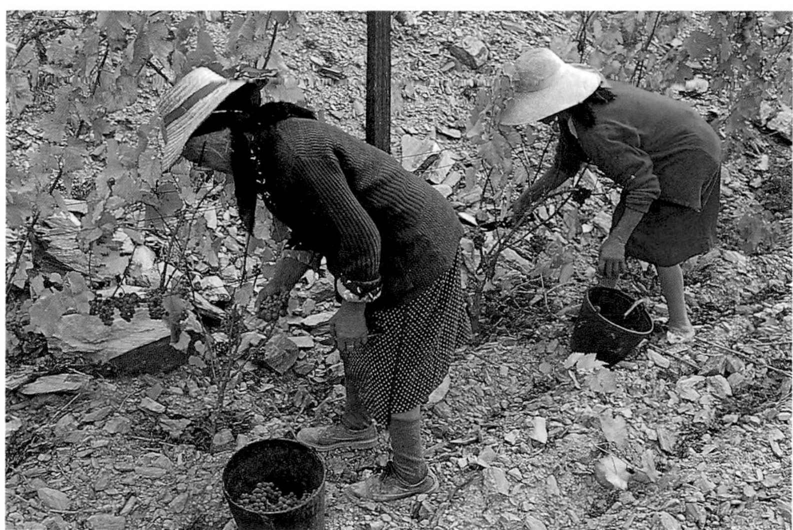
LOW VINES MAKE THE HARVEST BACK-BREAKING WORK.

On arrival at the quinta, the freshly picked grapes will have been roughly crushed and loaded into large granite troughs, called *lagares*. After their respite the pickers will change into shorts and climb into the thigh-deep mass of grapes and tread for four hours. The first two hours is the *corte* or "cut," treading being regimented and thorough to ensure the grapes are broken. Like a drill sergeant the foreman will call out *um-dois* (one-two) or *esquerda-direita* (left-right) and shout at any treader who seems to be slacking. Along with the shouts, a drum sounds a monotonous beat. After two hours, *liberdade*, or "freedom," is called, and the music livens up. Hard work becomes a merry party as the treaders dance until midnight to the sounds of either fife and drum or, more and more, a cassette player on full volume. The party atmosphere is helped by regular sips of the rough local brandy or the quinta's port. Ideally there should be two treaders for each

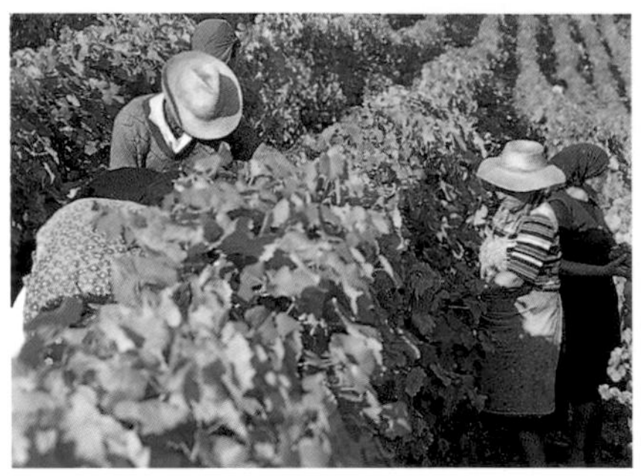

THE GRAPES ARE PICKED ...

... AND THEN LOADED INTO GIGOS AND CARRIED TO THE QUINTA.

pipe (barrel) of lagar capacity, but this is increasingly difficult to achieve as people pursue less physical jobs in towns and cities.

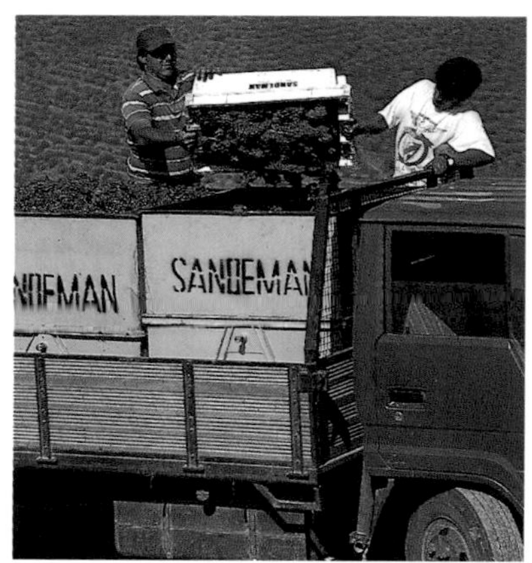

FRESHLY PICKED GRAPES READY TO BE TRANSPORTED TO THE LODGE.

Port wine makers are presented with a dilemma. The problem is that fermentation for port is short, arrested as it is by the addition of spirit halfway through, yet the wines are expected to age for many years – decades, in many instances. The extraction of color and tannin must be thorough and rapid since these are found only in the skins of grapes, which are discarded before fortification. The human foot is the best method, but each year fewer and fewer people are prepared to do the work. A manpower crisis in the 1960s and '70s, largely a result of Portugal's colonial wars in Africa, resulted in the introduction of self-circulating autovinifiers. These are concrete vats which use the pressure of the carbon dioxide gas released by fermentation to circulate the fermenting must, thus extracting the color. The subsequent introduction of reliable electric power has enabled many producers to turn to more modern fermentation vats.

The rich, half-fermented must is then run off while it is still sweet in order to be fortified with neutral grape brandy, which kills the yeasts. The result is a sweet, stable product: embryonic port.

The young wine is rough and tannic, with the raw spirit offensively obvious in the early stages. Port needs a long time to mature, two or three years in the case of the most basic rubies, and a similar number of decades for the best vintages and tawnies. Maturation can be either in bottle or wood (each vessel has its own unique effect on the style of the wine), and for shorter or longer periods of time.

TREADING IS STILL USED FOR THE BEST PORTS.

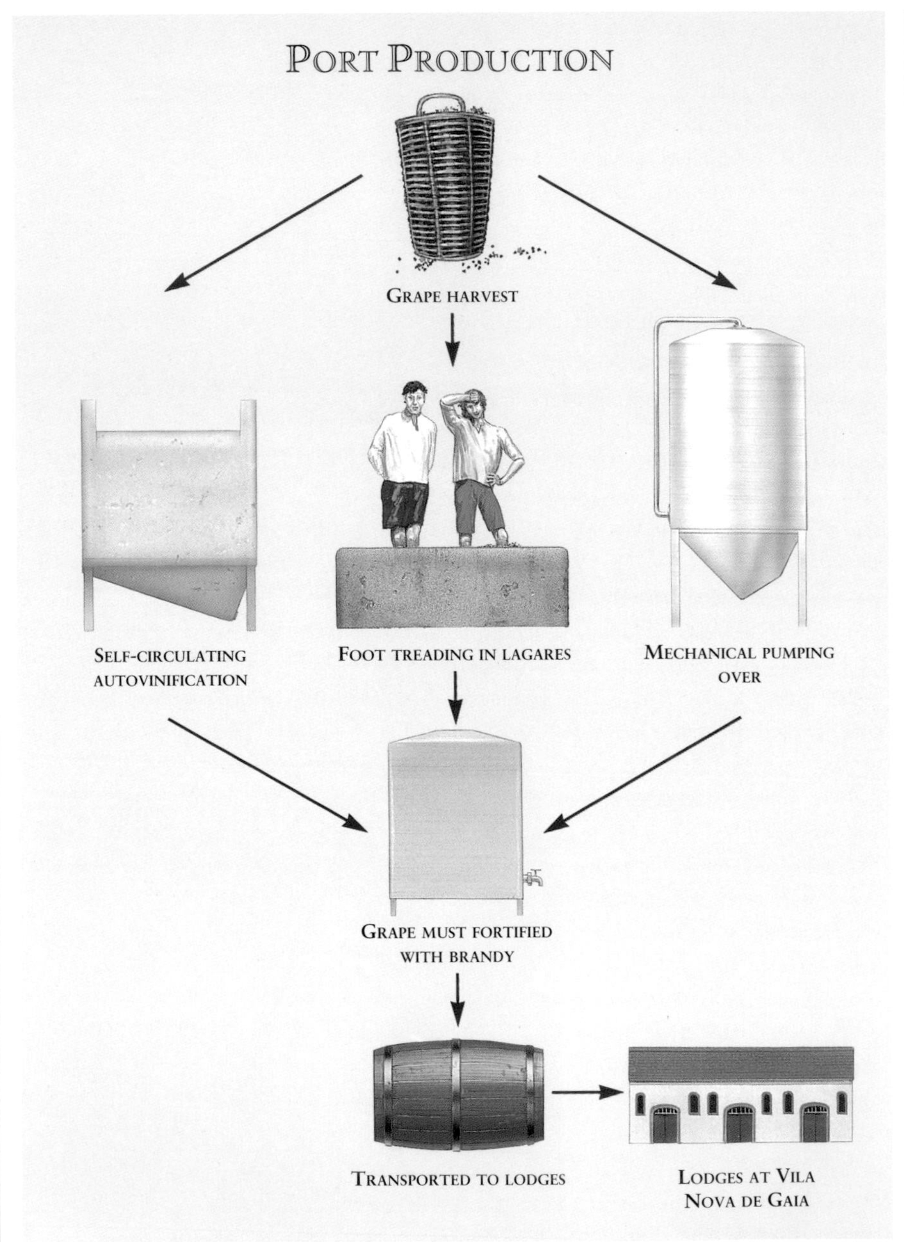
PORT PRODUCTION
GRAPE HARVEST
SELF-CIRCULATING AUTOVINIFICATION
FOOT TREADING IN LAGARES
MECHANICAL PUMPING OVER
GRAPE MUST FORTIFIED WITH BRANDY
TRANSPORTED TO LODGES
LODGES AT VILA NOVA DE GAIA

THE PORT WINE ROUTE

For centuries the Douro region was almost cut off from the rest of the world by the mountainous terrain and communication difficulties. Hotel accommodations were rare, so the only tourists were day-trippers, whose journey from Oporto, the nearest city, took three to four hours. The train ride from Oporto was and still is wonderfully scenic, but the train is very slow and the service has never been frequent. Traveling by road was even worse than taking the train. Some of the world's most scenic vineyards were effectively unreachable by drinkers of the port wine produced there.

European Community membership, and more recently European Union grants, have improved the infrastructure of the whole of northern Portugal. Roads are infinitely better than they once were. The journey from Oporto to the Douro region can now take as little as two hours, if one avoids the horrendous Oporto rush hour.

As the area has become more accessible and people are increasingly interested in agricultural, and specifically wine-related, tourism, a Port Wine Route (*Rota do Vinho do Porto*) has been established. Farms along the route are open to the public, giving visitors an intimate feel for what the area and its wines are about. Some quintas are open for tours and tastings, and often there is the opportunity to purchase wines as well. Some port firms, like Sandeman, have established and opened museums; Fonseca has installed an audio-visual presentation at Panascal, and other quintas offer accommodation. Finding lodging is easy, and accommodations are clean, welcoming, and simple in the bed-and-breakfast tradition. You can open your bedroom shutters in the morning to look out over terraced hillsides. Breathe in the fresh air, gently scented with the smell of wood smoke, as wood is still the main fuel used for cooking here.

Bear in mind that quinta houses are small and often may only have a few rooms. Booking in advance is essential, particularly in high season. Visitors may want to give some consideration to the climate of the region. In the summer the Douro is very hot, while spring and fall are more comfortable and presents the area at its best. In spring the hillsides are covered with the wild flowers that grow here in abundance; in the fall the area comes alive with the sounds and smells of the harvest.

If a quinta is on the Port Wine Route, it has been mentioned in the Directory. However, since wine tourism is very new in the area, the facilities available are still improving and the number of quintas joining the route are increasing every year. Full details of which quintas are included can be obtained from Portuguese tourism offices or the IVP (Instituto do Vinho do Porto) in Oporto. Many of the lodges in Vila Nova de Gaia and the hotels in Oporto have the latest information and you can also contact the offices of the Rota do Vinho do Porto (see page 221).

MATURATION AND THE LODGES OF GAIA

Fortification takes place in the fall and in the following spring, most of the wine is transferred to the shippers' warehouses, or lodges, in Vila Nova de Gaia. Here, on the south bank of the Douro opposite Oporto – almost on the Atlantic coast – the more temperate climate is better suited for long, slow, and even maturation. Wine stored in the Douro valley can take on a particular taste, known as "Douro bake," a result of high summer temperatures accelerating the wines' development.

Historically the wines were brought down the river in barcos rabelos, the flat-bottomed boats that have become the trademark of Oporto and the port industry. In days of yore, intrepid boatmen would brave the rapids of the Douro River, swollen by winter rains, to bring their cargo of port from the vineyards each spring. Now these boats are maintained only for publicity purposes and set sail only during races held each summer, from the bar of the Douro to the Dom Luis bridge. The fast-flowing Douro has been tamed to reduce the once-frequent flooding in Oporto and to produce hydroelectricity, so it is no longer navigable. Nowadays the wines are transported to Vila Nova de Gaia by road tanker across the Marão.

RED-TILED LODGES OF VILA NOVA DE GAIA.

Gaia is a difficult place to work. The old lodges are built on a steep hill, overlooking Oporto. Just as the Douro is demarcated, so is Vila Nova de Gaia and, until 1986, only wines that matured here were officially designated "Port." With Portugal joining the European Community in 1986, new rules were implemented to end the Gaia shippers' monopoly of port sales. Since then individual quintas have been able to export their wine directly, without going through the shippers and without having lodges in Gaia. After a slow start a large number of these wines are now available; for details see the Port Directory on page 186.

In Gaia the roads are narrow and mostly cobbled, but full of traffic as lodge staff and tourists try to negotiate the steep hills and tight corners, always aware that around the next bend there might be a parked truck collecting a port consignment. The lodges on the river front, Cálem, Sandeman, and Ramos Pinto among them, are the most accessible but are also at greater risk of flooding. Many lodges, particularly those on the front, offer guided tours, always followed by a tasting that introduce visitors to the region and the wines. Wherever possible the Port Directory gives details of opening times and telephone numbers.

The long, red-tiled lodges of Gaia house thousands of elongated old oak casks, called "pipes," a corruption of the Portuguese *pipa*. New wood is never used; chardonnay and new oak may be a perfect combination, but no one wants port to reek of vanilla. Larger vats of wood may also be used, especially for the red styles of port that require very slow aging. The smaller the cask, the greater the effect on the wine due to the higher amount of wood in contact with the wine. Tawny ports are kept in pipes, rubies in large vats holding thousands of gallons. The many different styles of port on the market vary depending on the quality of the wine, whether it is the product of a single year or a blend of several, and how it has been aged.

A PIPE OF PORT

Today few people can afford to lay down a pipe of port for a favorite niece or nephew, but the term is still in general use, if often misunderstood by laymen. A pipe is simply a barrel, but the port trade also uses a pipe as a standard measurement. Confusingly, there are two different possible sizes. A vineyard owner will talk of a vineyard yield in pipes of 145 U.S. gallons, but to sales and marketing people, the measure is 141 U.S. gallons or 712 bottles. The casks used for maturation vary in size from 145–172 U.S. gallons.

Pipes are an unusual shape – longer and narrower than most barrels used elsewhere. The reason, like the reasons for so many things in the Douro, is historic. In the days when wine was shipped down river in barcos rabelos, the pipes were carried to and from the river in ox carts along narrow twisting and very steep tracks. The narrow barrel evolved to match the terrain.

PIPES OF PORT MATURING IN A LODGE.

Port Styles – The Hierarchy

BASIC RUBY, WHITE, AND TAWNY

The vast majority of port produced is basic young ruby, white, and tawny. Ruby is a young, medium to full-bodied wine that is blended to a house style. Non-vintage wines are aged in wood, though not necessarily pipes, and normally sold at around three years old. Ports labeled "vintage character," or sometimes "reserve," are better-quality ruby wines. They are aged in large vats or pipes for approximately four to six years.

White port is made from white grapes. In recent years the styles have diverged, with some producers turning to pale, crisp, apéritif-style wines made like white wine but fortified just before the end of fermentation. This style is available at either 20 percent volume or the lighter 16 to 17 percent. The more traditional style is deeper in both color and taste, and is made in the lagar like red ports and subsequently aged for anywhere up to 10 years in pipes. Both dry and sweet traditional styles are made, but usually only the dry ones say so on the label (the assumption being that port is sweet). Both Ramos Pinto and Churchill Graham make outstanding examples of traditional dry white port. White port, well chilled, makes an interesting alternative apéritif; it can also be turned into a refreshing drink with ice and lemonade or tonic.

Young tawny, usually labeled "fine tawny," is a lighter style of wine than ruby. It is made by blending ruby and white, or by accelerating the aging process by storing the wines in lodges in the Douro itself.

These are the everyday ports. Rarely outstanding, they are wines to be enjoyed, but not debated and discussed. Far more interesting to the connoisseur are the aged tawnies and vintage wines where factors like provenance and maturation come to the fore.

AGED TAWNIES

Ports aged in wood for extended periods in pipes lose their original ruby red color and, through gentle oxidation in the cask, turn a reddish-brown, tawny shade. A number of different wines are made and sold with different names. The style depends on the length of time in the cask, coupled with the initial quality of the wine. Initially fruity, ruby red wines tend to retain some fruitiness after 10 years, developing a taste of nuts and dried fruit by the time the wines are 20 years old. At 30 the wines take on a distinctly mature character of spice, still nutty, and sometimes reminiscent of dried figs or dates, which continues to increase until the wines have spent 40 years in wood.

Only a few "old tawny" ports are still being made. Once a staple of all merchants, these wines have largely been replaced by tawnies that give a specific indication of age, which are far more marketable than the vague term "old." Extended aging in casks allows the color to change to topaz brown, while the nose becomes more like nuts, citrus peel, and dried fruit. The exact age of these wines is impossible to tell, but varies

Port colors vary dramatically, from the pale white ports, to the rich dark vintages.

from 8 to 25 years, depending on the producer and brand. Cockburn's Directors' Reserve, a blend approximately 12 to 15 years old, and Berry Bros. & Rudd Ltd.'s William Pickering are excellent examples of the type.

Because consumers are less willing to let the merchant choose the wine, specific ages and dates on the label are becoming *de rigueur* – hence the increasing success of tawny ports with an indication of age. Only four categories are permitted: 10, 20, 30, and over 40 years old. Unlike scotch, the age is an average, not a minimum. Top producers concerned for the reputation of their firm normally exceed the weighted average by a year or two. Aged tawnies are very different from vintage ports but are of an equivalent quality level, as they come from the best vineyards. In addition, they are often produced by treading and then careful nurturing in the relative cool of Gaia, or, more and more, in the quintas themselves.

Another type of tawny is colheita, pronounced "col-yate-ta." Colheita means "harvest" and, by extension, "vintage." These, however, are not vintage ports. The wine of one year's harvest only, these are aged in pipes for many years before they are bottled, effectively making them old, vintage tawnies. The youngest colheitas are bottled in their eighth year, but many are not bottled for much longer. To avoid confusion with vintage port, the label must clearly state that the wines have been aged in casks. Colheitas can be excellent, as is proved in the Port Directory, but the wine has to be excellent to start with. Aging alone will never make a poor wine good.

VINTAGE AND SIMILAR STYLES

Wine lovers everywhere owe a debt to port producers; the concept of mature vintage wine began with port. The technique of storing wine in inert glass, thus allowing the extended aging required for the finest wines, was rediscovered by the Portuguese and British shippers living in Portugal in the late eighteenth century, bringing back a practice lost when the Romans stopped using sealed amphorae (ceramic wine containers).

For the English-speaking world, vintage port is the pinnacle of the port hierarchy. It is the product of an exceptional year and is typically from the best vineyards. One of the most long-lived wines produced, vintage port is bottled when it is only two years old; it continues to mature slowly and reductively in the bottle for decades. Very full and fruity with huge levels of tannin when young, the best vintage port will not reach its peak for 20 years. During bottle maturation, it will throw a heavy deposit, called a "crust," and must therefore be decanted. The decision of whether or not to "declare" a vintage is that of the shipper or quinta owner, although that decision has to be ratified by the Port Wine Institute (Instituto do Vinho do Porto).

While vintage ports have always been considered to be the premium port wines, waiting for them to mature and then having to decant them, apart from considerations of cost, makes them strictly special occasion wines to be savored and discussed. For other occasions, late bottled vintage port (LBV) is the answer. Wines from a stated vintage, but produced virtually every year, LBVs are aged in casks for between four and six years before bottling, at which time they are filtered and stabilized to a far greater degree than vintage ports. Taylor's was the first to market LBV in a big way, creating a market that most other producers are now fighting for a share of. Modern LBVs, such as Graham's and Taylor's, are usually aged for six years and are meant to be consumed when released; they will not improve in the bottle. A traditional style also exists, which is bottled after four years and continues to improve, throwing a sediment, and therefore requires decanting.

Crusted, or crusting port, has always been a specialty of the British wine trade. Never recognized by the authorities in Oporto, crusted is a very high-quality ruby wine, blended from a few vintages and bottled young often by wine merchants in the United Kingdom. It forms a sediment, or crust, while it matures in the bottle and must be decanted. At the time of this writing the future of crusted port is in doubt due to the establishment of mandatory Portuguese bottling. Since crusted port cannot be bottled in Portugal, it may be an endangered species.

TERROIR-ISM AND SINGLE QUINTAS IN THE DOURO

In Burgundy the best wines theoretically come from the best plots of land; in Bordeaux from the best estates, each being carefully mapped out and tended by the château owner. The reason, it is said, is the *terroir*, a word that translates to "soil," but encompasses far more. Terroir is the combination of soil, both chemically and physically, its drainage or water retention, the aspect, and the specific climate of the vineyard. Whether a vineyard faces north or south, is steep or flat, near water or a forest – all will affect the terroir and, to a greater or lesser extent, the wine.

Wines from single quintas are increasingly becoming available.

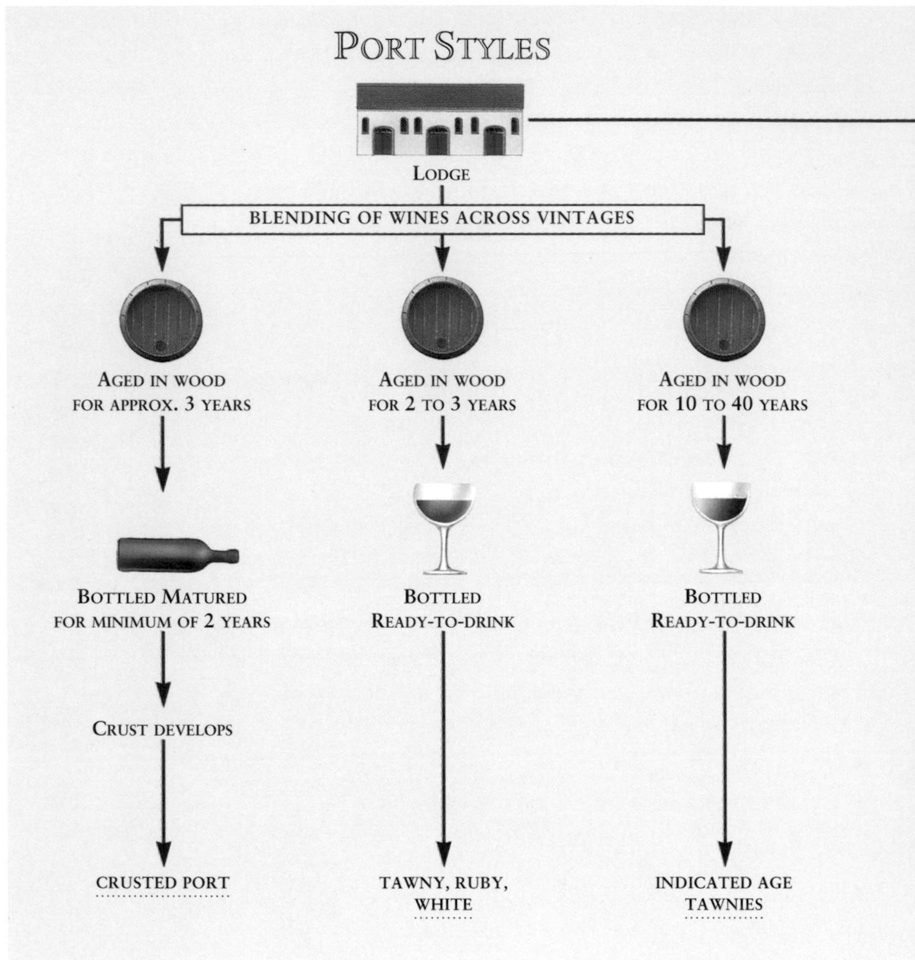

Most shippers have long agreed that the quality of top vintages comes from the complexity afforded by blending the wines from a number of quintas to produce the house vintage. Until recently few vintage ports gave any clues to the wine's provenance other than the name of the shipper and the vintage year. This was not always the case; the wine of Quinta de Vargellas was established in the first half of the eighteenth century. But apart from Quinta do Noval, single quinta wines were the exception rather than the rule.

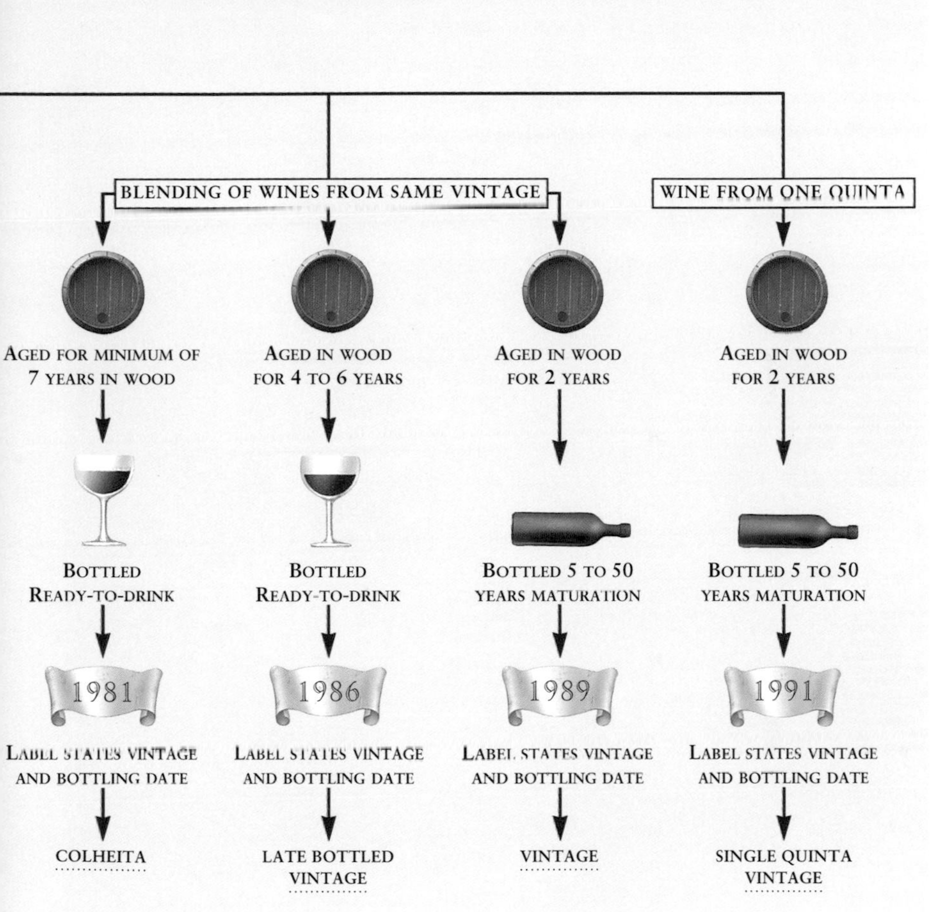

Recently more significance has been given to the quintas. All styles are available, from rubies and tawnies to full vintage wines. The 1986 ruling for shipping port, permitting individual estates to export directly without having lodges in Vila Nova de Gaia, has encouraged single quintas to sell their wines directly rather than through shippers' firms. Because of the time needed for maturation, some of these single quinta wines are only just coming on the market. These wines are meant to reflect the individual character of the estate and its terroir as much as the house style. This is perhaps most apparent with single quinta vintage ports. Often the product of a shipper's flagship vineyard, these wines are normally offered in years when a "full vintage" is not declared (those years in which the wine forms the backbone of the vintage blend). However, like vintage port, they are not made every year. Single quinta wines are frequently released when they are ready to drink, in contrast to the shipper's main vintage port.

The importance of single quinta wines can be judged by the many examples in this book. Large numbers of single quinta vintage and aged tawnies are now on the market as producers and consumers look for more variety in the wines they drink.

Taylor's Quinta de Vargellas.

DECLARING A VINTAGE

Unlike claret and burgundy, vintage port is not produced every year. Only when conditions are right, both in terms of weather and the equally variable marketplace, is a vintage "declared." On average these factors combine successfully only about three times every decade for the better shippers. It must be admitted that some houses make vintage port far more often than this, but these houses tend to have less of a reputation for vintage wines.

The decision to declare a vintage is entirely the choice of the individual house; no instructions come down from on high. The authorities, the Instituto do Vinho do Porto in this case, must ratify the decision, as they must for all wines. However, they cannot insist on any year being a vintage. As a result some shippers miss what are otherwise generally declared vintage years. Thus potential buyers will look in vain for, say, Cockburn's 1977, though both 1967 and 1975 (not great years) are available. Agreement among shippers can happen, but this usually occurs only in the greatest of years. Most companies declared 1991 a vintage year, but others, including some of the most highly regarded names, preferred 1992. On the other hand, 1994 was almost unanimously declared a vintage year.

The perfect vintage port year starts with a wet winter. The summers are hot and dry, so reserves of water accessible to the vines are essential since irrigation is prohibited. Warm, sunny, but slightly breezy weather is desirable when flowering occurs in mid-June, but from this point on hot sunshine is needed – hot, but not too hot. If the temperature gets too high or the ground too dry, the vine effectively closes down to preserve its precious water supply, stopping photosynthesis and thereby halting the accumulation of sugar in the berries so that the grapes do not ripen. Generally, heat is needed to ripen all fruit; but paradoxically, in the Douro very hot years result in sugar levels that can be too low.

Excessively wet weather in the fall will result in underripe and dilute grapes. However, it has long been recognized that a brief period of light rain just before the harvest can be very beneficial. The 1991 and 1994 harvests were both improved by showers in mid-September, refreshing the fruit, plumping it up, and giving a final spurt to the ripening. George Sandeman is on record as having written off the 1866 vintage, having witnessed the shriveled fruit on the vines. But between seeing the vineyards and reporting his findings, the rains came, improving the fruit to the extent that commentators of the day called these wines one of the best vintages ever. An English port shipper was expected to stick to his word, however; Sandeman did not declare a vintage wine that year.

AN ASSESSMENT OF RECENT VINTAGES

1960 Generally declared (by 24 shippers), this year has been underrated but the wines are now coming across well. However, there are few signs of any great future potential. The wines will maintain their quality for some years if correctly stored, but will not improve.

1963 This vintage, declared by 25 shippers, is one of the finest of the post-war years. The lighter wines have been ready for some time; the fuller-bodied ones reached their peak in the mid-1990s. The wines are drinking well and the best are not yet fading.

1966 The '66s have been unfairly set against the outstanding '63s for too long, and sales have suffered as a result. Declared by 20 shippers, the wines are of generally very high quality. All of the wines are ready to drink now and the best, Fonseca and Dow among them, will live for a very long time to come.

1967 This year was by no means an outstanding vintage. Declared by a mere five shippers, the wines have now either reached their peak or are on the decline. Any remaining stocks should be consumed.

1970 Since the beginning of the 1990s, this year, declared by 23 major shippers, has been the vintage of choice for port shippers. A classic vintage with good grip, the wines are now ready for drinking, but will improve well into the twenty-first century. Because mandatory Oporto bottling was introduced for vintage ports in the early 1970s, the '70s vintage was the last to be shipped in bulk to the United Kingdom for bottling by Bristol or London wine merchants.

1972 This is one of the poorest post-war vintages. Declared by only two shippers, the wines are already at the end of their peak.

1975 This year was declared by 17 major shippers as much for political reasons as anything else. This was the *verão quente*, or "hot summer," following the 1974 revolution, when the tail end of the Salazar right-wing regime was replaced by the Communists. Some wines are still drinking well – Cálem, Dow, and Fonseca in particular – but many are already past their peak.

1977 Along with 1963, this is one of the outstanding post-war vintages. Declared by all but three of the main shippers, the best wines may be ready for drinking by the late 1990s. However, they will probably not be at their finest until the second decade of the twenty-first century. Recent tastings have shown that the lesser wines of this vintage are ready to drink now.

1978 This was not a great year; the wines offer about the same quality as 1967 and 1975. Declared by only two shippers, and with a few second labels produced (lighter wines often released when mature, made when a full vintage is not declared), the wines are drinking well now but hold little future potential.

1980 Initially underrated as a vintage, the wines are comparable in quality to 1960 or 1970, although they lack the structure and therefore the staying power of the '83s or '85s. Prices are still fairly low so this is a smart choice for those who want a mature port without paying the prices of the 1970 vintage.

1982 Together with 1983, this year was a split vintage; some producers declared one, the rest, the other. In hindsight, those who chose 1982 made a mistake. This is a light vintage, now ready for drinking. None has much potential beyond the late 1990s.

1983 Considerably better than the '82s, to which this vintage is inevitably compared, 1983 produced big, powerful wines with firm structure and huge fruit, ensuring a long life. Not yet ready, most of these wines are still in a very closed state and will come around only well into the twenty-first century.

1985 Declared by most leading shippers and considered better than the 1983 vintage, these wines are best as long-term prospects; it would be a crime to open many of them before about 2010. Following four fairly close vintages the '85s were followed by a long gap in vintage declarations. Not until 1991 was there another generally declared year, though a few producers declared 1987.

1987 This vintage does not stand comparison with the '85s. Declared by only a few shippers, the wines are very light but some are nonetheless attractive.

1991 Declared by most shippers (with one or two notable exceptions who preferred the following year), this first general declaration since 1985 was very much welcomed by the trade. These are good wines for medium- long-term drinking.

1992 This year was declared by only a handful of shippers – mostly those who did not declare the '91s. In early tastings, the house styles rather than quality levels have distinguished the two years, making them difficult to judge against each other.

1994 Another generally declared year, 1994 had a textbook weather pattern. Abundant rain in 1993 continued through the winter, cold weather at flowering reduced the number of grape bunches, but this ultimately improved quality. Initial tastings show these to be very full, firm, long-lived wines with more complexity than the '91s.

1995 The decision as to whether to declare 1995 a vintage year will be made public in the spring of 1997. A number of producers were already enthusiastic at the time of the harvest, so there may be some single quinta wines. Full vintages are less likely, coming so soon after the '91s and '94s.

1996 This was a cool and damp year. Most grapes were harvested at about 11 degrees Beaumé (the scale used for measuring sugar content of grapes or wine) compared with the normal 13 or 14. Very few producers were happy with the wines. Niepoort, on the other hand, harvested very late. By this stage the weather had changed for the better and fully ripe grapes were brought in.

READING PORT WINE LABELS

Port labels are relatively easy to understand provided that you know the basic styles of wine produced. Most port labels, and certainly all premium port labels, will give a clear indication of how the wine has been made and thus the style you might expect.

Vintage port has the simplest of labels. Apart from the mandatory information required in different countries, the label usually states only the name of the shipper, the year, and the designation "Vintage Port." Care needs to be taken with colheitas, because although these are not at all like vintage port, the labels can be confusingly similar. If you want a true vintage port, look out for the term "Vintage Port." Colheitas may not use the term vintage and will say "matured in wood" somewhere on the label. Also, do not confuse late bottled vintage (LBV) with full vintage port. Read the label carefully.

At the other end of the scale, ruby and white port labels clearly state the port style. Note that white port with no other indication of style on the label is medium sweet. Remember the term "Vintage Character" means up-market ruby, not vintage port.

Tawny port labels can be a little less clear. Basic, young tawny port will state "Tawny" on the label. The confusion comes with the indicated age wines. For example, a "10 Year Old Tawny Port," is just as likely to be labeled "10 Years Old Port," leaving it up to the consumer to work out what style it is. Only wines of 10, 20, 30, and over 40 years old are permitted.

One word which is overused by the port trade and which can cause confusion is "Reserve." Always indicating a better than average wine, the word can be and is applied to red and tawny ports alike. For example, Cockburn's Special Reserve is a premium ruby and Romariz Reserva Latina is a high quality tawny. In neither case is there anything else on the label to help the confused buyer. Here you have to rely on the advice of your wine merchant or make sure you have this book with you to refer to.

SINGLE QUINTA AGED TAWNY

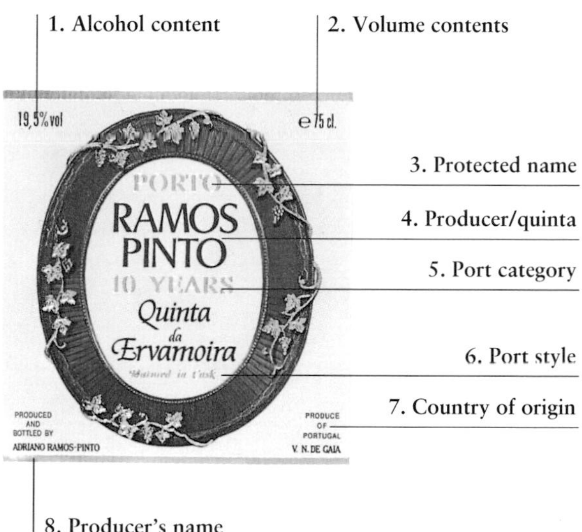

1. Alcohol content – 20% volume is standard for port, although the content can range from 19–21% alcohol by volume.

2. Volume contents – for the United States this measurement must be in milliliters (ml). For European Union countries both milliliters and centiliters (cl) are permitted.

3. Protected name – "Porto" is the internationally recognized and protected name. In the United Kingdom the name "Port" is similarly protected.

4. Producer/quinta – if a quinta name appears on the label, then the wine must come from grapes grown only on that quinta.

5. Port category – this wine is an aged tawny. Confusingly, one is expected to know that a 10-year-old port is tawny, not red. Some producers give more explicit information on their labels.

6. Port style – long aging in wood is the clue to the style.

7. Country of origin – real port can only come from Portugal.

8. Producer's name – the producer's name should always appear on the label.

Buying, Storing, and Serving Port

Port is stocked by all liquor stores and the range they offer highlights the big sellers: ruby and basic tawny with an LBV or two for good measure. Increasingly the stores' own brand selections have moved away from just a simple ruby to a whole assortment, including LBV, tawny, and even aged tawny. These are often considerably cheaper than the branded alternatives and represent good value. But a very cheap port is rarely worth the money. Shops with a "budget" image are likely to cut corners, so it might be better to pay a little more for a brand or a different store brand label. Close inspection of the label will show that many store brand ports carry the name of the major shipper that actually produced the wine. Avoid the trap of thinking that a store brand LBV made by shipper "x" is the same wine as the LBV sold under the shipper's name. Store brand buyers are looking for ways to save money, so they will use wines that are not as good. The better lots are reserved for the shipper's branded product.

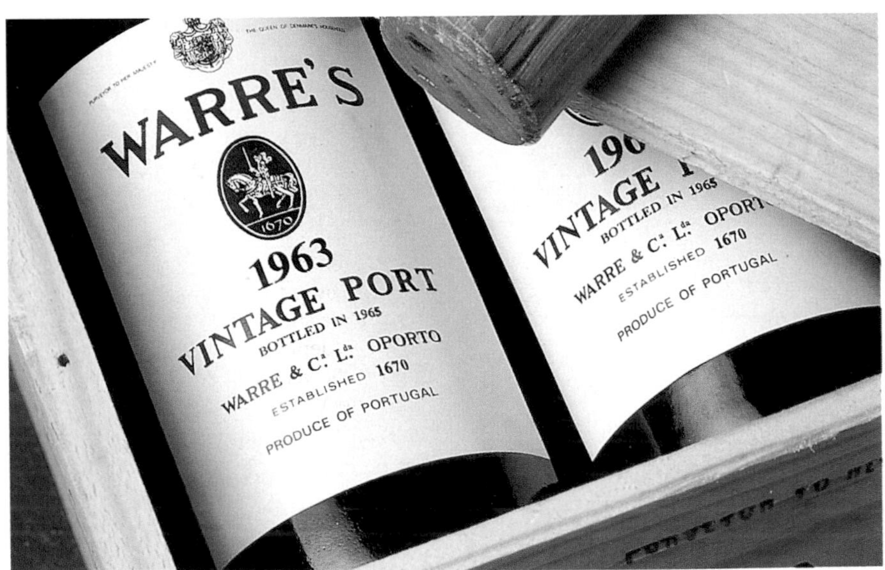

Premium vintage ports are sold in wooden cases.

Specialty wine stores generally stock a range of fine tawny and vintage wines, and can normally order particular wines if you want to buy a whole case (12 bottles). The traditional merchants are the main purchasers of vintage port when it is first released. A small amount of wine is made available for immediate sale, but most will be aged in perfect conditions and sold many years later. For the consumer, purchasing vintage port when it is mature is a relatively expensive option, but if the merchant is reliable one is at least assured of getting wines kept in optimum condition.

A merchant who needs more stock of older wine will buy at an auction which consumers can also attend. Here you will get the equivalent of the "trade" price – up to a third cheaper than the merchant's price, but not without drawbacks. The lots usually consist of many cases of the same wine. If 10 cases of port seem like a lot, get together with some friends to form a wine-sharing syndicate. Auctions can be risky. If the wine is out of condition, there is no recourse, so go to the pre-sale tasting if you can and always find out where the wine has been stored. Before you go, decide what you want and how much you are prepared to pay and stick to that figure. Also, don't forget that in addition to the basic selling price, a buyer's premium and taxes are payable.

PROPER STORAGE

The image of port is one of dusty bottles maturing for decades in cobwebby cellars under stately homes, as well as cut-crystal decanters and great ceremony. The producers like to cultivate this image, which is, after all, good for sales. But reality simply is not like that; the vast majority of port is ready to drink when it is bottled and there is no advantage to storing it.

A DARK CELLAR IS NEEDED FOR LONG-TERM STORAGE.

The exceptions are the bottle-matured ports: vintage, traditional LBV, and crusted. These wines will benefit from medium- to long-term cellaring, as will the checkbook, since young vintages are usually far cheaper than mature ones. The ideal cellar is cool and dark, has an even temperature (consistency is more important than the specific temperature), and is free from vibrations – storing wines near a central heating boiler is not a good idea.

Bottles should be stored on their side to keep the cork moist, with the white flash or label uppermost. (Vintage port used to be marked with a splash of white paint at bottling, a practice that is now quite rare.) Placing the white flash or label topmost ensures that the sediment, known as the "crust," always forms on the opposite side of the bottle, which simplifies decanting. Ideally the wines should be cellared before the sediment forms and disturbed only to be decanted, perhaps 20 or 30 years later for the best wines. In such bottles the crust that forms is a large, fairly firm, homogeneous mass that holds together and, being heavier than the wine, falls cleanly to the bottom of the bottle.

Aged tawnies and colheitas are generally made to be consumed when released, though they will certainly stay in good condition if stored in a cool place for a couple of years. Some examples of very long bottle-aged tawny wines have proven to be delicious, but this is risky since most will gradually fade.

Other ports – rubies, tawnies, and modern LBVs that are closed with stopper corks – should remain upright for the brief time they are in stock. These wines will keep for a few months, maybe even a year or two after bottling, but are not designed to be stored. It is far better to buy these by the bottle than by the case, so they can be enjoyed at their optimum moment of freshness.

Few people today can devote the necessary space to create a proper wine cellar. Cellar space is typically too valuable to use for wine storage; instead it becomes another living area or a utility room and home to the washing machine, central heating boiler, and work bench. A number of options are open to wine collectors in this position. Merchants often offer a cellarage service for a remarkably low cost. The wines are kept in temperature- and humidity-controlled conditions and the collection is insured for its replacement value. Cases can be drawn off as required and the merchant will arrange delivery. This service is only feasible for large collections, since the cost of administering small numbers of bottles is excessive.

For more modest collections, but where cost is not a problem, special storage units are available. These are rather like very gentle refrigerators – fitted with wine racks – that maintain the correct temperature. Details can be found in the small ads of most wine magazines.

However, even this option may be beyond the means of most people, but this does not mean that you cannot store your port successfully. If you cannot arrange ideal storage, then try to reduce negative influences as much as possible. Light and heat are the main enemies of wine, so a cool, dark cupboard is better than an open rack in the kitchen. To maintain a consistent temperature, choose somewhere mild rather than the attic or garage, where it might be cool in the winter but very hot in the summer. Remember the basic rules. Keep bottles on their side with the label uppermost and in their own wooden boxes (if you have purchased vintage port by the case). You should still be able to keep your ports in reasonable condition.

DEMYSTIFYING DECANTING

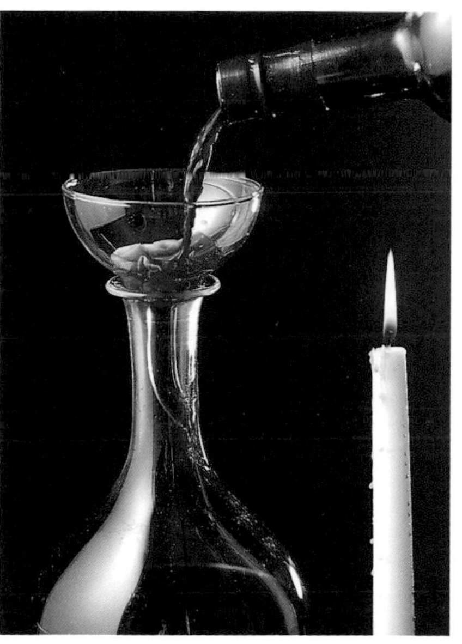

DECANTING VINTAGE PORT IS A SIMPLE PROCESS.

Many people are intimidated by the idea of decanting, a seemingly black magic ritual involving dark cellars, candles, and strange pieces of equipment that would not look out of place in a torture chamber. Complex corkscrews and red-hot tongs, mahogany and brass decanting candles, and silver-plated funnels all have their place in the operation, but none is essential.

Decanting is simply a matter of pouring wine into another bottle in order to leave the sediment behind. In its most basic form, the only requirements are a means of opening the bottle and a spare clean bottle, although most people prefer to use an attractive decanter. The bottle should be retrieved from the cellar and placed upright in the room in which it will be decanted 24 hours before opening. This allows the sediment to fall cleanly to the bottom of the bottle. A few hours before serving, the neck should be carefully wiped and the cork pulled. The wine can then be poured gently from the bottle into the decanter in one slow, easy, continuous movement. Do not stop in the middle as this will disturb the sediment. A candle or any other bright light source placed behind the bottle will show you how far the sediment has moved. When the sediment reaches the neck, stop pouring.

Port tongs can be useful for very old bottles if you suspect the cork might be too old and crumbly to withstand a corkscrew. The method is to heat the tongs until they are red-hot and then clasp them around the neck of the bottle, leaving them there for a few seconds. Very carefully wipe the heated glass with a damp cloth when the tongs are removed. This results in a clean break with remarkably few shards of glass, which would be removed through decanting anyway.

If you are not decanting, all that is needed is to remove the top section of the foil capsule with a sharp knife and then the stopper cork. No special tool is needed to reseal these bottles; the stopper cork is the ideal solution. Keep in mind, however, that faults can occur in any cork.

Corkiness, sometimes called "musty taint," is a potential problem for all wines. It is particularly problematic because it can affect one bottle from a batch, or a whole batch, and no one knows until the cork is drawn. Bacteria can react with the chemicals used to sterilize the cork to produce a most unpleasant taint, variously described as musty, chemical, or chlorine-like. Once a wine has been tainted there is no way of removing it and the only solution is to take the bottle back to the store you bought it from.

Some producers use driven corks in wines other than vintage and traditional LBV. For these a corkscrew is required, and the cork is difficult to reinsert. Various reusable stoppers are available for use, but a decanter, while not strictly necessary, looks much more attractive.

A SIMPLE CORKSCREW AND A PAIR OF PORT TONGS.

The wine trade recognizes that there is a problem with corks and all respectable merchants will take back faulty wine. If your merchant doesn't, buy elsewhere. However, keeping a wine for 20 years only to find it is then undrinkable is one of the gambles of wine drinking. If the merchant you bought the wine from is still in business he should still replace the bottle, although you may have difficulty proving where the wine was bought.

HOW TO SERVE PORT

Most port can be served directly from the bottle in which it was bought. Rubies and modern LBVs should always be served at room temperature (but not too warm, since they will seem excessively alcoholic), and tawnies either at room temperature or, as in Portugal, chilled. A glass of chilled 10- or 20-year-old tawny cleans the palate wonderfully; port shippers often use it almost as a mouthwash to remove the taste of food before serving vintage wine.

White port, whether dry or sweet, should also be served chilled. The lighter and drier the wine is, the colder the temperature should be. It can even be mixed with tonic, lemonade, or carbonated water. After a day of heat and dust on the Douro vineyards, there is little that revives workers more on returning to the quinta than a long, cold drink of white port, tonic, and ice. This may seem like heresy, but if the people who make port drink it like that, then who can argue? This is a modern variation on the drink that made port so popular in days of yore, the port 'n' lemon that women drank in pre-

MOST PORT NEED NOT BE DECANTED.

World War I English pubs, although in those days they would have used basic ruby port, while their men supped ale.

GLASSES, DECANTERS, AND PASSING THE PORT

Because it is higher in alcohol than most wines, port should be served in small glasses. It is typical to get six glasses from a standard bottle of wine; 10 to 12 glasses is appropriate for port. Small Paris goblets or small versions of the savoy glass are nicely suited for the drink, as is the International Standards Organization (ISO) tasting glass. When the Austrian glass maker Riedel turned his attention to port he came up with two glasses: one for vintage and the other for tawny. Both are very similar, but one is slightly taller than the other. They are also remarkably similar to the ISO version, but ISO glasses cost a great deal less. The worst glass for port is the one most often found in restaurants and clubs, the Elgin glass. Not only is this glass far too small, it is also the wrong shape for wine appreciation, as the sides slope out and, therefore the all important bouquet is lost.

SAVOY, PARIS, AND ISO GLASSES ARE ALL SUITABLE FOR PORT.

Whatever glass is used, it should not be filled more than two-thirds full, but preferably less, so the wine can be swirled around the glass and the flavors slowly savored. It is far better to take a small amount and refill your glass when the decanter reappears than to mar the taste by having a too-full glass.

Traditionally port is always passed to the left. In a formal setting the host will fill the glass of the guest to his right, then his own glass, and then the decanter will circulate around the table in a clockwise direction, with each guest taking some as it passes. In the past, there have been numerous theories as to why this tradition arose; explanations involved the direction of the orbit of the earth or even the occult. In fact, the reason is quite simple. With the majority of the population being right-handed, it is easier to pass a bottle to the left. As the decanter reaches each guest, he or she should refresh his or her glass and immediately pass it on; the only time it should come to rest is in front of the host. There are even special decanters with round bases that can be put down only in a special cradle, which ensures its continued circulation.

APPRECIATING PORT: THE TASTING

Port tasting is no different from any other wine tasting. The purpose is the same: to assess the wine's quality and maturity and, perhaps most important, whether or not it is to your taste. Tasting is also an essential part of quality control, a check to ensure that the wine is in good condition.

Only a small amount of wine is initially needed in the glass. Overfilling the glass – more than about one-third full – makes tasting more difficult because the wine cannot be swirled as easily. For this reason it is better not to use too small a glass. When comparing a number of wines, it is important to fill each glass to the same level. That way, the depth of the wine will not affect your assessment of the color.

Tasting involves a combination of three senses: sight, smell, and taste. The first stage involves looking at the port. Holding the glass at an angle over a white surface, look down on the wine, checking for clarity. The wine should be bright; if it is dull or cloudy, it may be faulty. Long bottle-maturation will result in a harmless sediment, but the port itself should be clear. You will see a gradation of color from the center to the rim; for red ports, the broader and browner the rim, the more mature the wine.

As for color, port is purple – almost black in young vintages, and matures to ruby and garnet. Aged tawnies can be russet or brown while white ports might be the color of an old tawny or the palest lemon yellow, depending on the aging. Most ports are meant to be drunk when bottled and should be a consistent color. However, the color of vintage port will change with time.

The sense of smell is perhaps the most important part of tasting. Smell and taste are very closely linked; think of how little you can taste when you have a cold. Indeed, the palate only confirms the flavors detected by the nose. Swirl the wine in the glass to release the aromas and sniff gently but deeply. The port should smell appealing. Any hint of mustiness or vinegar will tell you the wine is faulty and should be rejected. Imperfections can happen, even with the best wine, particularly if the cork is faulty or if storage was less than perfect.

The climate in which the grapes are grown and the high alcohol content usually give port a pronounced nose, rich and full; the aromas that come out of the glass should encourage you to taste. Red ports tend to have fruity aromas, with black fruits and even chocolate notes are predominant when young. Tawnies tend to have a nuttier character.

Just as appearance can provide a clue to the wine's age, so can the nose. In vintage port the primary fruit aromas give way to an aged bouquet. The fruit fades but additional layers of flavor develop with complex spice and herb characters, making the wine all the more interesting.

Not only should the palate confirm the nose, it should also reveal the wine's structure. On tasting, the first sensation one should be able to detect is sweetness. Nearly all ports are sweet, but there are degrees. Sweetness must be balanced by acidity, an important

Elegant decanter and glasses.

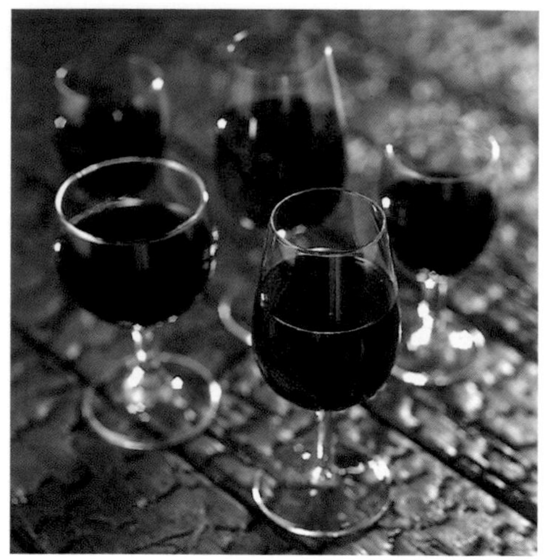

A SELECTION OF PORT WINE GLASSES.

component of all wines, but critical for sweet wines. Acid balances the sweetness and stops the wine from being cloying. Acidity manifests itself as a mouth-watering sensation, a freshness in the mouth.

By contrast there is tannin, a component extracted from the grape skin in red winemaking. Whereas acidity makes the mouth water, tannin makes the mouth dry. Tannin can be felt on teeth, gums, and tongue. It can make a young vintage port seem harsh, but it is a vital preservative that enables the wine to keep for decades. As the wine matures the tannins soften and the wine becomes more balanced. The sediment that forms as vintage port ages is largely tannin and coloring matter.

Different parts of the mouth detect different components of taste. It is important to take a reasonable mouthful and swirl it around, "chewing" it so it contacts all parts of the mouth. Additionally, taking in air through pursed lips will help release extra flavors, though this might make an unsociable noise. The wine should then be spat out.

Evaluating port will add to your knowledge and enjoyment and help you get every ounce of flavor and pleasure from the wine. Because memories are fallible, many enthusiasts write tasting notes for each wine as they taste it, building over the years a worthwhile encyclopedia of wine evaluations. A cellar book can be used to list wines in stock and to note your impressions of them, providing a record of which wines you have tasted, when, and with whom. This will help you monitor the progress of a wine and know when it is ready to drink, essential for protecting your investment.

Professional tastings are always done in neutral conditions – with good daylight, clean white surfaces, and no distracting odors – and before lunch, when the palate is freshest and the mind most alert. (Obviously this is not an appropriate hour for social drinking; port usually ends a dinner late in the evening.) While the decor cannot be completely clinical, and one can hardly avoid the aromas of food or cologne, a few small considerations will help. Simple effects like a white tablecloth or napkin and a sensibly shaped glass, not too full, will go a long way toward improving the pleasure one can get from wine.

APPRECIATING PORT: THE TASTING

Assess the color and appearance.

Swirl the wine to release the aromas.

Nose the wine.

Taste the wine.

Take in air to release extra flavors.

TASTING GLOSSARY

Body The weight and feel of the wine in the mouth. Not necessarily related to the alcohol content. Most ports are full-bodied in the overall scale of wines but as with sweetness, there are degrees of intensity.

Character The flavor of the wine, detected mostly on the nose.

Color Port varies in color depending upon the style, from very rich, dark purple to red through tawny or white. Generally as ports age they lose color, becoming more brown; however, white ports actually gain color, becoming deeply golden.

Dumb Some wines, particularly young ones, go through a phase of their development when they are "dumb" or "closed" when it is difficult to detect the character and aroma on the nose.

Grip Full-bodied red wines, including port wine, often have considerable amounts of tannin which, along with acidity and fruit, give the wine its structure. A wine with a firm structure is often said to have "grip."

Length/Finish The period of time after swallowing a wine during which you can still taste it. Generally the longer the length, the better the wine.

Nose The smell of a wine. This reveals the wine's character and gives some indication of its maturity.

Rancio Very aged and mature nose rather like very old cognac. The wine can take on a smell rather like mushrooms or rotting leaves. It is a style, not a fault.

Rim The edge of the wine in the glass held at an angle over a plain surface. The rim indicates the true color of the wine.

Sulking Wines can go through a "sulking" phase in the early part of their maturation, during which time they do not show their full potential.

Tannin A number of different chemicals extracted from the grape skin which have a mouth-drying sensation. They can appear tough and unyielding when young, but are important to preserve the wine.

PAIRING PORT AND FOOD

More and more people are becoming interested in wine and food matching. The old simplistic rules of white wine with fish and red wine with meat are now being questioned and adhered to less rigidly. Today we are more willing to try new combinations, often with surprising results. It would take a very strong constitution to drink port throughout a meal, but it does make a confident partner to many foods.

Classically port is served with Stilton cheese, as the strong flavor of the wine is a good match for the pungency of the cheese. This is the key to pairing food and wine; the intensity of flavor should be the first consideration. The marriage of port and Stilton works with a full-flavored red port, but venerable vintages with fragile flavors can be easily overpowered by too strong a cheese. Here a milder cheese, such as a good Cheddar, might be a better choice. In the Douro a local cheese, fuller in taste but similar in texture to Edam, is offered with a firm quince jelly – the sweet-sharp flavor combination complements the sweetness of port perfectly. Yet port, while sweet, is not a great match for most desserts. Port is rarely very sweet, so when set against the sweetness of a dessert, it can seem thin and tart.

Appetizers pair very well with white port.

Cheeses and desserts come after a meal – what does one choose for before and during dinner? A preprandial selection of appetizers goes very well with chilled tawny or white port. Particular favorites are cured hams, such as Serrano and Parma, full-flavored salamis, and similar sausages. The nutty character of an aged tawny is perfect with lightly salted, roasted almonds, another Douro specialty.

The old white ports (of which there are remarkably few) and tawnies also rival sherry and Madeira as accompaniments to soups, especially consommés. One of the most surprisingly successful combinations is young vintage port with rare steak, which is the suggestion of one port producer. The protein in the meat softens the tannins in the wine, and the strength of flavor matches very well.

Don't be afraid to experiment. Myriad savory dishes contain sweetness in some form or another, which is nicely balanced by the sweetness of port. Also, don't be put off by port's alcoholic content. Many cabernets and chardonnays are 13 or 14 percent alcohol, yet they tend to be consumed in much larger measures.

PORT IS A CONFIDENT PARTNER TO MANY FOODS, PARTICULARLY CHEESES.

PART TWO

THE PORT DIRECTORY

The directory covers port shipping companies, cooperatives, and single quintas. Most of the company profile information has been supplied by the firms themselves through questionnaires and interviews. Other published sources (see Bibliography, page 222) have been used to provide background details, particularly about the quintas. Finally, research trips to the Douro have been invaluable. The information here is as up-to-date as possible, given publication lead times, but remember that companies and vineyards are bought and sold, blenders and blends change, and product ranges alter.

PRODUCTION KEY

 *Quintas owned by the company.*

 *States whether company buys in grapes/wine. Where possible gives how much of annual production these sources supply.*

In wine tasting, a "vertical" tasting involves sampling a range of vintage wines from the same producer. For a "horizontal" tasting, wines of the same vintage year from *different* producers are tasted together. For this book, wines of the same age have been tasted together whenever possible. Thus, for example, all the 1991 vintages were tasted horizontally; the 10-year-old tawnies were tasted in batches, as were the LBVs. This gives a better impression of where the producer's wines fall within the overall quality spectrum.

Most of the samples have been supplied specifically for this book so they were, at least in theory, in the best possible condition. In addition, ports were tasted both in London and in Portugal. All the tastings took place during 1996 and 1997. Keep in mind that wines do change, particularly the vintage-dated ones; immature vintages will develop and allowance must be made for maturation. Even undated wines can change, through extended or improper storage, or through a deliberate change to the blend. Buy carefully from a reputable supplier, and do not keep stopper-corked bottles for too long.

Each entry in the Directory has an information box. Details are given on whether you can visit their lodges and quintas and recommended wines are good within their type, but may not necessarily be the best wine that a producer makes. Finally, each company is given an overall rating, providing a general guide to the quality of their wines. There is also another useful feature in the "Port Shipping Firms" section which gives information on whether the company owns any quintas and whether they "buy in" grapes or wine from other quintas.

OVERALL RATING

★ *Companies generally making sound, reliable wines, but which tend not to be exciting.*

★★ *Companies producing high quality wines.*

★★★ *An excellent producer.*

SECTION ONE

PORT SHIPPING FIRMS

The Portuguese wine industry has always been made up of a vast number of growers and a handful of merchants selling the wine. Whereas in Bordeaux one looks for the name of the château, with port the shipper's name is still all-important. The reasons for this are historical. Portugal operates the Napoleonic laws of succession, whereby on the death of a vineyard owner, his or her estate is divided up among the heirs, instead of giving everything to the eldest son. The result is an ever increasing number of vineyard plots and vineyard owners.

There are currently over 85,000 separate vineyards registered in the Douro region, most of which are far too small to provide enough wine to justify a full-scale winery, with all the investment that it would require. As a result, most growers sell their grapes, or wine that has been made in that most basic of manners, by treading, to the shippers, or through the co-operatives (see page 186).

Shippers often have long-term contracts with growers, stretching back for generations, often the only formal agreement is the shake of a hand. At vintage time a senior member of the shipping firm will visit each supplying farm to see how the harvest is progressing and talk over the problems of the year, invariably over a glass of very old tawny from the proprietor's private stock. In days gone by, when members of the shipping firm traveled by horse, only three or four farms could be visited a day. Now the car is the more normal means of transport, and they can reach up to a dozen farms.

As well as buying wine from quintas, shipping firms also own prestige properties, mainly the larger farms in the Cima Corgo and the Douro Superior. These vineyards form the backbone of the shipper's vintage blends, and in good-but-less-than-perfect years will often produce a single quinta vintage port. Single quinta wines made on shippers' quintas are listed here under the shipper, rather than under the quinta name.

Aida Coimbra Ayres De Mattos E Filhos, Lda.

Rua de Alcântara, 221
4300 Porto, Portugal

The Ayres de Mattos family has made Galafura, near Régua, its home for seven generations; they are descended from a family who lived in the region in the 1600s. The family's wines were winning awards as long ago as 1900, but the laws set in place in this century made it impossible for them to sell their wines directly, a situation that turned around when the regulations changed in 1986.

Always involved in agriculture and viticulture, the family owns a number of quintas; Quinta da Costa, Quinta das Condessas, Quinta da Laceira, Quinta de Fojo in the Douro, and another near Penafiel.

Information

Visiting *By appointment only. Tel. (351–2) 481540 (Oporto office).*

Recommended Wines *20 Years Old, Colheita de 1958.*

Overall Rating ★★

The main port quinta is Quinta da Costa, just inside the Cima Corgo. Neighboring it are a number of other vineyards, including one called Valriz, the origin of the brand name. The company itself is more commonly known as Porto Valriz. From here visitors can get one of the best panoramic views in the lower part of the Douro region, and see one of the few remaining *feitoria* markers. These are carved granite signs indicating the limit of the demarcated region, which dates from the days of Pombal. The vineyard is quite small, only about 27 acres, and in the middle is an ancient *armazem*, or winery, bearing the date "MDLXXV" (1575). An etching of this building appears on the company's labels.

The present vineyard is much newer, as all of the land has been replanted in the last 20 years using a combination of the two modern methods, patamares and vinha ao alto. The wine is made at the company's Adega do Rosca, literally the "winery of the boozer," near Régua. All wine is produced entirely by autovinification; it is then matured in the Douro region in large old vats made of chestnut wood. A small amount of very old wine, over 100 years old, is kept for blending and for very special guests. The commercial range is almost all tawny, either indicated age or colheita. A modern style of light, dry white port at 17 percent alcohol by volume is also made.

ADEGA DO ROSCA – TYPICAL OF MANY DOURO WINERIES.

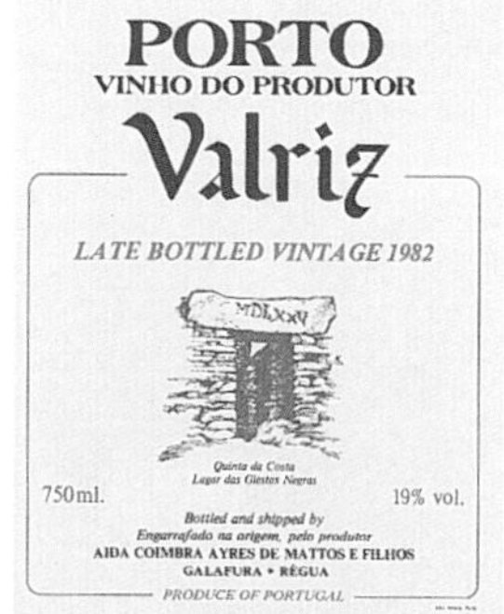

TASTING NOTES

10 YEARS OLD Vivid red-brown in color, remarkably youthful-looking. Pronounced fruity nose of raisins and plums, only slightly spirity, with a smoked ham hint. Sweet and spirity palate with reasonable fruit, but a little baked and mildly cloying. Good length and weight.

COLHEITA DE 1958 This wine, bottled in 1984, has had 26 years in cask and a further 12 in bottle at the time of this writing. Light, delicate herbal nose, with wood smoke and roasted nuts. Medium sweet with very fresh, crisp acidity. Has a fine and delicate palate, yet one with concentration and great length.

AGED TAWNY

20 YEARS OLD Like the 10-years-old equivalent, the company has – unusually – released the details of the blend. In this case it is a blend of the 1970 and 1969 vintages. Amber tawny in color, not totally clear, a certain amount of natural cloudiness, which indicates the wine has not been over-filtered. Hot and baked nose, but very pleasantly so. Not as sweet as the 10 Years Old, with a better balance of acidity and fruit. Concentrated, mature palate with a good, if spirit-dominated, finish.

PRODUCTION

 *Including Costa, Fojo, Laceira, Valriz.*

 *Not applicable.*

Sociedade Agricola Barros

Rua Sporting Club de Coimbrões, Apartado 101, 4401 Vila Nova de Gaia Codex, Portugal

This company's wines are sold under the name "Vista Alegre," which is the shipping brand of Sociedade Agricola Barros, or the Barros Agricultural Corporation. This is a totally separate company from Barros, Almeida & Ca. Vinhos, S.A. One of the newest port wine names to appear on the shelf, Vista Alegre wines were only introduced into the marketplace in 1994. Wine production by the company and its forebears, however, goes back some five generations.

INFORMATION

VISITING *Yes, to Quinta da Vista Alegre and to the lodges in Régua. Tel. (351–2) 3707252.*

RECOMMENDED WINES *Reserve Port.*

OVERALL RATING ★

Long-time landowners in the Douro, the Barros family's estates – in Pinhão, Tabuaço (on the Távora, south of the Douro), Santa Marta (near Régua) and Sabrosa (at the top of the Pinhão valley) – were taken over by the newly formed Sociedade Agricola Barros in 1973. The company's shareholders are direct descendants of the original owners, so the change brought about a new company out of a family holding, while maintaining the Barros family's involvement.

The company owns four estates: Quinta da Vista Alegre (from which the brand takes its name), Quinta de Valongo, Quinta de Vilarinho, and Quinta da Lameira. Combined, these estates supply about four-fifths of the 79,000 U.S. gallon annual production, with the remainder bought in. Lagares are used for a small volume of wine, while pumping over is used for the majority. There are still some autovinifiers here as well, but these are used only when there is an excess of production. The maturation of the wines takes place in the Douro region, with lodges situated at the quintas and in Régua. They are, therefore, one of the very few entirely Douro-based companies.

PRODUCTION

Lameira, Valongo, Vilarinho, Vista Alegre.

One-fifth of annual production.

TASTING NOTES

RESERVE PORT An old tawny, aged for some five to eight years in oak before bottling. Pale onion-skin-brown in color with a full marzipan and cooked walnut nose. Sweet, in the slightly sticky way that many of the Douro-matured ports can be, but with balanced acidity, full weight and smooth finish.

20 YEARS OLD Medium depth walnut brown color. Light nose, strongly spirity with dried fruit and wood smoke. Sweet and a little cloying but full-bodied and good flavor, if a little cooked in character.

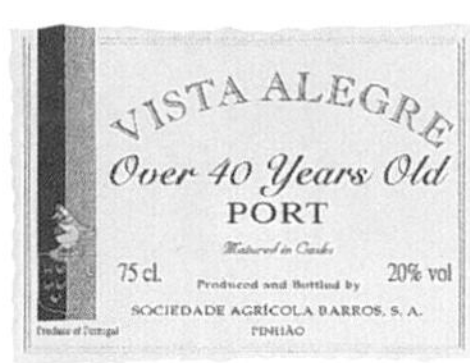

Barros, Almeida & Ca. Vinhos, S.A.

Rua D. Leonor de Freitas, 1802,
P.O. Box 39, 4401 Vila Nova
de Gaia Codex, Portugal

> **INFORMATION**
>
> **VISITING** *Yes, to the lodges. Tel. (351–2) 302320.*
>
> **RECOMMENDED WINES** *Colheita 1966.*
>
> **OVERALL RATING** ★★

Barros, Almeida is one of the largest of the Portuguese port shippers, responsible for about 6 percent of total port sales. However, it is not very well known, largely due to the diversity of its brands. Currently trading under four names – Barros, Almeida & Ca. Vinhos, S.A.; C.N. Kopke & Ca. Lda.; H. & C.J. Feist Vinhos, S.A; and Hutcheson, Feuerheerd & Associados Vinhos, S.A. (see separate entries); the company has grown through acquisitions and owns a number of companies and their brands. Rocha, Douro Wine Shippers, Vieira de Souza, A. Santos Pinto, and Almeida are all part of the group, although since 1996 the latter has been incorporated into Hutcheson, Feuerheerd & Associados Vinhos, S.A.

The company started in 1913 when Manoel de Almeida started Almeida em Comandita, a port shipping company. Almeida was joined by Manoel Barros, who is reported to have started as an office boy in the company, but married Matilde de Almeida, sister of the company's founder, and soon became a partner. The company name changed to its present title at the same time.

After Barros joined the firm it became far more aggressive in its approach. Careful management during the 1920s, and on through the Depression of the '30s, allowed Barros to buy other ailing firms. Despite the problems to trade caused by World War II, the company managed to keep afloat and it was not long after the end of hostilities that they were on the acquisition trail again, buying C. N. Kopke & Ca. Lda., who were the oldest port firm at that time.

Barros owns a number of quintas in the Douro region. The most important quinta is São Luiz, which is almost exclusively used for the Kopke brand. As well as extensive vineyards, São Luiz is the main vinification center for the Barros companies. This facility supplies about half the company's needs.

It is not surprising, given the size of the Barros production, that their main production is basic ruby and tawny wines sold to the Netherlands, France, and Belgium, where they are drunk as aperitifs. Along with the basic wines, however, they produce the old tawnies and colheitas, which date back to the mid-1930s. Their vintage wines are not as good; Barros and the companies in the group tend to declare vintage years frequently, but the wines tend to be light and mature early, even those from the best years.

Production

Including Alegria, Dona Matilde, Mesquita, São Luiz.

95% of annual production.

Tasting Notes

COLHEITA 1966 Pale tan brown color, fully mature. Full, fresh, mature nose of nuts and aged spirit. A hint of smoke and spice makes for a complex and quite interesting nose. Medium sweet with high but balanced acidity, medium weight, and great concentration of mature flavors. An excellent wine.

VINTAGE 1985 Pale garnet red, already the color of quite a mature wine, despite the concentration of the vintage. Delicate mature bouquet of dark fruit, spirit, and spice with a little of the smoke that has appeared in a number of the Barros family wines. A light palate, medium sweet with ripe tannins, and fairly concentrated fruit. An elegant wine which is at its peak now. Although it will hold for a number of years, it will not improve further. This is unusual for so hot and ripe a vintage.

Sociedade dos Vinhos Borges e Irmão, S.A.

Av. da Républica, 796, Apartado 66,
4401 Vila Nova de Gaia Codex, Portugal

Borges is a name any visitor to Portugal gets to recognize, not because of port but because of banking – the Banco Borges & Irmão is part of the same group as the wine company. Borges – the port makers – is one of Portugal's most important producers, with quintas and wine brands in many other parts of the country. Other international brands owned by the company include Gatão Vinho Verde and Trovador Rosé.

Initially a general trading company, dealing in products as diverse as currency to matches, Borges was started in the 1880s by two brothers, António and Francisco Borges. The wine trade became more important in the 1890s, but it was not until the first decade of the twentieth century that they first opened a lodge in Vila Nova de Gaia. Also at this time, they bought their first quintas, Quinta da Soalheira and Quinta do Junco.

Quinta da Soalheira, literally "noon-day heat," is in the Rio Torto valley, a long and difficult drive from the main road. The lagares here are unused, as the grapes are currently vinified at Quinta do Junco. The 10-year-old tawny carries the brand "Soalheira" (not, however, Quinta da Soalheira). Quinta do Junco and Quinta da Casa Nova, bought by Borges in 1926, are in the Pinhão valley, just upriver from Eira Velha and Foz. The premium wines, aged tawnies, and vintages, all come from these three quintas. Junco is the main vinification center for all three company quintas. Wines not made in lagares are made by autovinification. Unlike Soalheira, the Pinhão valley quintas were included in the original demarcation of the port wine region back in 1756.

Borges vintage wines tend to be light, and are meant to be consumed when young. The tawnies are a little more interesting.

INFORMATION

VISITING *The lodge in Gaia welcomes visitors; it is open Monday to Friday. Quinta visits are possible by arrangement. Tel. (351–2) 305002.*

RECOMMENDED WINES *Soalheira 10 Years Old.*

OVERALL RATING ★

Tasting Notes

WHITE Very pale lemon yellow, paler than most white ports, and looks very young. Rather neutral nose of apples and other green fruit. Off-dry palate with good acidity, making the wine refreshing. However, it lacks fruit flavor. A good base for a mixed drink.

LATE BOTTLED VINTAGE 1992 Very deep purple-ruby red with a young nose of black fruits – black currants and wild blackberries. Sweet with balanced acidity and soft tannins. Only light to medium weight, not as full as either the color or the nose might lead one to expect. A modern style of LBV meant for early consumption.

SOALHEIRA 10 YEARS OLD Deep russet brown color and a full, rich, ripe nose of dried figs and prunes. Mature yet still with some fruit. Very sweet, with only just balanced acidity. Full flavored and quite viscous in texture, which makes the wine a little cloying after the first or second glass.

Tasting Notes

RUBY

RUBY Medium ruby red with a light, youthful nose of red fruit and spirit. Sweet and slightly jammy on the palate, not as fresh as the nose suggests. Medium weight and length.

WHITE

WHITE (see page 72)

AGED TAWNY

SOALHEIRA 10 YEARS OLD
(see page 72)

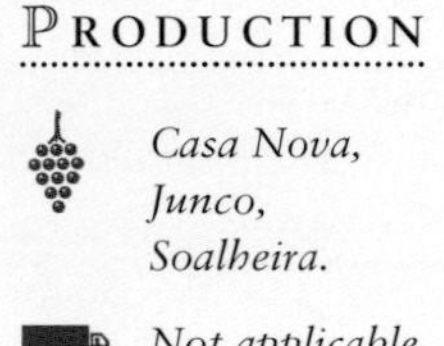

LBV

LATE BOTTLED VINTAGE 1992
(see page 72)

VINTAGE

1994 VINTAGE Deep-colored wine with a very spirit-dominated nose, rather like very young cognac. Medium- to full-bodied; medium sweet with quite firm tannins, but without huge fruit concentration. A reasonable medium-term wine.

J. W. Burmester & Ca. Lda.

Rua de Belomonte, 39–1°
4000 Porto, Portugal

Burmester is a lesser-known house that is well worth becoming familiar with. A fairly small firm, Burmester specializes in limited quantities of high-quality aged tawny port. Because they are small and still entirely in the hands of the founding family, they can afford to be meticulous in maintaining quality and tradition.

> **INFORMATION**
>
> **VISITING** *Trade and press visits only.*
>
> **RECOMMENDED WINES** *Indicated age tawnies, traditional LBVs.*
>
> **OVERALL RATING** ★★

The company was officially established in 1750, but the history of Burmester can be traced back another 20 years to 1730. As with so many of the early firms, port was not their only original product. Port became the main product in 1750; the Burmesters have, at one stage or another, been involved in insurance, navigation, shipping, and banking, and were among the founders of the National Westminster Bank in the United Kingdom.

One of the ancestors of the present family was *burgmeester* (mayor) in his hometown of Möelln, near Lübeck, in northern Germany. Escaping religious persecution, the family fled to England in the fifteenth century. It was the British section of the family that later, in 1730, established links with an Englishman named John Nash. Together they founded the firm of Burmester Nash in Portugal and set up two bases, one in London and one in Oporto. Two brothers were in charge, Edward in London and Frederic in Oporto, although at the time of the Napoleonic invasion both retired to the safety of London.

JOHANN WILHELM BURMESTER.

Johann Wilhelm Burmester took complete control of the firm in 1861 and, having become the sole owner, changed the name to its present one. The directors today include his grandchildren.

Historically, Burmester bought its grapes in the Pinhão valley and around the parish of Sabrosa. In 1991 the firm bought Quinta Nova de Nossa Senhora do Carmo, a "class A" vineyard in Sabrosa that now supplies nearly one-third of their needs. This historic vineyard covers an area of about 297 acres and has about 111 acres planted with the top five port grapes. Traditional suppliers continue to sell their grapes to Burmester, who prefer to use the grapes to make their own wine, rather than buying ready-made wine. Just under one-fifth of the wines are made by treading.

PRODUCTION

Nova de Nossa Senhora do Carmo.

Two-thirds of annual production.

The Burmester lodge is right in the heart of Vila Nova de Gaia, not far from Taylor's. Here, cleanliness is the order of the day, not just in the tasting room or in the laboratory, but throughout the building.

Burmester tawnies are among the best available. Generally lighter in style than some, the vintages appear to be suitable for early drinking, yet the 1963 is still showing very well. Burmester is one of many to claim their LBV was a first, since they produced a 1964 (and rules permitting the style were published in 1962). The Burmester LBV is the traditional style that throws a sediment and requires decanting. The 1964 vintage is still commercially available, albeit in small quantities. More recent vintages include 1982 and 1985.

QUINTA NOVA DE NOSSA SENHORA DO CARMO.

Tasting Notes

10 YEARS OLD Medium ruby red color, resembling a mature burgundy more than a tawny port, showing only a very little age. Roast nut and dark orange marmalade nose; just a hint cooked. Very sweet palate but with a cleansing acidity; rich, smooth, viscous feel to the wine, with a long finish.

OVER 40 YEARS OLD Deep amber tawny color with an intense aged and very nutty bouquet. Only slightly spirity. Medium sweet with quite low acidity, and a rich, rounded, smooth palate of nuts and dried peel.

COLHEITA 1937 Deep brown with a vivid yellow rim, like an old Madeira. Pungent, mature nose of toffee and fudge, hardly typical of port; sweet and very full. The years have concentrated the flavors, making a complex mouthful.

TASTING NOTES

LATE BOTTLED VINTAGE 1992 Massively full and very youthful nose of black currants and mint. Very sweet with firm tannins, balanced acidity, and great length. An outstanding wine (though the sweetness might become cloying after a few glasses if consumed without food) and one to keep for a few years to enjoy at its best.

LATE BOTTLED VINTAGE 1964 This vintage-quality wine has been in cask for five years instead of two. Garnet red in color, showing considerable maturity, with a mature but remarkably fruity nose and with some spirit and spice. Silky-soft palate with just a hint of residual tannin and an enormously long, delicate length.

VINTAGE 1991 Medium to deep ruby with a very open, pronounced nose of sweet, ripe fruit and molasses. Rich, sweet style, with soft fruit and only moderate tannins and balanced acids. Not unpleasant now, but will be much better in another five or ten years. Not a great long-term wine, however.

TASTING NOTES

AGED TAWNY

10 YEARS OLD (see page 76)

20 YEARS OLD Medium orange-red tawny color with a clean, aged, nutty and slightly perfumed fruit character, with hints of smoke and caramel. Medium sweet; spirit not too obvious and a long, nutty finish. One of the very best 20-year-old tawnies tasted.

OVER 40 YEARS OLD
(see page 76)

COLHEITA

COLHEITA 1987 Tasted alongside the 10-year-old tawny, this wine was somewhat less complex, with a toffee and fruit nose carrying hints of roast nuts. Very sweet and quite thick in the mouth. A very full-flavored port.

COLHEITA 1937 (see page 76)

LBV

LATE BOTTLED VINTAGE 1992
(see page 77)

LATE BOTTLED VINTAGE 1985 It is interesting to compare the LBV and vintage wines from the same house and vintage, especially since this LBV has had a reasonable degree of bottle age. The LBV is, as might be expected, more forward; garnet rather than ruby, with a full, completely mature nose of spice and dried fruit rather than the plummy hints of a young wine. The tannins are softer than in the vintage, and the wine generally lighter, but they are both good-quality wines within their respective classes.

LATE BOTTLED VINTAGE 1964
(see page 77)

VINTAGE

VINTAGE 1994 Medium to deep ruby color with a rich, ripe, and very open nose for a wine so young. Sweet, ripe, plummy fruit on the palate with relatively soft tannins. A wine for medium-term drinking rather than the long haul.

VINTAGE 1991 (see page 77)

VINTAGE 1985 Medium-depth ruby color with only the slightest hint of maturity showing; not as deep a wine as some. Intense, rich nose of dark chocolate and plums, with a little wood smoke as well. Sweeter than medium but with enough acidity to balance it, and a strong backbone of tannin, more so than the color implies. Powerful and concentrated fruit, but not a blockbuster. Very good wine for the medium to long term.

VINTAGE 1970 One of the lighter wines from this outstanding vintage; already fully mature with raisins and dates on the nose. Sweet with moderate acidity and negligible tannin, and with good fruit concentration on the palate. Good now, if lighter than some; without potential for further development.

VINTAGE 1963 Pale to medium depth, clearly mature, with a spice and raisin nose. Medium sweet to sweet palate with very soft tannins; a silky feel to the palate that comes of long aging. This wine is good now and will not improve, but is unlikely to fade too soon.

VINHO DO PORTO
VINTAGE
1992

BOTTLED IN 1994
BOTTLED AND SHIPPED BY
J. W. BURMESTER & CA., LDA.
PORTO - PORTUGAL
750 ML PRODUCT OF PORTUGAL ALC 20% BY VOL.

BURMESTER
OPORTO
VINHO DO PORTO
VINTAGE 1985
EXTRA
SELECTED

BOTTLED AND SHIPPED BY
J. W. BURMESTER & CA., LDA.
750 ML. BOTTLED 1987 Alc. 20% by vol.
Product of Portugal

A. A. Cálem & Filho, Lda.

Rua da Reboleira, 7–4000
Porto Portugal

> ## INFORMATION
>
> **VISITING** *The lodges are open to visitors throughout the year. Tel. (351–2) 2004867. (The correct way to pronounce the name is something like "Car-laign," rather than "Kale-em.")*
>
> **RECOMMENDED WINES** *Vintage 1970 and 1994, colheitas.*
>
> **OVERALL RATING** ★★

Port is only one of many Cálem (pronounced something like "Car-laign," rather than "Kale-em") interests; others include numerous other drinks agencies, other Portuguese wines, and even the local agency for Ferrari sports cars. The present head of the company, Joaquim Cálem, is the direct descendant of the Cálems who founded the port firm in 1859.

It is often said that the heart of the Douro region is the area around Pinhão. If this is the case, then Cálem is in an ideal position, since the best of their wines are sourced from Quinta da Foz. *Foz* is Portuguese for "confluence," or river mouth, and this quinta is right on the corner where the River Pinhão flows into the Douro. The quinta was reduced in size very slightly to make way for the railroad, and today guests enjoying a quiet dinner on the quinta terrace are often surprised by the appearance of one of the occasional Douro trains, so close one might be on the station platform. Quinta da Foz is sold as a single quinta vintage in less-than-great years.

Adjoining Foz, and also owned by Cálem, are the quintas Sagrado, Santo António, and Vedial. These, as well as Foz, have been undergoing considerable renovation as the old terraces have been bulldozed to make way for patamares. Once it is fully operational, this collection of vineyards will be able to supply the firm with over 300 pipes of class A wine, one of only a handful of single sites to be able to produce so much.

These top quintas supply only about one-tenth of the total production; as a large producer, Cálem has to buy in grapes from a number of different growers. The

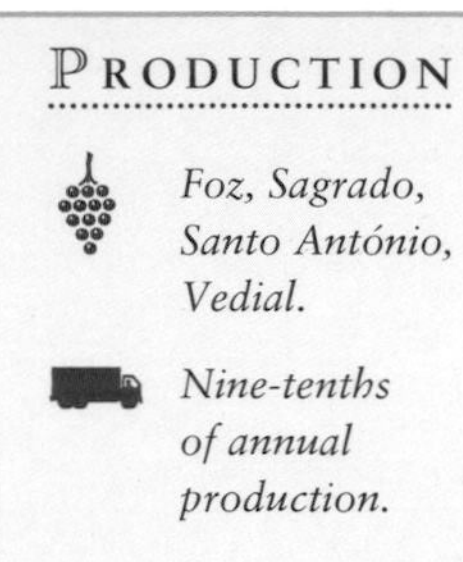

quinta wines are trodden by foot, but most of the purchased grapes are processed at Santo Martinho de Anta, not far from the famous Mateus palace about 15 miles away. This is a modern winery with easy access for the grape trucks. It is equipped with stainless steel remontagem vats and concrete autovinifiers, which still make over half the wine.

In the late 1980s and early 1990s, wine making and blending were under the control of Jeremy Bull, formerly of Taylor's, where he had spent most of his career. Jeremy has now retired, but his influence will continue to be felt, particularly in the 1994 vintage that he was in charge of making (but not blending). This vintage is currently showing very well.

Some excellent vintages have been produced, and Cálem has made a specialty of colheitas, but the majority of the company's sales are in the categories rated as "current" ports by the IVP. Cálem's biggest market is Portugal itself, where they have the largest single brand, Velhotes.

Like Sandeman, Cálem is one of the first shippers most tourists in Oporto visit, as their lodge is the first one reached after crossing the lower level of the Dom Luis Bridge. In the past this made for easy transfer of the wine from the boats to the lodge – no steep cobbled streets for the ox carts to negotiate to reach Cálem, just a short journey over the road. Taking advantage of their position, Cálem has established a sharp public relations campaign by offering guided tours around the lodge. Visitors to the lodge are shown one of the real disadvantages of working here: flood marks on the lodge wall, some well over head height, and some very recent. The stands for the pipes in the lower part of the lodge are equipped with hooks and chains that can anchor the casks when floods are predicted.

QUINTA DA FOZ.

Tasting Notes

10 YEARS OLD Medium to deep orange-brown, still quite youthful looking. Full, dried fruit and spirit nose, not as mature as some 10 year olds, but with a full, sweet palate, balanced acidity, and good length. A very well made, if uncomplicated, wine.

COLHEITA 1987 Pale topaz orange; very bright. Light and fresh nose, really not giving much away. Everything is there on the palate, however. Full, powerful flavors of marizipan and almond oil, medium sweet with very crisp acidity, which is still in balance.

LATE BOTTLED VINTAGE 1990 Deep ruby red, full fruitcake nose, quite youthful but complex. Sweet, fresh palate with firm, ripe tannins and a great length. This, like most, is an LBV to be consumed when bottled. (A bottle that was stored accidentally for a few years faded dramatically.)

Tasting Notes

QUINTA DA FOZ 1992 Very deep purple red with a closed nose. Fullish palate with huge tannic structure, on the drier side. Full fruit, with plums and vanilla. Good length. Not as good as the 1994; a wine for the mid-term.

VINTAGE 1994 Very deep purple color. Full and very open, if slightly spirity nose, very intense black fruit on nose and palate. Full-bodied with a very firm structure. Great weight and length; a wine that will be excellent in years to come – one to keep. (Bottle shown is a tasting sample.)

VINTAGE 1970 Still very youthful color, less developed than many 1970s. Deep ruby red with a touch of maturation on the rim. Very open, intense nose of fruit and spice, with just a hint of spirit. Full, more mature palate; medium sweet with crisp acidity and still remarkably firm tannin. A very long finish.

Tasting Notes

RUBY

FINE RUBY Medium depth, vibrant ruby red color with wonderfully young, fresh fruit flavors; soft, red fruits like cherry and raspberry rather than the dark fruits so often found. Medium sweet and well-balanced palate. Good for its type (the sample was straight off the bottling line and very fresh). Wines of this sort do not keep and lose their freshness fairly rapidly.

VINTAGE CHARACTER This is a serious ruby, quite deep garnet in color and with a fruit and spice nose showing some maturity. Medium sweet and rounded with soft tannins and balanced acidity, and a very good length for a wine of this level. Very conveniently Cálem has brought this wine out in a small-sized bottle, under the brand "Port for Two."

WHITE

FINE WHITE Pale-colored white port with a youthful, if rather nondescript nose: slightly fruity and floral, but difficult to pin down. Medium-dry style with balanced acidity and a reasonable length.

TAWNY

VELHOTES Aged for about five or six years, this is a pale garnet ruby with a fresh fruit nose and palate. Medium sweet and medium-bodied with low tannin and balanced acidity. A pleasant, easy-drinking style of port.

AGED TAWNY

10 YEARS OLD (see page 81)

COLHEITA

COLHEITA 1987 (see page 81)

COLHEITA 1962 Fully brown, as expected; intense, mature nose of old wood, spice, and nuts, slightly musty quality as well. Sweet but not cloying, good acidity, and great concentration of flavor. Excellent.

LBV

LATE BOTTLED VINTAGE 1990 (see page 81)

SINGLE QUINTA VINTAGE

QUINTA DA FOZ 1992 (see page 82)

QUINTA DA FOZ 1990 Slightly baked, cooked fruit on the nose and palate make this wine less attractive than some of the other vintages. It does, however, have a good concentration of slightly jammy fruit and a moderately powerful structure that will keep it for some years.

VINTAGE

VINTAGE 1994 (see page 82)

VINTAGE 1991 Medium depth; open, ripe nose of chocolate and fresh fruit. Medium to full weight and clean, fresh-tasting palate with a good length. Remarkably pleasant now, this wine needs a further 10 years or so to be at its best. It is not the long-term keeper that the 1994 is, however.

VINTAGE 1985 This wine seems to be going through a very dumb phase. It was hard work to get any characteristics off the nose at all, and the palate seemed remarkably light, almost austere. And yet there is concentration. The color is still very deep, and there are firm tannins giving a powerful structure.

VINTAGE 1970 (see page 82)

Churchill Graham, Lda.

Rua da Fonte Nova, 5
4400 Vila Nova de Gaia, Portugal

> **INFORMATION**
>
> **VISITING** *To lodges by appointment, and for small groups only. Tel. (351–2) 3703641.*
>
> **RECOMMENDED WINES** *White, Traditional LBV.*
>
> **OVERALL RATING** ★★

Most of the companies – and the producers – discussed in this book have long traditions. Even the single quinta ports, which have only recently hit the market, have histories that go back hundreds of years. In contrast, Churchill Graham is the new kid on the block.

Johnny Graham, of the family that once owned British shipper W. & J. Graham & Co., took the brave decision to leave his relatively safe employment at Cockburn's to set up his own port house in 1981. (It had been more than 50 years since a new British company had entered the market.) Graham wanted to produce port in the traditional manner, with an emphasis on quality rather than quantity. But almost immediately, he clashed with the Symington group over the use of the name "Graham" on the labels, as Graham's is one of Symington's best brands. The solution was to call the company Churchill Graham but to label the wines "Churchill," after his wife Caroline Churchill.

Initially the firm ran on very tight finances, buying in all their wine and maturing it in a small lodge rented from the Taylor-Fonseca group. The quality of the wines soon showed and the venture deserves to do very well.

As yet Churchill does not own any quintas, but buys their grapes from three premium sites. The backbone of the Churchill blend comes from Quinta da Manuela, a southwest-facing vineyard in the upper Pinhão valley; the south-facing Quinta do Água Alta, on the north bank of the river Douro at Ferrão, and the third main supplier is Quinta do Fojo, also in the Pinhão valley.

Since the company started only a relatively few years ago, there are no truly old Churchill ports on the market. A 10-year-old tawny has just been released, but up until now there have been only whites and reds, vintages, and LBVs available. As a note of interest, repeated tastings of some of the early vintages have revealed a significant degree of bottle variation. Some were quite volatile, so much so that the character was masked.

Tasting Notes

WHITE Deep amber in color, with a full, rich nose of dried peel and honey. The palate is dry, with intense fruit and a very long length. Best served chilled, but not too cold or the flavor will be numbed. This makes an interesting pre-dinner drink or accompaniment to a not-too-sweet dessert.

1987 VINTAGE QUINTA DA AGUA ALTA Still very deep-colored, with a pungent smell of plums and figs and just a vague hint of leather. Beginning to come around but still youthful; capable of a good few years of further aging.

1991 VINTAGE Very deep-colored wine with a slightly spirity nose of ripe damson plums. Fairly soft, open style with quite firm tannin, which will preserve the wine for the medium term.

Tasting Notes

WHITE

WHITE (see page 85)

LBV

TRADITIONAL LBV 1990
Remarkably good value for the money; fuller and more complex than most LBVs of the same price. Still very deep in color, almost black in the core with a narrow purple-ruby rim. This plummy wine has enough tannic structure to permit some aging, although it is exceptionally fine for drinking now.

SINGLE QUINTA VINTAGE

1987 VINTAGE QUINTA DA AGUA ALTA (see page 85)

1986 VINTAGE QUINTA DO FOJO
Already quite pale with red fruit hints on the nose; medium sweet with only a little tannin remaining. Johnny Graham calls this a "pretty" wine, not an adjective often applied to port, but true in this case. Pleasant now; unlikely to develop further.

VINTAGE

1994 VINTAGE Medium depth of color and weight with a leaner, more austere, slightly less ripe fruit character than some, but with firm tannin and a good length. A medium-term wine for those who want a less gutsy but perhaps more elegant style of port.

1991 VINTAGE (see page 85)

1985 VINTAGE A particular Churchill's favorite so far. Very rich and ripe with the upfront fruit of the vintage, but with enough structure to allow it to age. This is eminently drinkable now, but will reward long cellarage.

JOHNNY GRAHAM.

Not applicable.

Buy from Agua Alta, Fojo, Manuela.

Cockburn Smithes & Ca. S.A.

Rua das Corados, 13, Apartado 20
4401 Vila Nova de Gaia Codex, Portugal

Established in 1815, Cockburn's is hardly known in Portugal. However, Cockburn's is the brand leader for the United Kingdom market, accounting for over one-third of all port sold, more than five times its nearest rival.

Exports have always been important to Cockburn's. The first London office was set up by the founder's sons only 15 years after Cockburn's was established. Robert Cockburn, son of a Scottish judge, originally set up the company as Cockburn Wauchope & Co., a name it retained only until 1854, when one member of the Smithes family, Henry, became a partner in Oporto. He soon returned to the London office, but his younger brother, John T. Smithes, stayed in Portugal. The Smithes were in charge of the Portuguese side of the company until John Henry Smithes retired in 1971, although he was so involved with the business that he stayed on as a consultant for a further dozen years. John Smithes has always been held in great regard by the growers he has dealt with and by his competitors, who consider him as having one of the finest palates in the trade.

> ### INFORMATION
>
> **VISITING** *The lodges can be visited Monday to Friday between 9:30 and 5:00. Telephone first. (Visitors traveling by taxi should note that Cockburn's is not well known locally; most Oporto cab drivers will try to take you to one of the waterfront lodges instead.) You can also visit the vineyards in the Douro; by appointment only. Tel. (351–2) 3794031.*
>
> **RECOMMENDED WINES** *Most vintages.*
>
> **OVERALL RATING** ★★★

The third family in Cockburn's history is the Cobbs. Frederick Cobb joined the London company in 1863, and by 1939 Reggie Cobb was running the company's Oporto branch along with John Smithes. There are neither Cockburn nor Smithes descendants on the staff these days, but Peter Cobb, nephew to Reggie, is still a Cockburn's director.

Cockburn's became part of Harvey's of Bristol, the wine merchant and sherry shipper, in 1962, a year after Harvey's had acquired Martinez Gassiot. The two companies merged and are now run as essentially the same company. However, each has its own range of wines, which are marketed separately. Both Harvey's and Cockburn's are part of Allied

QUINTA DOS CANAIS.

Domecq Spirits and Wines – one of the biggest companies in the world drinks industry – giving Cockburn's access to an enviable international distribution network.

For many years the backbone of Cockburn's vintages has been Quinta dos Canais, a spectacular farm at the lower end of the Douro Superior, not far past Valeira and just opposite Taylor's Vargellas. A vast quinta, once the venue for shooting parties and lavish balls, Canais is difficult to reach by road. Visitors are usually brought here by boat, a reminder of the days when the river was so vital to the trade. Canais was bought in 1942 by Sr. Sobral, who sold his wine to Cockburn's. In 1989 he retired, and Cockburn's bought the property to protect their supplies. Nearly two-thirds of the vines were over 25 years old, and therefore on old terraces. A replanting program was immediately established both to increase production from under 100 pipes to over 300, and to reduce costs by installing patamar terraces.

Quinta do Tua, in the Cima Corgo, has been in the company far longer. Now one of Cockburn's "wine centers," or central wineries that process grapes bought in from other vineyards, Tua was bought from Dona Antónia Ferreira in 1889 after its output had been annihilated by phylloxera. Soon after buying it, John Smithes began experimenting with different grafting and pruning methods as well as different grape varieties. Tua is thus considered to be one of the earliest experimental vineyards in the region.

QUINTA DO TUA.

There are half a dozen other vineyards on the company's books, but the most impressive for any student of viticulture is Atayde. Heading up toward the Spanish frontier, Atayde is in a wide valley, allowing vines to be planted without terraces. Since it is virtually flat here, mechanization is possible to an extent not even considered elsewhere – to the point of attempting mechanical harvesting (though without much success). This vineyard is particularly healthy, having been planted with specially grown virus-free stock.

About 10 percent of the wine produced is trodden by foot, mostly where wine is bought from small growers. Unusually, Cockburn's installs full time technicians from Gaia to supervise the wine making at each quinta for the duration of the vintage, which ensures the best possible product. Autovinifiers, the self-circulating vats beloved of many, are not used at all. The company's view is that autovinification takes control away from the winemaker. The remaining 90 percent of the wine is therefore produced by remontagem, mechanical pumping over. However, other methods have been tried.

The rotary "vinimatic," a machine that mixes the fermenting must and grape skins with a movement rather like that of a cement mixer, had limited success but thermoextraction, whereby the grapes are heated briefly to help extract color, is used for some of the rubies.

Cockburn's excels at making large volume, reliable mass-market wines in huge quantities. Fine ruby, tawny, and the vintage character brand Special Reserve are excellent examples of their class. Cockburn's also makes relatively small volumes of premium wines, vintages, and aged tawnies, which can be among the best.

Cockburn's has made some very odd decisions about vintage declarations in the past. They preferred the 1967 to the 1966, and never sold any 1977, which was a classic vintage year. More recently they have been largely in line with the rest of the pack, declaring 1983, 1985, a single quinta vintage from Tua in 1987, a 1991, another single quinta wine from Canais in 1992, and a full vintage in 1994.

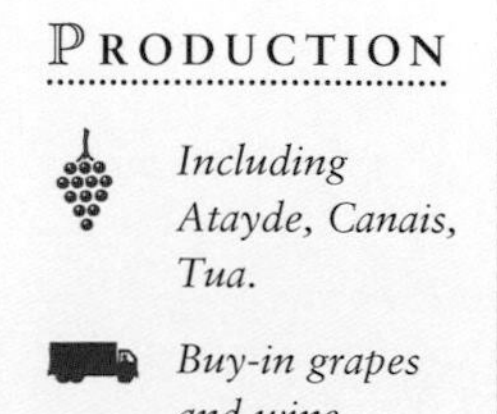

PRODUCTION

Including Atayde, Canais, Tua.

Buy-in grapes and wine.

COCKBURN'S FLAGSHIP BRAND, SPECIAL RESERVE.

Tasting Notes

SPECIAL RESERVE This is Cockburn's flagship brand that carries the slogan: "Always special, so why reserve it." It is among the top sellers in all of Cockburn's markets. More youthful and fruity than many vintage character wines; a soft, fruity wine with a nose of cooked plums and light fruit jam, without any hint of being baked.

10 YEARS OLD Orange-tawny in color, still fairly red, with a full fruit and nut nose of figs, raisins, and almonds; a little more spirity than the red ports. The jump in quality between fine tawny and this is enormous, and for a relatively small increase in price.

ANNO LATE BOTTLED VINTAGE 1992 At the time of this writing the vintage was changing from 1990 to 1992. The 1990 is truly brown at the rim and showing considerable bottle age. Previous tastings have shown this to be a good wine, but it is tiring now. The 1992 has medium depth only, is still very young with red fruit flavors, and has fairly low tannins.

TASTING NOTES

RUBY

SPECIAL RESERVE (see page 90)

TAWNY

FINE TAWNY Fine tawny is usually uninteresting in the extreme as it is a simple blend of ruby and white ports. Bought fresh, since this is not a wine to age, Cockburn's is a medium-sweet wine with enough flavor to put it above most of its peers. Refreshingly fruity; pale pink rather than brown, with a raspberry and toffee nose. Not a great wine, but a very good example of its type.

AGED TAWNY

10 YEARS OLD
(see page 90)

LBV

ANNO LATE BOTTLED VINTAGE 1992 (see page 90)

SINGLE QUINTA VINTAGE

QUINTA DO TUA 1987 VINTAGE Still very closed; ripe plum character with some chocolate. An excellent wine for medium-term drinking, probably coming around in the first decade of the twenty-first century.

VINTAGE

1994 VINTAGE Moderately deep color with better than average intensity on the nose, with a fruity plum and blackberry character. The palate gives more than the nose, fuller and riper than expected. Medium to sweet with a firm grip of tannin and balanced acidity. This wine will still be drinking well in 25 or 30 years' time. One of the best of the 1994s.

1991 VINTAGE A less than great vintage from Cockburn's; slightly vegetal and not up to the usual standards.

1985 AND 1983 VINTAGE Of these two concentrated wines, the 1985 is preferred – it is big and full, yet with the pungent richness of the vintage that makes it rather too drinkable now. Both wines should be kept until about 2000 to 2010.

1975 VINTAGE These generally should have been consumed by now. Never great wines, they have reached their best. They will certainly not improve, but rather will start to disintegrate shortly.

1970 VINTAGE Still doing very well and now fully mature. Garnet in color with a fine mature nose and moderately firm palate. Not the best 1970 vintage but good all the same.

1967 VINTAGE Only a few shippers preferred 1967 to 1966; oddly, Cockburn's was one. The wines are still attractive, if rather delicate and fragile. They should be consumed now.

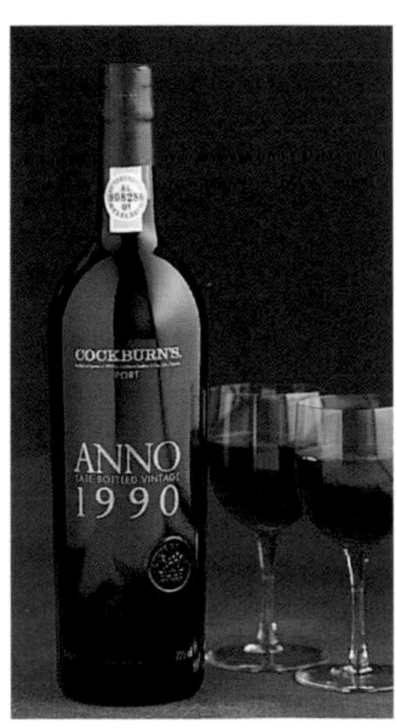

COCKBURN'S CALL THEIR LBV, "ANNO."

Croft & Ca. Lda.

Largo de Joaquim Magalhães, 23
Apartado 5, 4401 Vila Nova de
Gaia Codex, Portugal

With a history dating back to 1678, Croft is one of the oldest of the port firms. The Croft family, originally from Lancashire, England, can trace their lineage back more than seven centuries. The wine trade connection only started when they became connected, through marriage, to the Thomsons of York, who were already trading with Portugal.

The first Croft to become involved in the wine trade was Thomas, who married Frances Thomson. It was their third son, John, who established the port firm. John had no heirs but his nephews all joined the firm, keeping the name alive.

> **INFORMATION**
>
> **VISITING** *Available to the trade only.*
>
> **RECOMMENDED WINES** *Distinction, 20 Years Old.*
>
> **OVERALL RATING** ★★

The Croft family has produced a number of influential people. John Croft wrote *A Treatise on the Wines of Portugal*, published in 1788. This was the classic book of its day, remaining the most important book on the subject until this century. His son, also John Croft, was of invaluable help to Wellington during the Peninsular War, in recognition of which he became a baronet.

Fame and titles do not bring wealth; that comes from hard work and shrewd business sense. The Crofts were not lacking in either of these qualities. By the early part of the nineteenth century Croft was one of the top four exporters of port. Even at this early stage Croft began developing markets other than Britain; America, France, and the Benelux countries were already important customers. The international trade continues, with brands available worldwide, largely the benefit of being part of a major drinks group. In 1911 Croft became part of Gilbeys, who have since become part of International Distillers and Vintners (IDV).

Quinta da Roêda, the company's flagship quinta, has been described as the diamond set in the golden ring that is the Douro River. It is located immediately east of the town of Pinhão, right in the heart of the Cima Corgo. The quinta was established in 1811 and brought by Taylor's in 1844; it passed to Croft in 1875. Its reputation has been excellent since the Taylor's days, and some single quinta vintages are available. It is a large, terraced vineyard, but on a more gentle slope than most, so that on some of the very widest terraces it seems like a conventional vineyard.

The quinta house, a small version of the tea planters' style of bungalow at Quinta do Bomfim, is on the lower slopes, not far from the river. Between the house and the river are lawns and the winery. Here grapes, both from the quinta and bought in from Ribalonga and Vale de Mendiz, are processed. Lagares are used only for small, experimental batches; mechanical pumping over dominates all the commercial production here.

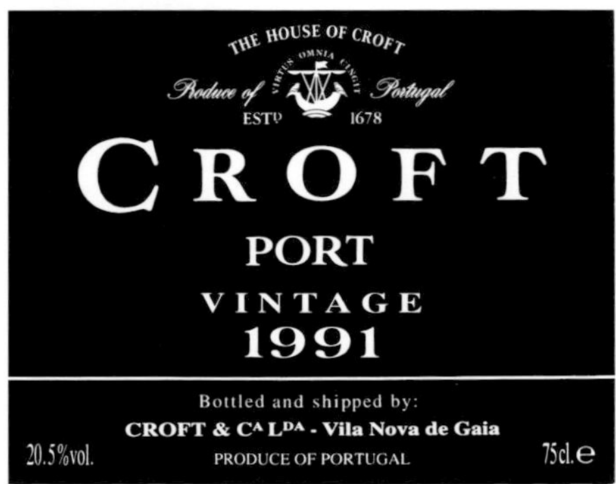

Tasting Notes

LATE BOTTLED VINTAGE
Experience has shown that this is one of the more consistent LBVs, not varying very much from one vintage to another. Croft produces a modern, filtered LBV; deep ruby in color, with a rich fruitcake and spice nose. Full generous palate with good weight; medium sweet with enough acidity to give it balance.

QUINTA DA ROÊDA 1983
Medium to pale ruby garnet color with a fuller nose than the Croft 1975; very mature for a wine so young. Dried fruit with figs and dates and noticeable spirit. Medium-bodied and medium sweet with some light tannins remaining. A pleasant enough wine that will hold for a further few years.

VINTAGE 1991 Medium depth of color but, of course, very purple. Ripe damson plum fruit; still very closed. Not overly intense tannins, but a firm and elegant structure. Powerful fruit on the palate, which will make a good medium-term wine.

Tasting Notes

AGED TAWNY

DISTINCTION The company's premium tawny brand, aged for about eight years before bottling. No age or date is given on the bottle. A red-tawny hue with a full nose that has just enough maturity to be interesting, while still retaining the rich fruit of youth. Medium weight with a full fruit and nut palate and a long length. Distinction is a reliable brand of tawny, one of the better wines in its class.

10 YEARS OLD Really quite young-looking wine, red-orange rather than tawny, with hazelnut and dried fruit character. Medium weight with moderately intense fruit and a reasonable length.

20 YEARS OLD Altogether a more serious wine than the 10 Years Old. Still redder than some of the competition, but a fully mature nose and much more intense palate of dried figs and dates, with almond or marzipan character.

LBV

LATE BOTTLED VINTAGE
(see page 94)

SINGLE QUINTA VINTAGE

QUINTA DA ROÊDA 1983
(see page 94)

VINTAGE

VINTAGE 1994 One of the paler 1994s, already ruby rather than purple. Fairly light, forward, and open nose of black currants and pepper. Very sweet, surprisingly so, with very firm tannins. A strange combination of a very intense palate, yet a short finish – perhaps the wine is just going through a phase. A wine for the medium to long term .

VINTAGE 1991 (see page 94)

VINTAGE 1985 Another wine developing quite soon. Deep ruby-garnet red with a rich, fruitcake-like nose, very open, which seems to be characteristic of the whole vintage at the moment. It has soft tannins and medium acidity. Drinking well now but will improve for a few more years; however it is not as long-lived as many examples of the vintage.

VINTAGE 1982 In this split vintage, Croft chose '82 for the full vintage and '83 for the single quinta wine from Roêda. The 1982 is already looking quite old, pink in color and quite pale, with a soft nose of raisins and petals. The palate delivers more than the nose implies, medium-sweet with very soft tannins, but good levels of acidity and quite a full flavor, if rather light on structure. At its peak now, this is unlikely to improve dramatically, but it will hold.

VINTAGE 1975 Pale garnet red in color with a very mature nose, slightly high-toned and volatile, with mature dried fruit and spirit. Medium sweet with balanced acids and soft tannin, and a reasonable length. This wine is fully ready now, and has been for the last few years. It will not improve any further and should be consumed before it fades.

VINTAGE 1927 Pale orange-pink, not in any way brown; full and, of course, mature nose with floral characteristics. Sweet and very fragile palate, creamy and silky, with very little noticeable tannin with the soft acidity. Great length of flavor. This wine is not going to improve, but it has lasted nearly 70 years so far. If you have some, there is no rush to drink it up, unlike some of the more recent vintages. This was tasted in 1993 through the generosity of Mr. Peter Hasslacher of Deinhard Ltd.

Roêda.

Buy from Reibalonga and Vale de Mendiz.

Delaforce Sons & Ca. – Vinhos, Lda.

Largo de Joaquim Magalhães, 23
Apartado 6, 4401 Vila Nova de
Gaia Codex, Portugal

Now part of International Distillers and Vintners (IDV), along with the firm Croft, Delaforce was founded in 1868 by George Henry Delaforce, the son of John Fleurriet Delaforce, who had joined the port trade in 1834 as a worker in the lodge of Martinez Gassiot. George Henry Delaforce established the business and began trading with many other European countries, including Russia, England, Ireland, Germany, France, and Scandinavian countries. The company of Delaforce Sons & Ca. was started in 1903 when Henry and Reginald Delaforce took over the company.

Information

Visiting *Trade only, by appointment, to the lodges. Tel. (351-2) 302212.*

Recommended Wines *His Eminence's Choice Tawny.*

Overall Rating ★★

As is so often the case in port firms, the family links have been maintained, even through international takeovers and mergers. The current managing director of port brands for IDV is David Delaforce, who is responsible for the marketing of both Croft and Delaforce in the world marketplace. His son, Nicholas, the sixth generation of the Huguenot family to be involved in the firm, is a port blender.

Delaforce does not own vineyards. Instead, they have a long-term contract and exclusive rights to Quinta da Corte, a dramatic vineyard in the Rio Torto, just downriver from Ramos Pinto's Bom Retiro. Corte is mostly walled terraces, with both old and new styles being used. Because of its position – on one side of a narrow valley – and the immaculate state of its vineyards, pictures of the vineyard appear in almost every book and leaflet about port to illustrate perfectly the kind of terrain that the vineyards are in and the problems of working them.

Currently, Delaforce vintages tend to be medium-term wines, although some of the older wines are still showing very well. The wines are available in most markets, but are particularly strong in Germany, where they are the market leader. Other important markets are the Netherlands and the United Kingdom, as well as the United States.

TASTING NOTES

QUINTA DA CORTE 1984 VINTAGE Now showing some age on the rim, with a spicy fruit nose and light palate. Good grip of tannin and a long, elegant finish.

1985 VINTAGE Still quite deep with very open and full nose; much more forthcoming than many at the moment. Ripe, hot palate with reasonably high but ripe tannins, and good power of flavor.

THE DELAFORCE LODGE IN VILA NOVA DE GAIA.

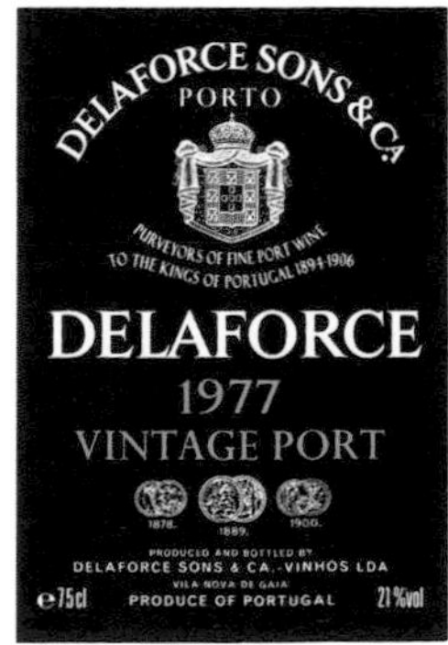

GRAPES FOR THE PREMIUM PORTS ARE GROWN AT QUINTA DA CORTE.

TASTING NOTES

AGED TAWNY

HIS EMINENCE'S CHOICE TAWNY The company's flagship brand. Aged for about eight years in cask, it is only just freeing itself of the ruddiness of youth. Slightly high-toned nose of exotic spices combined with a sweetish, fairly full, and complex palate make it a particularly pleasant drink.

LBV

LBV Dark ruby in color; full, rich body and flavor with reasonable fruit. Not a wine to keep, but a good example of its type.

SINGLE QUINTA VINTAGE

QUINTA DA CORTE 1991 VINTAGE Medium depth of color; full, rich nose of plums and chocolate, plus a little smoke. Ripe, sweet palate with softer tannins than expected, and a good length.

QUINTA DA CORTE 1984 VINTAGE (see page 97)

VINTAGE

1994 VINTAGE Very intense black core with the narrowest of rims; however, nose and palate not up to the promise of the depth of color. Moderately powerful only on the palate; fairly light and fruity on the nose. An elegant wine for the medium term.

1992 VINTAGE Moderate depth of color with an intensely plummy and very open nose; already developing. Full and sweet palate with firm tannins and a good length.

1985 VINTAGE (see page 97)

Not applicable.

Quinta da Corte is their main supplier.

H. & C.J. Feist – Vinhos, S.A.

Rua D. Leonor de Freitas, 180/2,
P.O. Box 39, 4401 Vila Nova de
Gaia Codex, Portugal

Feist was set up in London as a port trading firm under the name H. & C. J. Feist by two German cousins, in 1836. By 1870 the business had expanded to the extent that a Portuguese office was required and Carl (C. J.) Feist moved to Oporto to set up a new branch of the company. The Portuguese half of the company remained very much a family business with the son-in-law and later the grandson of the founder being directors in their turn.

INFORMATION

VISITING *Yes, to the lodges. Tel. (351–2) 302320.*

RECOMMENDED WINES *1963 Colheita.*

OVERALL RATING ★

During World War II the London office was destroyed in an air raid. So bad was the damage that it never reopened, leaving just the Portuguese end of the business. Trading as H. & C. J. Feist – Vinhos, S.A., it was later taken over by Barros, Almeida, one of the largest of the port wine groups (see page 69). Feist has now become a brand within the company; it does not enjoy the autonomy of its sister company Kopke.

The vast majority of grapes for Feist wines are bought in; only a very small amount come from the company's own Quinta da Fonte Santa, which adjoins Kopke's Quinta de São Luiz. Like its sister companies, the Feist specialty is colheita, with a long list of wines available, dating back to the 1937 harvest. As with Barros, Almeida itself, vintages tend to be declared frequently – six were declared in the 1980s, and are early-maturing wines.

PRODUCTION

Fonte Santa.

Buy-in majority of their grapes.

Tasting Notes

20 YEARS OLD Pale orange color, very bright. Light nose of smoke and candied peel. Sweet and cloying palate where the sweetness dominates, only held up with the alcohol. Lacks fruit.

1963 COLHEITA Dark walnut brown color with a full, mature, and very oxidative nose. Spirit, roast nuts, and dried fruit, along with toffee or fudge. Very sweet and toffee-like on the palate but with balanced acidity and great concentration of flavor. Good long finish. Big, gutsy, and powerful, if lacking a little elegance.

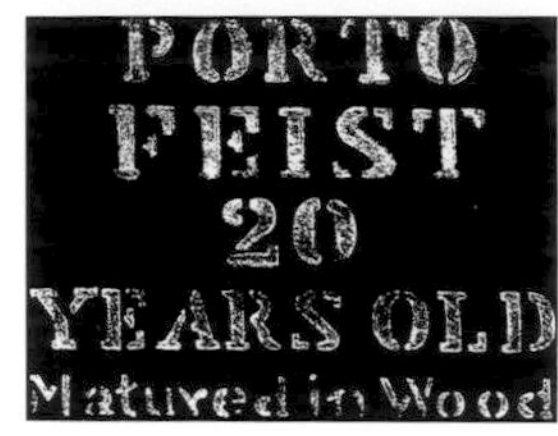

A.A. Ferreira S.A.

Postal Address
P.O. Box 3002, 4301 PORTO CODEX
Offices and lodges
19/105 Rua da Carvalhosa – 4400
Vila Nova de Gaia, Portugal

Ferreira is among the greats of the port world. An enviable collection of vineyards and a long history of viticulture put the company in the ideal position to produce premium-quality wines.

The vineyard holding predated the formation of the shipping company; growers first and shippers later; the shipping firm was established in the middle of the eighteenth century by José Ferreira. José's life reportedly came to an end by way of a bullet from Napoleonic troops, who heard his fluent French and mistook him for a deserter. José's sons, José and António Barnado, extended the vineyard holdings considerably, laying a better foundation for the firm. But it was one of their descendants, Dona Antónia Adelaide Ferreira, who built up the company's reputation to what it is today. Dona Antónia, nicknamed Ferreirinha, or "little Ferreira," was the grande dame of the port industry and Portugal's answer to Veuve Nicole-Barbe Clicquot-Ponsardin, one of the most famous names in the Champagne industry.

Information

Visiting *The lodge is open all year Monday to Friday from 9:30 to 5:00 (closed for lunch). It is also open Saturday from 9:30 to 12:00, April to October. No appointment is needed. The quintas can be visited by prior arrangement with the company. Tel. (351–2) 3700010.*

Recommended Wines *Quinta do Porto 10 Years Old, Duque de Bragança 20 Years Old, 1982 Vintage.*

Overall Rating ★★★

Widowed in her early thirties, Dona Antónia, like Veuve Clicquot, devoted her enormous energies to her company. Dona Antónia was one of the first to invest very heavily in the Douro, buying quintas in the Cima Corgo and Douro Superior, and building the infrastructure of roads to improve access. When she died in her mid-eighties, she had amassed two dozen quintas and founded hospitals and clinics in this remote area.

Ferreirinha was always held in great esteem by the locals, and there were many instances of mutual assistance. One story relates to the 1868 vintage. The harvest was particularly large and the glut of wine left the farmers with unsold stock. Although it was not needed, Dona Antónia bought a considerable amount of the wine and put it into storage. Phylloxera arrived shortly afterward, devastating the vineyards and leaving most shippers with nothing to sell. Ferreira, of course, had plenty.

Quinta da Leda in the Douro Superior.

Ferreira still owns three superb farms. On opposite sides of the Douro, near Pinhão, are quintas Porto and Seixo, and up toward the border with Spain lies Quinta da Leda. Maintaining the traditions started by Dona Antónia, Ferreira is still very much at the forefront of innovation in the area. Along with Ramos Pinto, they were the first to use vinha ao alto planting to a great extent and, like Ramos Pinto, are vigorous defenders of the system. Quinta do Porto is still mostly terraced; however Quinta do Seixo has over half of its vines planted in vertical rows, an unusually high proportion in such a large quinta in this part of the Douro.

Ferreira was owned by the family until the late 1980s when it was bought by the Sogrape empire, most famous for the medium-dry rosé brand Mateus. As with many port firms, descendants of the family are still at the helm.

As the biggest brand in Portugal (despite prices that are some 15 percent higher than the competition), it is not surprising that Ferreira has an enviable reputation for their tawnies. Some experts tend to dismiss the vintages, which is a great pity since they are mostly very elegant wines and still have excellent staying power. Ferreira vintages can seem very delicate when compared with some others, but they should not be written off as lightweights. The gentler extraction the company prefers results in fewer harsh tannins, but there is still plenty of backbone in most of the wines. About 70 percent of Ferreira's production is standard ruby and tawny, and a high 17 percent is white. The white is made in three styles: dry, medium-sweet, and *lagrima*, a very sweet dessert wine.

Quinta do Porto, near Pinhão.

TASTING NOTES

DONA ANTÓNIA FERREIRA PERSONAL RESERVE This is a different style of wine from the other rubies tasted for this book. Aged in a vat for about six years, it has taken on some of the spicy characteristics that come with maturity. Not as full and fruity as the others, but more complex.

VINTAGE CHARACTER This wine has real charm; more elegant and riper than the ruby, deep in color with an intense, full-bodied palate. Still a very youthful style.

WHITE PORT A pleasant wine, pale in color, with a fresh peach or apricot nose and more character than most. Medium-sweet to the taste, with refreshing acidity for a clean finish.

Tasting Notes

QUINTA DO PORTO 10 YEARS OLD This south-facing vineyard's exposure to the sun results in great ripeness and richness in the wine, which is deep orange-brown with a nose reminiscent of warm fruitcake, richly fruity and spicy. Sweeter than some, but the wine makers have been able to retain enough acidity to balance the sweetness.

1985 VINTAGE Just beginning to show some age on the rim; still a very dense ruby color. The nose is stewed fruit with some spice character. Not yet at its peak; beginning to reach maturity but will continue to develop for a number of years.

DUQUE DE BRAGANÇA 20 YEARS OLD Longer aging has resulted in a wine that is paler than the 10 Years Old, and definitely brown rather than orange. The blend can include wines up to 40 years old, which shows in the complexity of flavors containing hints of dried fruit, figs, or dates, and exotic spices. There is no fresh fruit flavor here but the sweet palate is supported by a remarkable freshness, giving an elegant wine with a lingering finish.

TASTING NOTES

RUBY

DONA ANTÓNIA FERREIRA PERSONAL RESERVE
(see page 103)

RUBY The basic ruby is a faultless, fruity young wine, obviously very carefully made but not as interesting as the Vintage Character and the Dona Antónia.

VINTAGE CHARACTER
(see page 103)

WHITE

WHITE PORT (see page 103)

AGED TAWNY

QUINTA DO PORTO 10 YEARS OLD (see page 104)

DUQUE DE BRAGANÇA 20 YEARS OLD (see page 104)

VINTAGE

1994 VINTAGE Showing very well against the others of the vintage. Full and with firm structure but perhaps not as firm as some, with a massive concentration of fruit. This is a medium- to long-term wine and is unlikely to come around in much less than 20 years.

1991 VINTAGE When first tasted, just after bottling, this had a full and fruity character with a strong but not harsh structure; it has since closed up. When tasted again in 1996, the wine was dumb and difficult to get anything from. However, the concentration still showed. Not as full as the 1994, this is going to be a medium-term wine that will probably come around in 15 or so years.

1985 VINTAGE (see page 104)

1982 VINTAGE Remarkably youthful ruby color and vibrant raspberry and strawberry fruit, not showing any sign of age whatsoever. Medium-sweet with still amazingly youthful fruit, and a firm but not at all harsh structure. One of the best of the 1982s; certainly one of the least developed.

VINHA AO ALTO PLANTING AT QUINTA DO SEIXO.

PRODUCTION

 *Leda, Porto, Seixo.*

 *85% of annual production.*

Fonseca Guimaraens – Vinhos S.A.

Rua Barão de Forrester, 404, Apartado 13
4401 Vila Nova de Gaia Codex, Portugal

There is no doubt that Fonseca makes some of the best ports available. Even among their competitors in the industry, Fonseca is held in the greatest esteem. If Châteaux Pétrus and Le Pin are the top Pomerols, then Fonseca and its sister company, Taylor's, are the port equivalents. Although now owned by Taylor's, the Fonseca Guimaraens family continues to control the day-to-day operation of the vineyards and wine making. Bruce has recently semi-retired as estate manager, but his son David is the wine maker for the firm.

Information

Visiting *Visitors are welcome both to the lodges and to Quinta do Panascal. Tel. (351–2) 304505.*

Recommended Wines *Fonseca Guimaraens 1976, Fonseca 1985, Fonseca 1994.*

Overall Rating ★★★

The company dates back to 1822, when Manoel Pedro Guimaraens bought a merchant company based in Oporto called Fonseca & Monteiro. Shortly after the purchase Manoel found himself supporting the "wrong" side in a vicious political rivalry and was forced to flee his homeland, escaping to England hidden in a port cask. While he was in exile the reputation of the firm flourished, becoming one of the largest port wine exporters.

Re-established in Britain, it remained in London until 1927, when the headquarters returned to Oporto. In 1948 the partners of the firm sold their shares to Taylor, Fladgate & Yeatman, who were by this time related through marriage, and who still own the company.

Production

Cruzeiro, St. António, Panascal.

Buy-in grapes.

Combining forces has certainly been beneficial to both companies. Taylor's gained an extra string on their bow and Fonseca has gained marketing power and expertise. This has been accomplished while still maintaining the two different house styles – similar and certainly complementary, but different nonetheless.

Fonseca's flagship vineyard is Panascal in the Távora valley, about a 10-minute drive from Pinhão. This was one

QUINTA DO PANASCAL, IN THE TÁVORA VALLEY.

of the first quintas to open its doors to the public, running audio tours throughout the year. Here tourists can see how port is made – in lagares, as it has been over the centuries – and also tour the vineyards to view the terraced vines and dramatic Távora scenery. Panascal is mostly south-facing, providing a perfect aspect for the vines; much of the land has recently been replanted with patamar terraces. Although it was bought only in 1978, the estate had been an important part of the Fonseca blend for many years.

Other quintas owned by Fonseca are St. António and Quinta de Cruzeiro in the Vale de Mendiz. These are all class A vineyards, and have been supplying grapes for longer than they have been in the company portfolio. These are, like most quintas, just working farms, and are not open to the public.

All the grapes from the company quintas are trodden by foot; indeed, Fonseca probably has the newest lagar in the Douro, installed at Panascal to accommodate the increased production of the 1990s. Building the lagar has created extra space that has been put to good use: the quinta dining room was extended.

The wine making has been in remarkably few hands. For 100 years, with only one exception, all the vintage wine has been made by two people. Frank Guimaraens was responsible for wines made from 1896 until 1948, and Bruce, who retired at the end of 1995, for everything since (except the wines of 1955, which were made by Bruce's aunt, Dorothy Guimaraens). Bruce is one of the great characters of the Douro. A big man with a bigger personality, he is very much a man of the vineyards, and never happier than when he is "up country" in the demarcated area. His retirement, however, does not signal the end of the Guimaraens involvement. Not only does he still pop into the lodge to offer advice as needed, but in addition his eldest son, David, trained by Roseworthy in Australia, has taken over the wine making. Another son, Christopher, is also likely to join the firm.

With its long history of trading from London, Fonseca firmly considers itself to be a British rather than a Portuguese house. The style of the wines is definitely British, with elegant, long-lived vintages and fruity tawnies. When two houses are part of the same group, it is tempting to compare the different styles. Whereas Taylor's produces very strong, structured wines, the Fonseca equivalents are somehow bigger and gutsier, and perhaps a little more perfumed. Both houses are equally good.

A note about the vintage wines: wines of the very best years are declared "Fonseca" vintages. When the wines are good, but not spectacular, the second label, "Fonseca Guimaraens," is used. These are normally released only when they are ready, or are at least approaching maturity. In effect, they are the same as most companies' single quinta brand, but with the option to blend from more than one site. Fonseca Guimaraens vintages represent very good value for money, given their price when they are released and their maturity.

Confusingly, in recent years the occasional single quinta Fonseca wine has come from Quinta do Panascal. These are typically less complex than the Fonseca Guimaraens wines, either as a result of young vines at Panascal (as vines get older their production falls in quantity, but improves in quality and complexity) or simply because they come from one site. On the other hand, these give consumers the chance to drink bottle-matured Fonseca wines more affordably than even the Fonseca Guimaraens vintages.

Tasting Notes

BIN NO. 27 FINE RESERVE This is the Fonseca vintage character, or premium ruby wine. Rich and plummy, with a very deep color and remarkably strong structure, this is one of the best of its type.

20 YEAR OLD RICH TAWNY Pale orange-brown wine with a powerful dried fruit aroma, especially apricot and dried apple; only slightly nutty. Medium-sweet with a concentrated, elegant flavor of dried fruit and nuts. Very long finish.

FONSECA VINTAGE 1985 Very deep purple-ruby rim on a black-cored wine. Floral nose of violets and rose petals, with intense black fruit as well. When people describe Fonseca as perfumed, this is what they mean. Alcoholic and tannic on the palate, with totally undeveloped fruit. Needs a long time before it is truly ready.

TASTING NOTES

RUBY

BIN NO. 27 FINE RESERVE
(see page 109)

AGED TAWNY

20 YEAR OLD RICH TAWNY
(see page 109)

SINGLE QUINTA VINTAGE

QUINTA DO PANASCAL 1984 VINTAGE Already mature in appearance, but a more youthful nose than the garnet color implies. Still fruity, with hints of cherry and red fruit. The palate is attractive if rather lighter than the other wines from the same company, with soft tannins. Ready to drink now, not one to keep.

VINTAGE

FONSECA VINTAGE 1994 Black with the narrowest of purple rims. Closed nose of hugely concentrated fruit, plums and prunes, with some tobacco hints. A big mouthful, medium-sweet with very firm tannins and massive concentration.

FONSECA VINTAGE 1992 Blue-black color on rim, hardly changed since first tasted on release. Still very closed; more delicate on the nose than some of the 1992s, but with a fullish palate of ripe, dark fruit showing the class of the house.

FONSECA VINTAGE 1985
(see page 109)

FONSECA GUIMARAENS 1984 VINTAGE Deeper color than the 1982 and 1978, though still a fairly mature ruby garnet. Mature spice and tobacco nose, spirity but not unpleasantly so. Medium weight with firm tannins and good concentration. One of the best of the recent run of Guimaraens wines, though not as good as the 1976.

FONSECA VINTAGE 1983 Still deep, but with a ruby rather than purple rim. Pungent, if raw, nose of black fruit; medium-sweet with massive tannins and good balancing acidity. Huge, gutsy dark fruit flavors and a long, powerful finish. A classic wine that needs time. Not as great as the 1985, but an outstanding wine all the same.

FONSECA GUIMARAENS 1982 VINTAGE This is very forward for the vintage; already pale garnet, verging on the color of a young tawny. The nose is of spice and old wood, only moderately pronounced, not as powerful as one might expect from a vintage port. Medium-sweet with light tannins and balanced acidity. A wine for drinking in the next few years.

FONSECA VINTAGE 1980 Although pleasant enough, this is the most disappointing of the Fonsecas, although Bruce Guimaraens is adamant that it will develop into an interesting wine, given time. Light and mature in color with a mature spice and spirit nose; light and rather lacking fruit.

FONSECA GUIMARAENS 1978 VINTAGE Pale garnet red in color; clearly mature. Fine and delicate nose of fruit with some vanilla and old wood hints on the nose. Medium-sweet with detectable, but no longer huge, tannins, but with a long, mature finish. A wine to drink now; not one to keep. Very good in the short term.

FONSECA GUIMARAENS 1976 VINTAGE This is a good wine, whatever parameter it is judged by. Given the price, and the fact that its producer considers it a second-tier wine, it is stunning. Very deep in color, hardly showing any hint of age on appearance; a very full fruit and licorice nose with rich, meaty, almost gamey characters from age. Medium-sweet and very full-bodied, massive concentration of fruit and still quite firm tannins, which will keep this wine for many years. Perhaps not as complex as a classic Fonseca vintage, but as good as some, and better than many, other vintage wines from better years. (Interestingly, so far this wine has thrown very little sediment.)

FONSECA VINTAGE 1975 There are few 1975s still in good condition; most should have been consumed by now. This wine from Fonseca is an exception; it is one of the best wines of the vintage. Now fully mature, with a slightly fragile fruitiness once opened (do not leave it in the decanter too long), but with enough structure to hold for a few years yet.

Forrester & Ca., S.A.

Rua Guilherme Braga, 38, Apartado 61
4401 Vila Nova de Gaia Codex, Portugal

Joseph James (later Baron) Forrester was one of the great men in the history of port. He was a geographer, cartographer, and artist as well as an oenologist; his name is among the most famous in the industry. There is even a street in Oporto named after him. But despite all that acclaim, the company that bears his name, Forrester & Ca. Lda., uses the name Offley for its wines.

The Offley family came from the west of England, and the first William Offley was sheriff of Stratford from 1517; like Mr Christopher Smith of Smith Woodhouse, his son was Lord Mayor of London. However, it was not until 200 years later that the Portuguese connection was established, when the seventh William Offley set up a company in Oporto in 1737.

INFORMATION

VISITING *Trade visitors permitted only.*

RECOMMENDED WINES *Tawnies, particularly the 10 Years Old and 20 Years Old.*

OVERALL RATING ★★

Offley was joined in 1803 by Joseph Forrester, uncle of the famous Joseph James, who was involved with the company from 1831 until his death in the Douro River in 1862. After having lunched with Dona Antónia Ferreira at her quinta, the boat he left in capsized in the rapids at Valeira and he drowned, supposedly weighed down by a money belt filled with gold with which to pay the growers. His female companions in the boat floated to safety, buoyed up by their crinoline dresses.

The recent history of the company has also been checkered, the subject of a number of takeovers and share swaps. In the early 1960s it was bought by Sandeman. Martini & Rossi, the vermouth giant, acquired a partial interest in the firm, and in 1980, when Seagram took over Sandeman, Martini took over Forrester. Throughout these changes, the company has maintained the quality of the premium brands; however, the mainstream, cheaper wines are not exciting. The firm was sold very recently to Sogrape, who already own Ferreira, the brand leaders in Portugal. With Ferreira's premium brand position in the domestic market, it will be interesting to see how, or if, the company philosophy changes.

TASTING NOTES

BARON DE FORRESTER 20 YEARS OLD Fully brown with hardly a hint of red; pronounced nose of toffee and fudge with dried figs. Medium-sweet with crisp acidity and some tannin. Fruit very obvious and overt on the palate, giving a complex wine with a good length.

BARON DE FORRESTER 1975 RESERVE Offley does not specialize in colheitas in the way Gilberts or Noval do, but this is one for consideration. Quite a deep color; medium brown with no red now. A mid-power nose showing smoke and spice, with dried fruit and caramel. Medium-sweet with just balanced acidity; full body and concentration with a long finish.

BOA VISTA 1985 VINTAGE Still dark ruby; hardly any real signs of maturity. Full, rich, nose of plums and black pepper, just about developing now. Full flavor with quite firm tannins and balanced structure. A full wine that is only marginally less complex than some produced by the top houses. Beginning to drink well.

Tasting Notes

AGED TAWNY

BARON DE FORRESTER 10 YEARS OLD Deep russet brown with a light marzipan nose; spirit not too obvious. Medium-sweet with a little soft tannin remaining and a full, rich, concentrated nutty flavor that has considerable charm.

BARON DE FORRESTER 20 YEARS OLD (see page 112)

COLHEITA

BARON DE FORRESTER 1975 RESERVE (see page 112)

SINGLE QUINTA VINTAGE

BOA VISTA 1994 VINTAGE Medium-to-pale color, paler than most, with a light and fruity nose of red rather than black fruits; a little volatile. Medium-sweet with firm but not aggressive tannins, somewhat overpowering the fruit at the moment. When tasted, this had not been bottled for very long. Bottling often "shocks" the wine so the fruit may well expand during the next few months. This is most likely a medium-term wine, but it will be interesting to see how it develops.

Production

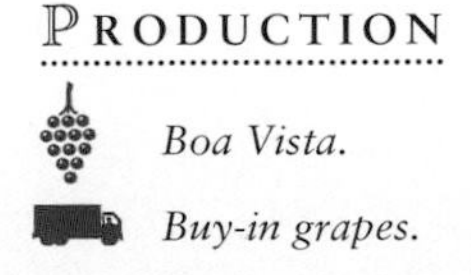

Boa Vista.

Buy-in grapes.

Coopers are needed to make and repair pipes.

BOA VISTA 1989 VINTAGE Dark ruby with hot, baked fruit and black pepper nose. Medium weight with firm tannins, but the fruit on the palate is a little too cooked, taking away some of its elegance. Not yet ready, but not a very long-term wine. Probably ready at the end of the decade.

BOA VISTA 1987 VINTAGE Relatively forward for a wine so young. Medium depth with a full fruit and spice nose; allspice comes across quite strongly. Medium-sweet and balanced, with only moderate acidity and medium weight. A medium-term wine, coming around now. Will probably reach its peak in a few years.

BOA VISTA 1985 VINTAGE (see page 112)

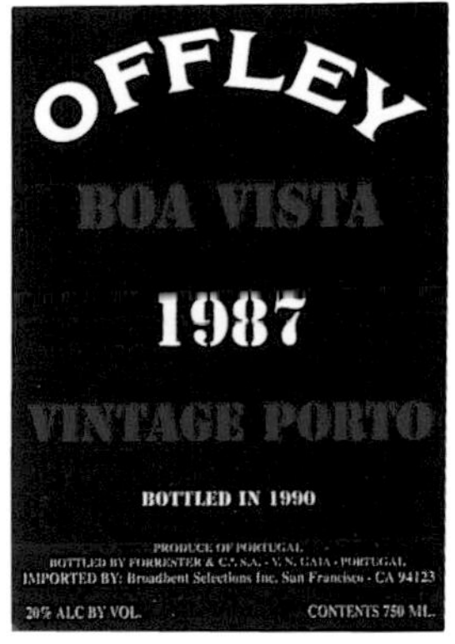

BOA VISTA 1983 VINTAGE A little less deep than the 1985, but with the same pepper character and full plummy fruit. Less concentrated on the palate, and more obviously lacking the complexity of the 1985. Having softer tannins, this wine is drinking well now and will continue to do so for a number of years yet.

Inside the Forrester lodge in Gaia.

Garrett & Ca., Lda.

Av. da République, 796, Apartado 27
4431 Vila Nova de Gaia Codex, Portugal

Garrett is a relative newcomer to the port market, set up by its sister company Sociedade dos Vinhos Borges (see page 71) in 1984.

Currently the range is very limited, only a young white, a basic tawny, and a ruby are being produced. Currently, they do not produce any premium grade wines at all. The wines produced are deliberately aimed at the "value" end of the market, thus protecting the Borges reputation for quality, while giving them a foothold in this important competitive market with reliable, consistent products.

INFORMATION

VISITING *No.*

RECOMMENDED WINES
White Port.

OVERALL RATING ★

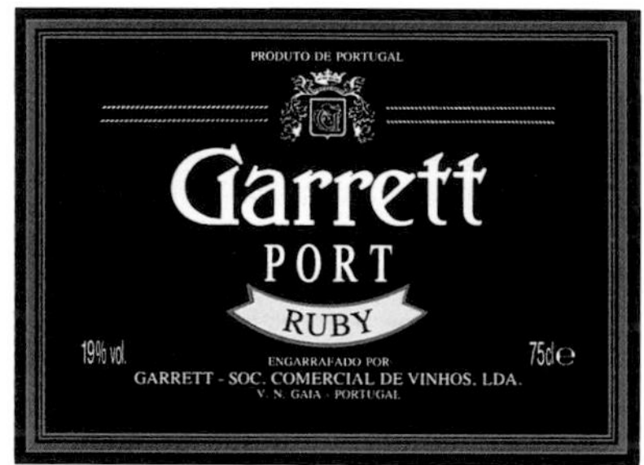

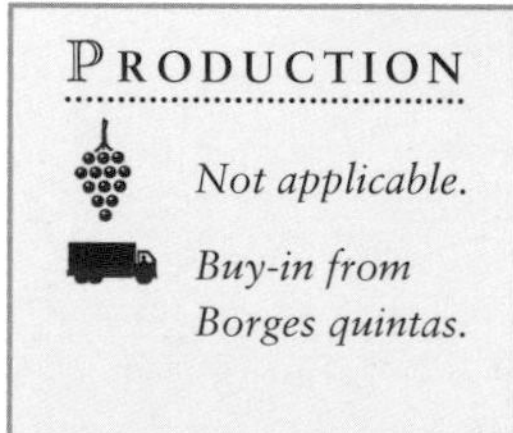

Tasting Notes

WHITE Medium-depth golden color with an open fruity and floral nose, very fresh and appealing. Medium-dry with crisp acidity and medium weight. Rather spirity on the palate, though not so on the nose, with a medium length. A pleasant enough sweeter apéritif or base for mixed drinks.

TAWNY Basic tawnies are expected to be red rather than brown, but this one is surprisingly red. It is a very deep ruby color for a tawny, with a light and fresh red fruit nose of cherries and raspberries. Medium-sweet with balanced acids and very little tannin. This is a pleasant and uncomplicated wine, light in body and flavor, without a great deal of character.

Gilberts & Ca., Lda.

Rua de Belmonte, 39–1° 4000
Porto, Portugal

In 1962 the originally German firm of Burmester bought a small, independent company called Alcino Correia Riberio, along with its stock of fine old tawny ports. The name was changed to Gilbert in honor of Karl Gilbert, a former partner and director of Burmester, and a descendant of the original Burmester family. The establishment date of 1914 printed on labels and letterheads refers to the original firm.

Karl Gilbert was born in Metz in Lorraine in France. His mother, however, was from Oporto and from the port trade, so it was logical that in his youth he should join the family firm. Apart from being a well-respected member of the trade, Karl Gilbert was the honorary consul in Oporto of the Austro-Hungarian Empire until 1918. The directors of the firm are all Gilberts or Burmesters, but Gilberts and Burmester are run as separate companies.

Since Burmester owns Quinta Nova de Nossa Senhora do Carmo, it is not surprising that most of the wine originates here. Gilberts, the associate company, does not have any vineyards of its own. The wines are matured in Vila Nova de Gaia to avoid the harsh summer weather of the Douro; the lodges are not open to visitors.

Like the parent company, Gilberts produces some vintage wines that are pleasant and well made. However, their wood-aged ports, the tawnies and colheitas, are far more interesting. Gilberts wines can be very sweet, which can overpower the flavors.

Information

Visiting *No.*

Recommended Wines *Colheita 1940, Vintage 1994.*

Overall Rating ★

Production

Not applicable.

Supplied by Quinta Nova de Nossa Senhora do Carmo.

Gilberts
PORT
colheita
1937
MATURED IN WOOD
TAWNY SWEET
75 cl. BOTTLED AND SHIPPED BY Gilberts & Ca. Lda. OPORTO 20% vol.
PRODUCT OF PORTUGAL

Tasting Notes

10 YEARS OLD Browner than the sister company's (Burmester's) example; tawny with a broad orange rim. Very full and spirity nose of wood smoke and dried peel. Very sweet with only just balanced acidity; smoky character coming through strongly on the palate with a long, alcoholic finish.

COLHEITA 1940 Clear, deep caramel color. A very intense, spirity nose with hints of dried peel and burnt sugar. This is a very mature nose that has lost all its fruit but has become highly concentrated, reminiscent of the very best, very oldest amontillado sherry. Extremely sweet palate, this is a wine for one's sweet-tooth. The sweetness really covers up much of the flavor.

VINTAGE 1994 Black core with a narrow purple rim. The nose is like fruit juice concentrate; very youthful and quite pungent. Sweet with firm tannins and a full body. Not as fresh and lively as some, but with all the components to make this a medium- to long-term wine.

Tasting Notes

AGED TAWNY

10 YEARS OLD (see page 117)

20 YEARS OLD Pale orange with a broad mature rim. Powerful smoky nose with orange and dried peel hints. Mature but not caramelly. Very sweet with marmalade-like fruitiness, cooked peel rather than nuts. Good, long finish, but not as concentrated as the Burmester equivalent.

COLHEITA

COLHEITA 1955 Deep walnut brown with a toffee and fudge nose, very mature and oxidized – deliberately, of course. Sweet, almost sticky palate with just-balanced acidity. Very concentrated flavor though, and rather medicinal in texture and flavor. Great length and complexity. This is almost too concentrated. A good wine, if you like the style.

KARL GILBERT.

COLHEITA 1940 (see page 117)

LBV

LATE BOTTLED VINTAGE 1985 Another traditional LBV, in need of decanting since it has thrown a great deal of sediment. Medium to deep garnet in color, quite mature in appearance, with a full spice and raisin nose, perhaps just a little coarse, but quite complex. Very sweet with soft tannins and balanced acidity.

VINTAGE

VINTAGE 1994 (see page 117)

VINTAGE 1985 Showing some maturity on the rim, this wine still has a youthful nose of prunes and figs. Medium weight; sweet with soft tannins and good concentration. Ready soon.

VINTAGE 1963 Fully mature, garnet red with a complex nose of old wood, spice, and fruitcake. Less obviously sweet than some of the Gilbert wines (due perhaps to the extra complexity of age), with a long and lingering finish.

Gilberts
PORT
LATE BOTTLED VINTAGE
1987

BOTTLED 1991
BOTTLED AND SHIPPED BY Gilberts & Ca. Lda. OPORTO
75 cl. PRODUCT OF PORTUGAL 20% vol.

Gilberts
PORT
VINTAGE
1992

BOTTLED 1994
BOTTLED AND SHIPPED BY Gilberts & Ca. Lda. OPORTO
75 cl. PRODUCT OF PORTUGAL 20% vol.

Gilberts
PORT
colheita
1987
MATURED IN WOOD
TAWNY SWEET
BOTTLED AND SHIPPED BY
Gilberts & Ca. Lda.
PORTO
PRODUCT OF PORTUGAL
75 cl. 20% vol.

Gould Campbell

Trav. Barão de Forrester, Apartado 26, 4401 Vila Nova de Gaia Codex, Portugal

Gould Campbell is one of the Symington group houses, along with Warre & Ca., S.A., W. & J. Graham & Co., Silva & Cosens Lda., Smith Woodhouse, and Quarles Harris. Founded in 1797, just before the Peninsular War, the firm has had a long history of producing quality port. It still makes good wine, as is often proved at blind tastings, but has been rather unfairly relegated to the position of a lesser brand. Even the Symington public relations department describes it as one of their second-tier brands.

Information

Visiting *To lodge, by appointment only. Tel. (351–2) 3796063.*

Recommended Wines *1983 Vintage, 1985 Vintage.*

Overall Rating ★★

Certainly Gould Campbell is not usually in the same league as the premium Symington brands – Dow's, Graham's, and Warre's – but to dismiss the wines as second-rate is to miss out on some very good ports.

In contrast to the three high-ranking Symington brands mentioned above, about 92 percent of Gould Campbell's production is made from bought-in grapes. Many of these come from small traditional farms where a row of vines contains a mixture of grape varieties, so it is impossible to determine what varieties are used. The remaining 8 percent comes from Quinta de Santa Magdalena, in the Rio Torto valley. This small farm, only about 20 acres in size, has been replanted under the World Bank scheme, so it is block planted on patamares.

Production

Santa Magdalena.

92% of annual production.

TASTING NOTES

1990 LATE BOTTLED VINTAGE In contrast to the Smith Woodhouse LBV, this is a modern style of LBV; medium to deep ruby with notes of fruit and spice. Medium weight with fresh, clean acidity and a rich, medium-sweet palate. A good example of a mid-range LBV.

1991 VINTAGE Very deep color with a rich, fruity nose. Just a touch lean on the palate, with a nice clean finish. Still far too young; this is a wine that needs a further 10 years or so to be at its best.

RUBY

FINE RUBY Pleasant, straightforward, youthful ruby wine, light- to medium-bodied, with balanced acidity and very low tannin. An easy-drinking port.

VINTAGE

1994 VINTAGE Tasted twice since declared. Medium depth of color with a slightly earthy, vegetal note at first on the nose, giving way to stalky fruit. Medium to light weight with rather lean fruit. A second bottle requested at the first tasting was found to be the same. A more recent tasting has not revealed any significant differences. Not a successful vintage for this house.

1985 VINTAGE Dark ruby red in color, still looks very young. Rich, full, and very ripe nose; full of plummy fruit. Medium-dry with firm structure and a good length. An excellent wine for the long term.

1983 VINTAGE One of the best Gould Campbell wines tasted. Still very deep in color with a full, ripe nose, massively fruity. Youthful, undeveloped palate with huge tannins, but enough concentrated fruit to outlive them. A wine for the very long term.

W. & J. Graham & Co.

Trav. Barão de Forrester, 85, Apartado 19
4401 Vila Nova de Gaia Codex, Portugal

Graham's is undoubtedly one of the best port shippers, producing some of the fullest and richest of all ports. Now part of the Symington empire, the company, which was founded in the early part of the nineteenth century, was originally in the textile business. Shipping port started only by accident.

Like many of the British shippers, Graham's is of Scottish rather than of English origin. Although the firm was Glasgow-based, it had an office in Oporto, which in 1820 accepted 27 pipes of port as payment for a bad debt. The wine proved popular, and soon the Scottish parent company was requesting further stock from the two managers in Portugal, the brothers William and John Graham. By the end of the nineteenth century, port had become their main trading commodity.

> **INFORMATION**
>
> **VISITING** *The lodge and museum are open 9:30 to 6:00 daily in summer; in winter they are closed weekends and at lunchtime (12:30 to 1:30). Tel. (351–2) 3796065.*
>
> **RECOMMENDED WINES** *LBV and full vintages, especially 1985 and 1994.*
>
> **OVERALL RATING** ★★★

Andrew James Symington joined Graham's when he arrived in Portugal from Scotland in 1882, but soon left to join Warres. The Symington connection was to be revived nearly a century later when, in 1970, the Graham family sold the company to the Symington empire.

Over the intervening quarter-century, careful protection of the brand image and style has been the hallmark of the company's management. The different companies in the group have their own very definite characteristics: in Graham's case, this means a full, rich, and quite sweet wine.

The company's flagship quinta, Quinta dos Malvedos, is in the Cima Corgo on the north side of the Douro River, just west of Tua. Today, the quinta overlooks the still waters of the dammed river; in the old days the rough water that flowed here inspired the quinta's name, which means "bad ways." Graham's bought the farm in 1890 at a time when many shippers were buying Douro properties. When the Symingtons bought

Graham's, they did not want the quinta, which was by now running at a great loss. It was offered back to the family, who turned it down after deciding against turning it into a citrus farm. In the end, it was sold to António Baltasar Baptista. However, the farm fell into further disrepair while production declined.

In 1982 the Symingtons, who were already using "Malvedos" (not, it should be noted, "Quinta dos Malvedos") as a brand bought the farm back and invested heavily in new planting and general improvements to the farm and winery. Virtually all the vines, apart from a small showpiece vineyard, are on patamares. It is a testament to the remoteness of the Douro that Malvedos was connected up to mains electricity supply only as recently as 1984.

Quinta dos Malvedos supplies about a quarter of Graham's annual needs; the remainder is bought in, particularly from Quinta das Lages in the Rio Torto valley, near Ramos Pinto's Bom Retiro. Lages has been selling its wine to Graham's for nearly 80 years, and this prime site has supplied the backbone of many a Graham's vintage. The quinta manager is proud, not only that his wines go to such a high-ranking house, but also because the relationship is based on trust and a handshake, not a written contract.

A very high percentage of Graham's total production is made the traditional way, as most of Malvedos and Lages grapes are trodden by foot. The remainder, a little over half, is made in autovinifiers, since the Symingtons prefer these to remontagem. Nearly two-thirds of the production is categorized by the Instituto do Vinho do Porto as "Special Category," i.e., premium ports. Their LBV has recently overtaken Taylor's as the largest seller in the United Kingdom and is very popular in the United States as well. However, it is the vintage wines for which the company is particularly – and justly – proud.

GRAHAM'S VINTAGE PORT.

Tasting Notes

SIX GRAPES The company's premium ruby blend. Very deep ruby in color with a youthful crimson-purple rim. Pronounced, very youthful berry fruit with black currant and cherry hints. Sweet, but with fresh acidity, soft yet noticeable tannins, and a reasonable length.

10 YEARS OF AGE TAWNY Deep russet brown; not as mature looking as some 10 year olds. Rich and very full nose of ripe plums and prunes, with dried figs and apricots. A fruity nose. Extremely full, powerful palate, quite sweet but with balanced acidity and a great length. A very good, if rather youthful, example of the type.

20 YEARS OF AGE TAWNY Much more mature appearance; now genuinely nutty with hazelnuts and Brazil nuts evident. Sweet with a silky texture that covers up the spirit on the palate, although it is very evident on the nose. One of those wines it is far too easy to drink too much of.

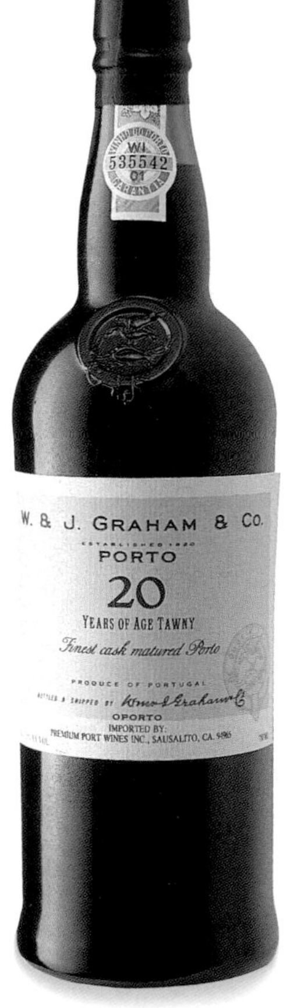

Tasting Notes

MALVEDOS 1984 Graham's do not use the term Quinta dos Malvedos, indicating that the wine can be a blend that includes other properties. Medium ruby garnet in color with a spicy and complex nose. Sweet with moderate tannin and good weight, this is a very pleasant wine for current and short- to medium-term consumption.

1994 VINTAGE Medium depth of color, though of course still very blue-purple. Light, rather unyielding nose at first, but eventually opening out to give a ripe, dark fruit and chocolate character. Vastly more intense on the palate. Sweet with massive structure and great concentration of fruit. A great wine for the long term.

1985 VINTAGE Very deep, still black appearance with only the narrowest of purple rims. Concentrated black fruit nose with tar and floral hints also present. Very sweet at first, but with enough acidity to balance that, and with enough tannin and fruit concentration to enable this wine to mature for another 20 or 30 years.

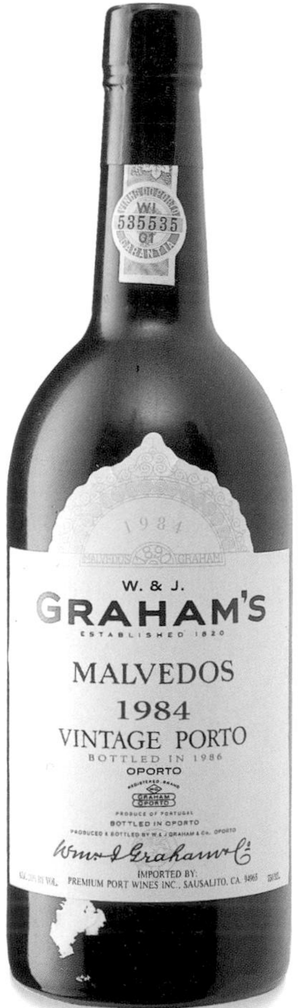

TASTING NOTES

RUBY

SIX GRAPES (see page 123)

AGED TAWNY

10 YEARS OF AGE TAWNY (see page 123)

20 YEARS OF AGE TAWNY (see page 123)

LBV

LBV 1990 This is one of the more consistent LBVs. Deep ruby red color with just a hint of maturity on the rim; very full, black fruit with a fruitcake and spice nose. Extremely powerful, sweet palate with balanced acidity and tannins, giving the overall impression of a huge mouthful of wine. This is one of the best modern-style LBVs, differing from Taylor's in style, being sweeter and a little less powerful, but of equal quality.

PRODUCTION

Malvedos.

75% of annual production.

SINGLE QUINTA VINTAGE

MALVEDOS 1984 (see page 124)

VINTAGE

1994 VINTAGE (see page 124)

1991 VINTAGE Like the 1994, this wine still gives little away on the nose, being closed and tight. Opening up dramatically on the palate, it turns out to be intensely rich with concentrated, plummy fruit. Perhaps not quite as concentrated as the 1994, but again, a long-term wine.

1985 VINTAGE (see page 124)

1983 VINTAGE Still very deep-colored with a pronounced nose of fresh and dried fruit, with plums, figs, and some fruitcake hints, and a peppery spirit. Full and rich in the typical Graham's style. Not as overtly fruity as the 1985 vintage, a little leaner somehow, but still full and with a very long finish. One of the best 1983s and a wine for the long term.

THE GRAHAM'S LODGE IN GAIA.

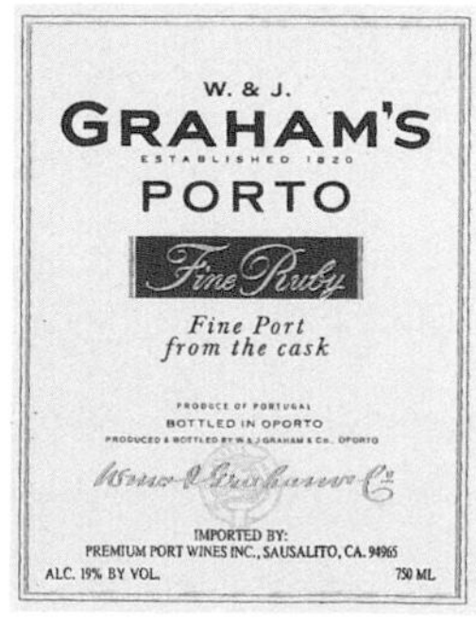

Hutcheson, Feuerheerd & Associados – Vinhos, S.A.

Rua D. Leonor de Freitas, 1802,
P.O. Box 39, 4401 Vila Nova de Gaia
Codex, Portugal

INFORMATION

VISITING *Yes, to the lodge. Tel. (351–2) 302320.*

RECOMMENDED WINES *Feuerheerd 1987 Vintage.*

OVERALL RATING ★

Hutcheson was established by two British traders, Thomas Page Hutcheson and Alexander Davidson Taylor in 1881. From the beginning they specialized in port, being a later generation of shippers than the likes of Warre's and Graham's for whom port was only one of many commodities.

Thomas Hutcheson retired in 1920, to be replaced by Augustus Bouttwood, who ran the company with Alexander Taylor until the latter's death in 1925. The instability of the company, with neither of the founders leaving any heirs, left it open for takeover. In 1927 the then-new company of Barros, Almeida bought the firm.

Feuerheerd has a longer history. It was established in 1815 by the ancestors of the Bergqvists of Quinta de la Rosa. At one point the Bergqvists owned both the Feuerheerd firm and the quinta, but when the shipping company failed in the 1930s, the quinta remained in the Bergqvist family and the shipping business was sold to Barros, Almeida.

Hutcheson and Feuerheerd merged in 1996. At that same time Barros, Almeida tidied up their portfolio of brands by joining Vieira de Souza, A. Pinto Santos Junior, Rocha, and Almeida together with Hutcheson and Feuerheerd, the associated companies in the firm's title. Consequently, a handful of port brands have disappeared as a result of the amalgamation.

Without Quinta de la Rosa to rely on, the company's wines come from Quinta da Santa Ana in the Baixo Corgo and Quinta de Dom Pedro, alongside the Kopke quinta, São Luiz, as well as bought in grapes. Over 90 percent of the company's production is basic rubies, tawnies, and whites, but a full range of colheitas is also available.

PRODUCTION

 *Dom Pedro, Santa Ana.*

 *Buy-in grapes.*

TASTING NOTES

SOUZA COLHEITA 1983 Deep ruddy brown color. Toffee and fudge nose; however, the spirit is a little overpowering. Very sweet caramel-like flavor which tends to be a little cloying if the wine is not well chilled, but has full body and reasonably long finish.

FEUERHEERD 1987 VINTAGE Deep ruby with a moderate ruby rim. Dumb nose, but has a medicinal quality, smoky and herbal. Sweet with only just enough acidity and moderate tannins. The palate is overly alcoholic, with the spirit showing through as a very hot aftertaste. Drink within the next five years.

RUBY

HUTCHESON CHRISTMAS PORT Deep, very youthful bluish ruby red with an unpronounced fruity nose of dark, bitter cherries and raspberries but with a hint of jam. Sweet on the palate without the structure to back up the sugar level.

HUTCHESON VINTAGE CHARACTER Deep ruby red with a pronounced nose of red fruit but with a background hint of grass, indicating the fruit might not have been as ripe as it needed to be. Sweet palate with enough acidity to balance the sweetness. Very soft tannins and a medium body and length of finish.

C. N. Kopke & Ca, Lda.

**Rua D. Leonor de Freitas, 180/2,
P.O. Box 39, 4401 Vila Nova de
Gaia Codex, Portugal**

> **INFORMATION**
>
> **VISITING** *Yes, to the lodges, 183 Rua Serpa Pinto, Vila Nova de Gaia. Tel. (351–2) 302420.*
>
> **RECOMMENDED WINES** *1991 Vintage.*
>
> **OVERALL RATING** ★★

The oldest foreign port house, and the oldest existing house, is the little known C. N. Kopke. Little recognized outside Portugal and the Benelux countries, Kopke enjoys a certain degree of autonomy within the Barros, Almeida group, and some of their wines have won coveted awards at international competitions. Despite this, the company could benefit from being better known and distributing the wines more widely.

The company's archives were destroyed by fire in 1882, so much of the detail of their history has been lost, but it is known that the firm was started by a German, Christiano Kopke, as early as 1638. Port wine was but one of the commodities that he traded in, but it has proved to be the most lasting.

The German Kopkes and the Dutch van Zellers seem to have intermarried on a number of occasions and through one of these unions Kopke took over the running of the famous Quinta do Roriz. Shipped by Kopke in the eighteenth century, Roriz was one of the first ports to be exported as a single quinta wine. The van Zellers still own Roriz, but the grapes from Roriz are no longer sold to Kopke.

The heart of the blend now comes from Quinta São Luiz, further downriver between the Torto and Távora tributaries. Acquired by Kopke in 1922, the quinta was bought with the shipping company by Barros, Almeida in 1953. Along with the neighboring quintas Lobata and Mesquita, these produce about 8 percent of the company's needs – but it is the important top 8 percent, as these are class A vineyards.

The traditional terraces are gradually being replaced with modern patamares or vinha ao alto, Barros being particularly proud of their commitment to modern viticulture. Similarly, only a very small proportion of the wine is now made in lagares; the majority is now made by pumping over.

Tasting Notes

1977 COLHEITA Medium tawny brown, with just a hint of red. Full toffee and burnt sugar nose, with nut oil and spirit as well. Sweet, perhaps over-sweet, with a full flavor of spirit and caramel on the palate. Very long finish. Full, sweet, and very mature, good quality, but lacks the freshness that gives this style of wine its elegance.

1991 VINTAGE Very deep ruby red with a narrow blue rim. Youthful and concentrated red and black fruit. Totally undeveloped as yet, of course. Quite a big, full wine on the palate. Sweet with balanced acids and firm tannins. Black fruits with chocolate overtones. A wine that will be at its peak from about the year 2000.

Production

Lobata, Mesquita, São Luiz.

92% of annual production.

Martinez Gassiot & Co., Ltd.

Rua das Coradas, 13, Apartado 20
4401 Vila Nova de Gaia Codex, Portugal

Sebastian Gonzalez Martinez, a Spaniard, founded the firm that bears his name in 1790. Initially the company bought and sold sherry, port, and cigars. In 1822 an Englishman, John Peter Gassiot, joined Martinez, adding his name to that of the company. At this time, Martinez was purely a London-based company that sourced wines from a number of shippers. The company's lodge in Vila Nova de Gaia was acquired in 1834, and would soon be run by John F. Delaforce, the father of George Henry Delaforce who would later start the firm of that name. Remarkably, Sebastian Martinez did not retire until 1849, at which time the day-to-day running of the company was taken over by Gassiot and his two sons, John and Charles.

INFORMATION

VISITING *By appointment only. Tel. (351–2) 300215.*

RECOMMENDED WINES *1970 Vintage, 1994 Vintage, 30 Years Old Tawny.*

OVERALL RATING ★★

The firm was made a public company in 1902. It is said that when Jonnie Teage, senior partner of Cockburn Smithes, was told about this, he was urged to visit London to see if any cooperation between the firms might be possible. He chose not to go, as he was busy with repairs to the Cockburn's lodge. Ironically, 60 years later, the two companies both found themselves under the umbrella of Harvey's of Bristol.

Cockburn's is the larger of the two companies; as a result, Martinez tends to be relegated to the role of own-label sales. When allowed to stand on their own, however, Martinez wines can represent excellent value for the money since the brand is less known.

Martinez is mostly sourced from the same vineyards as those used for Cockburn's, but additionally there is Quinta da Eira Velha. Owned by the Newman family, traders from the west of England, this quinta is managed by Cockburn's and Martinez, and the wine is sold under the Martinez label. Eira Velha is one of the oldest quintas in the area and has a well-documented history. The wine is often sold as a single quinta vintage.

Martinez vintage ports are sometimes sold, particularly in the United States, under the name of Harvey's.

Tasting Notes

VINTAGE CHARACTER Young, fairly pale ruby color. Moderately pronounced red fruit and herbaceous nose, slightly peppery. Juicy fruit; medium sweet with crisp acidity, making for a very lively and fruity style of wine. Soft tannins and medium weight with a clean finish.

30 YEARS OLD TAWNY Pale amber tawny with a light, very mature nose of spirit and wood smoke, with roast chestnut hints. Medium-sweet with a full flavor of dried fruits and nuts. Crisp, cleansing acidity and a very long finish.

VINTAGE 1985 Even after 10 years, still a deep crimson red with a powerful syrup of figs and fresh date nose. Quite sweet with firm tannins and a remarkable fresh acidity, almost like lemon juice – it freshens the palate in the same way as a sorbet. Unusual but not in the least unpleasant.

TASTING NOTES

RUBY

VINTAGE CHARACTER
(see page 131)

AGED TAWNY

30 YEARS OLD TAWNY
(see page 131)

VINTAGE

VINTAGE 1994 Very deep black-purple color with a highly intense nose, dominated by dark fruit. Extremely powerful palate with the concentration of very dark continental chocolate, firm tannins, and a great length. Most impressive when tasted in July 1996; rates as one of the best of the vintage. A wine that will live for ages.

VINTAGE 1991 Medium color rather than deep; fruity, if slightly volatile, acetone nose, very spirity. Soft, ripe fruit on both nose and palate, with an intense structure of tannin and acidity; capable of long aging. Tasted side by side, this is preferable to the Cockburn's 1991, despite the fact that they were made by the same team.

VINTAGE 1985 (see page 131)

VINTAGE 1970 Tasted in October 1996 from the lodge-matured stock, in a blind comparative tasting of three 1970s. This wine is now pale ruby with a broad tawny rim, but has a massively open and mature nose of pepper and spice. Full palate, still having firm tannins and with great concentration of flavor and length. At its peak now, but will hold for many years.

PRODUCTION

Not applicable.

Eira Velha an important quinta.

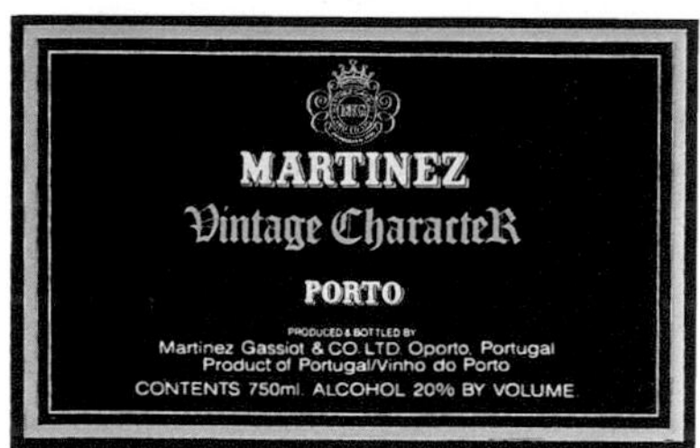

Sociedade Agricola E Comercial dos Vinhos Messias S.A.

Rua José Mariani, 139, Apartado 66
4401 Vila Nova de Gaia Codex, Portugal

Established in 1926, Porto Messias became involved in the port wine business in 1934. Sr Messias Baptista ran the firm from its inception until 1973, when it was taken over by his sons and grandsons.

The heart of the blends comes from Quinta do Cachão. Not far away is the company's other vineyard, Quinta do Rei. These quintas supply only a small fraction of the port they need, so most of the wine has to be bought in from surrounding farms, usually as grapes rather than wine.

Information

Visiting *Available to the trade only.*

Recommended Wines *Ruby.*

Overall Rating ★

Like many Portuguese houses, Messias is able to supply a long list of colheitas, in this case going back to 1947. However, they have an odd list of vintage declarations. Five vintages were declared in the 1980s, including 1982, 1984, and 1989, but 1985 is absent. Similarly, the firm decided to declare 1967 and 1968, but not 1966.

The wines tend to be light and rather bland, a style favored by Belgium, France, and the Netherlands, which are the company's main customers.

Production

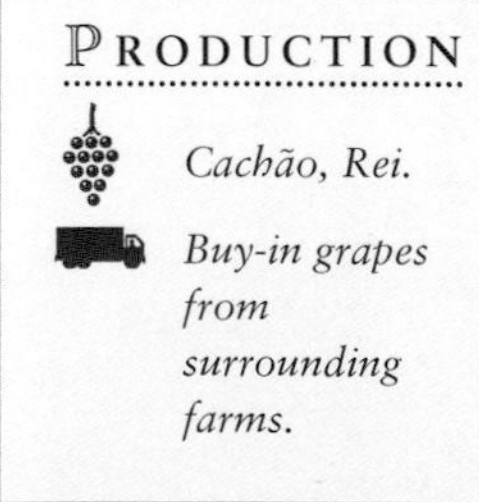

Cachão, Rei.

Buy-in grapes from surrounding farms.

The dramatic vineyards of Quinta do Cachão.

Tasting Notes

RUBY Pale ruby red with a very youthful, fresh nose of cherries and raspberries. Summer fruit smells. Sweet and light-bodied, lacking depth and concentration. Much better served chilled to highlight the freshness without worrying about the complexity.

COLHEITA 1980 Slightly hazy tawny color with a clean, fairly intense "vermouth spice" nose, similar to the herbal-spicy character of rosso vermouth. Sweet with low acidity, giving a spirity and sweet finish. Rather bland on the palate.

1982 VINTAGE Ruby turning to garnet color with a fullish plum and spice nose, lighter than most of the 1980s. Sweet with light structure, only moderate tannin and soft acidity; a slightly disappointing palate after the nose. Drink now.

Niepoort (Vinhos) S.A.

Rua Infante D. Henrique, 39–2°
4050 Porto, Portugal

> **INFORMATION**
>
> **VISITING** *No.*
>
> **RECOMMENDED WINES** *10 and 30 Years Old Tawny, colheitas, vintages.*
>
> **OVERALL RATING** ★★★

This tiny Dutch house, making only half a million bottles per year, is one of the least well known in the industry. Yet the wines deserve a far greater audience than they get.

Established in 1842, Niepoort is now run by the fourth and fifth generations of the Niepoort family, Relf and his son, Dirk, with the latter in control of the day-to-day wine making and vineyard operations. An intense, enthusiastic man, Dirk is unusually non-partisan, fascinated by wines from all corners of the world. Dinner with the Niepoorts is as likely to be preceded by Australian chardonnay or vintage champagne as it is by white port or Super Bok beer, two of the staples in this area.

Until very recently the company bought in all its grapes from small growers in the Cima Corgo, buying from only vineyards classified as class A on the Cadastro system, such is the Niepoort concern for quality. In the late 1980s the company, having survived for 140 years without a quinta, suddenly went on a buying spree and purchased three: Nápoles and Carril in 1988 and 1989 respectively, and Quinta do Passadouro in 1990. Among all three quintas, they supply about one-seventh of the company's needs.

Quinta do Nápoles should be the jewel in the crown. Located south of the Douro, on the east bank of the Rio Tedo, it is one of the oldest quintas in the region. It can trace its history back 500 years, but the house is currently in a state of disrepair (a situation seemingly unchanged for most of the last 50 years). Money has, however, been spent to replant the vineyards and to purchase stainless steel tanks.

Passadouro belongs to Dirk Niepoort and Dieter Bohnmann, an industrialist, as a joint venture rather than as part of Niepoort S.A. However, the wines are used in the company's blends as well as sold as a single quinta wine. Situated in the Pinhão valley, not far from Noval, Passadouro is made up of four small neighboring quintas bought at various times; the most recent purchase was a former Taylor's property. The main house

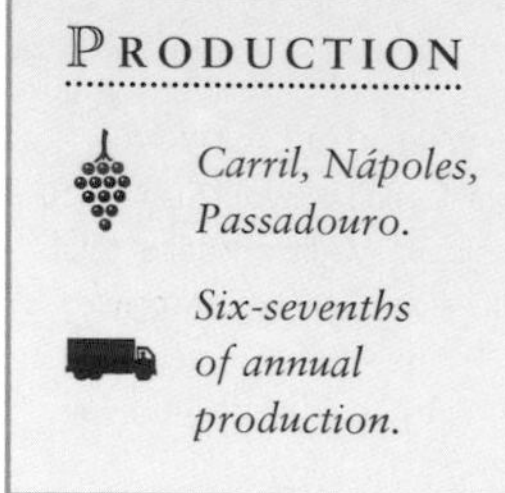

is now used as a guest house, although the very long and rough road leading to it is likely to put off all but the most inveterate travelers.

The majority of the Niepoort property is farmed organically, without pesticides or herbicides. In the parched Douro most growers try to avoid natural vegetation between the vines and on the terrace bank to avoid overstressing the vines and reducing yields. The Niepoort philosophy is to keep the weeds cut short and to manually remove them as needed at critical times. As a result the vines have a very low yield, sometimes as little as 9.4 U.S. gallons per acre, or about one-third of a bottle from each vine. In viticulture there is a generally held view that, within certain limits, quantity is inversely proportional to quality. Thus their policy improves the quality of the grapes.

Despite, or perhaps because of, Dirk's background in California as well as his frequent visits to other wine-producing countries, Niepoort is a thoroughly traditional, old-fashioned house. This is not the land of the technocrat; no gas chromatographs or electronic color measuring instruments are here. While most growers today use refractometers to judge ripeness, the Niepoort way is to taste the grapes. Dirk has a passion about riper tannins; in some years he will wait to harvest the grapes until far later than most companies in the hope that the tannins will ripen. Consequently, in youth the wines do not come across as astringent and brutal, despite being technically very tannic.

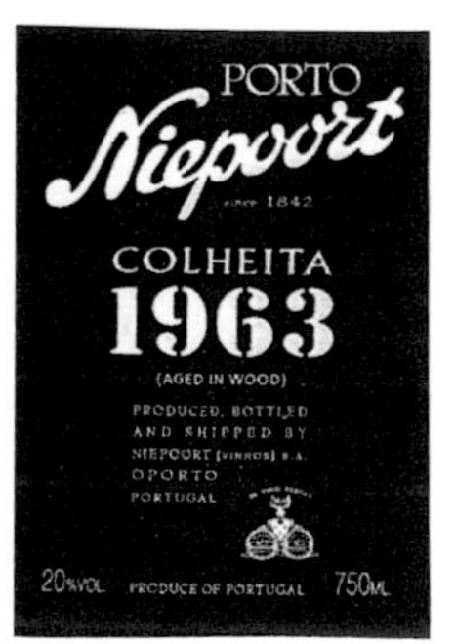

About 40 percent of the wine is trodden by foot; the remainder is made by mechanical pumping over, one small concession to technology. Even with treading, Niepoort takes a different tactic. The "standard," if there can ever be such a concept in a region as disparate as the Douro, is that one person per pipe must be in the lagar. Niepoort insist on two people; for example if 20 pipes are to be filled, 40 people must be in the lagar. This must make things a little crowded but it is an excellent method for extraction.

The lodge, too, is old-fashioned; small and cramped. The tasting room resembles a museum with its yellowing shelves packed floor to ceiling with sample and reference bottles – one from each cask or vat – as well as a reference library of wines from vintages long past. A high Dickensian writing desk and stool sit in the corner, not just for show but for daily use. One almost expects letters to be written with a quill.

TASTING NOTES

20 YEARS OLD TAWNY More complex and powerful than the 10 Years Old. Medium depth of color with a powerful, almost cognac style nose. Medium-sweet with a full nutty palate which retains an amazing freshness.

COLHEITA 1987 Fully tawny color with a fresh and quite delicate nose of nuts and dried fruit. Medium-sweet, with a light to medium palate. Balanced fruit, sweetness, and acidity with a long length.

LBV 1992 Deep color, great concentration of dark fruits on the nose and palate with a firm structure of tannin and acid which will allow this wine to mature for many, many years. This is one of the most traditional of traditional LBVs

TASTING NOTES

RUBY

RUBY Quite pale in color and light in style, with a very fresh, fruity, and spicy character; not at all jammy.

WHITE

DRY WINE Deep orange color with a citrus, spicy, candied-peel nose. A dry, light, white port, but one with enough backbone to be interesting. Niepoort white ports are trodden and aged in the same way as the reds, giving them extra complexity and interest.

TAWNY

JUNIOR TAWNY The basic tawny of the family. Pale ruby in color with a light cherry-like fruit character; a medium to light style with a freshness that makes for very easy drinking.

FINE TAWNY Despite the name, which usually indicates the most basic of tawnies, this is a fairly serious wine. At five years old it is more complex, richer, and a little sweeter than the Junior, but rather dumber on the nose.

SENIOR TAWNY A step up again, a wine with concentration and elegance in equal measure. More gutsy than the younger versions; one of the few Niepoort wines to come across as powerful on both the nose and palate.

AGED TAWNY

10 YEARS OLD TAWNY Medium orange-brown with a delicate hazelnut nose, hardly spirity at all, quite unusual for a tawny. Medium-sweet and perfectly balanced, with a very long, elegant finish.

20 YEARS OLD TAWNY
(see page 137)

30 YEARS OLD TAWNY This is an outstanding wine. By this age many ports are taking on a toffee and fudge character and getting rather thick and heavy – not always pleasant to drink. This is very fine and, despite its age, not at all cloying. Pickled walnuts and marzipan come through but the wine does not show everything at once. It is a wine to consider carefully, since only after a few tastes does the complexity come out.

COLHEITA

COLHEITA 1988 More red in color than the 1987, more fruity on the nose with a powerful and almost aggressive fruit on the palate. Medium-sweet with some tannin and a long finish.

COLHEITA 1987 (see page 137)

COLHEITA 1935 The 1935 (bottled 1977) has the deep walnut brown color of old oloroso sherry and the yellow rim of the finest Madeira. A spirity nose is followed up by concentrated dried fruit – raisins and prunes – and a great length.

LBV

LBV 1992 (see page 137)

SINGLE QUINTA VINTAGE

QUINTA DO PASSADOURO VINTAGE 1994 Deep color with strong fruit on the nose with an elegant palate; sweet with plenty of tannin and acidity to keep the wine for many years. Initially this seemed relatively light compared to many of the other 1994s, but this is more a result of the lack of aggressive tannins than anything else.

VINTAGE

VINTAGE 1970 Very deep ruby, full and rich nose, only beginning to show some of the spice associated with maturity. Sweet with crisp acidity and massive structure still of very firm but ripe tannins. A great length of finish.

VINTAGE 1945 1945 vintage ports are now very rare and have mostly reached the peak of their drinking lives. The 1945 Niepoort is still remarkably youthful, with a deep ruby color and an intense and powerful nose of dark, ripe fruit. Astonishingly concentrated, in no way reveals its age, still having firm tannins and plenty of fruit.

Osborne (Vinhos de Portugal) & Ca., Lda.

Rua da Cabaça, 37
4400 Vila Nova de Gaia, Portugal

> **INFORMATION**
>
> VISITING *The lodge is open all year to visitors. Tel. (351–2) 302648.*
>
> RECOMMENDED WINES *LBV.*
>
> OVERALL RATING ★★

The black bull of the Osborne wine company is well known throughout Spain, advertising their sherries and brandies, but far less famous is their port business. With the company's emphasis on education through the trade, this is set to change, but it will be a long time before Osborne ports have the fame of their sherries.

Although normally pronounced in the Spanish way, with the accent on the final "e" (Osborné), Osborne started as a British firm. It was established in 1772 by an Englishman from Exeter called Thomas Osborne. The Portuguese side of the business is much younger, however. The company first began doing business in Portugal in the 1960s and the company only got its own lodge in Vila Nova de Gaia in 1988, when Christiano van Zeller vacated the Noval lodge as part of their move upriver.

So far Osborne has been a trader, not a grower. They have their own winery, which makes nearly two-thirds of the wine they need, and the rest is bought in as wine. All the grapes come from the Cima Corgo and Douro Superior; nothing is sourced at Régua. About 40 percent of the production is bought from small growers who still tread the grapes by foot. Osborne is a moderate-sized operation, producing about a million bottles per year, of which 20 percent are premium categories. Osborne vintages are fairly light and fruity, but show considerable elegance.

Education has been highlighted as a way of getting the company better known in the right circles, particularly by the sales staff who will sell the wine. To this end they offer the Osborne Master of Port, a program to train sommeliers throughout the world, in association with the Union de la Sommelerie Français and Champagne Tattinger. Teaching sales people, especially those in a restaurant environment, can only help the sales of port in general, as well as Osborne's products.

Tasting Notes

MASTER OF PORT SPECIAL RESERVE An aged tawny. Deep orange ruby with a spicy nose reminiscent of cinnamon and allspice, with fruitcake and dried fruit. Medium-sweet and medium-bodied with overt spirit on the palate, rather hot on the mid-palate. Good depth of flavor, but not in the same class as the 10 year old.

10 YEARS OLD TAWNY Very pale color of topaz brown; mature nose of spirit and fruit, with some spice and a little caramel. Medium-sweet with refreshingly crisp acidity. Not very concentrated fruit, but a fine finish. A light and elegant wine.

LBV

LBV 1992 This has recently replaced the 1991 version. Deep purple-ruby hue with a full and concentrated nose of plums and dark chocolate. Full, rich palate with good structure for an LBV, with both powerful fruit flavors and enough tannin and acid to balance it. A very good example. Oxidizes quickly – drink up once the cork has been pulled.

VINTAGE

VINTAGE 1994 Medium to deep hue with a light, fruity, fairly closed nose. Firm tannins and fully sweet; medium- to full-bodied with balanced fruit and structure. A well-made elegant wine, but not a block-buster. Drink in the medium term.

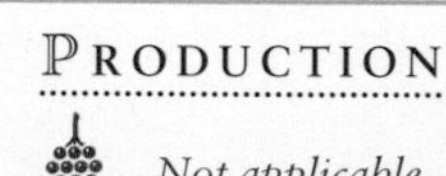

PRODUCTION

Not applicable.

100% of annual production.

Manoel D. Poças Junior – Vinhos S.A.

Rua Visconde das Devesas, 186,
Apartado 1556
4401 Vila Nova de Gaia Codex, Portugal

INFORMATION

VISITING *Trade only; contact should be made through a local importer.*

RECOMMENDED WINES *10 Years Old.*

OVERALL RATING ★

Selling its wines under the brands of Porto Poças, Pousada Porto, and Porto Seguro, Poças Junior is one of the few remaining family-owned Portuguese port shippers still in business.

The firm's founder, Manoel D. Poças, was a farmer's son who started work at the age of 12 as an errand boy for an insurance company in Oporto. His employer, Rawes, was an agent for Lloyds of London, insurers of both ships and cargo; therefore his work brought him into daily contact with shipping firms. When, at age 22 he was looking for a career change, it was logical to join a port shipper, the firm Ferreira.

At this time trade was in a recession, but as World War I drew to an end, business increased again in a boom that was to last until the worldwide Depression of the thirties. Seeing his opportunity, Manoel Poças went into business on his own with a company called Poças & Comandita. His partner and financial backer was his uncle, Manoel Francisco Gomes Junior, a former warehouse manager for the port firm Hunt, Roop, & Co. The partnership was to last only six years, after which the company took on its present name. Realizing that getting into the export field would be difficult, the firm initially specialized in supplying fortification brandy to other companies. With the rise in port sales, the demand for brandy increased.

But not all would be smooth sailing. Following a coup d'état in 1926, the new dictator, Salazar, imposed a government monopoly on the sale of brandy, effectively removing the reason for the company's existence. Only at this point did Poças move into wine sales. Fortuitously the company had just acquired, through a customer's bad debt, Quinta das Quartas, which they still own today. Good years followed, even through the 1930s, when many firms saw sales fall. However, World War II was to be catastrophic for everyone in the port business.

Poor trade continued through the years following the war, exacerbated by a poor deal that almost led to the end of the firm. Only in the 1950s did trade increase again, and was particularly good in the 1960s. Manoel retired in 1966, with other members of the family already having been brought into the partnership some years before.

PRODUCTION

 *Quartas, Santa Bárbara, Val de Cavalos.*

 *91% of annual production.*

Since then, with sales increasing and finances improving, the company has been able to invest in improvements to the vineyards and wine making facilities. Their own vineyards, Quintas das Quartas, de Val de Cavalos, and Santa Bárbara, supply about 9 percent of the total requirements. Quartas is small and entirely walled; substantial areas of the other two are more mechanizable. Only about 2½ percent of the wine is trodden by foot; the rest is produced by mechanical pumping over, another product of recent investment.

Small amounts of Poças ports appear in the English-speaking markets; the majority of exports go to Belgium, Spain, France, the Netherlands, and Denmark. Since the main markets are the Benelux countries and France, places where port is served chilled as an apéritif, the wines tend to be very sweet and slightly jammy in nature. Chilling freshens them up and gentle cooling is recommended, even if the wines will be consumed after a meal. In addition to the wines that follow, Poças also produces a range of colheitas dating back to the 1960s and a few vintages, but none of these were tasted.

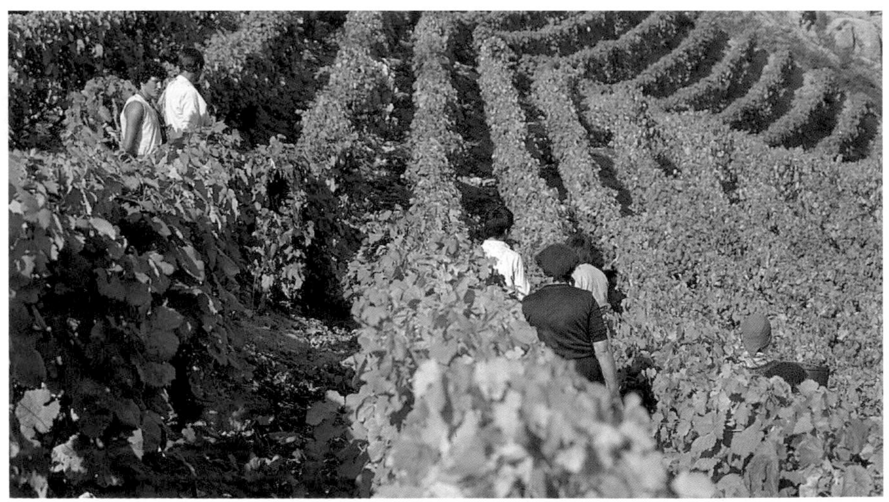

HARVESTING GRAPES FOR POÇAS PORTS.

TASTING NOTES

TWO DIAMONDS RUBY Light ruby red color with a very fresh, youthful nose of raspberries and cherries. Sweet, slightly jammy fruit on the palate, but quite light with a clean, refreshing finish.

10 YEARS OLD A gutsy wine, deep tawny brown in color, with a pronounced, herbal quality along with toffee and caramel. Very sweet and fat style with a rich, smooth palate and relatively long finish.

TAWNY

POUSADA TAWNY PORT Pale pinkish brown in color; initially youthful and fruity but developing in the glass to the more mature toffee and raisin nose that one would expect from a tawny. Very sweet with toffee and fudge character; can be a little cloying if not chilled.

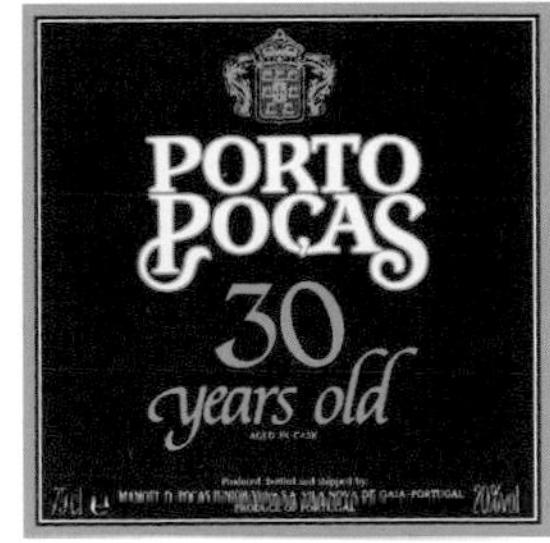

Quarles Harris & Ca, S.A.

Trav. Barão de Forrester, 85, Apartado 26
4401 Vila Nova de Gaia Codex, Portugal

Quarles Harris is one of the half dozen houses in the Symington group. The firm was founded in 1680, making it one of the oldest in the business. However, it is now rather obscure and unknown, as the not-inconsiderable marketing skills of the Symington family have been directed more toward the other brands in their portfolio.

Information

Visiting *To lodge, by appointment only. Tel. (351–2) 3796063.*

Recommended Wines *1994 Vintage.*

Overall Rating ★★

Unlike the main companies in the group, Quarles Harris has no vineyards of its own. The wines for the brand are made from bought-in grapes vinified at Bomfim or, since 1996, at a new winery a few miles downriver from Pinhão. A little is bought in as wine, and made in lagares.

Because Quarles Harris wines are not tremendously well known, the prices tend to be keen. However, there is no doubt that they are lesser wines than the greats – Dow's, Warre's, and W. & J. Graham's. In terms of sweetness, the wines tend to be on the drier side, more like Dow's than Graham's.

Production

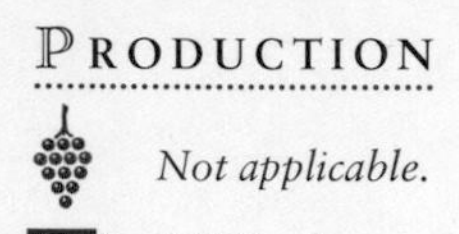

Not applicable.

100% of annual production.

The wines are vinified at Quinta do Bomfim.

Tasting Notes

20 YEARS OLD TAWNY Medium slightly pinkish brown, with a spirity and figgy nose of fruits rather than nuts; slightly medicinal and herbal, too. Medium-sweet with balanced acidity. Moderate weight; fresh with a pleasant finish, but lacking great concentration or length.

1991 VINTAGE Medium depth of color with a slightly spirity nose overpowering the fruit, which is still closed and sulking. Plums and chocolate on the palate, along with medium sweetness and moderate tannins. Attractive, if closed now; will benefit from a further 5 to 10 years maturation.

TAWNY

10 YEARS OLD TAWNY Reddish brown in color, very bright and clear. Powerful aromatic nose, but with a slight hint of solvent or varnish. Light weight on the palate; medium-sweet with crisp acidity and a medium, nutty length.

VINTAGE

1994 VINTAGE Extremely deep black wine with a very closed nose still. Black currant and mint notes. Medium- to full-bodied with firm but not aggressive tannins and balanced acidity. A good wine that will mature in the medium term, in about 10 to 15 years.

1985 VINTAGE This is one of the more mature examples of the 1985. Ruby red, medium depth with a rich, open nose of ripe, if hot, fruit. The palate is a little austere, drier than many 1985s, medium-bodied and with soft tannins.

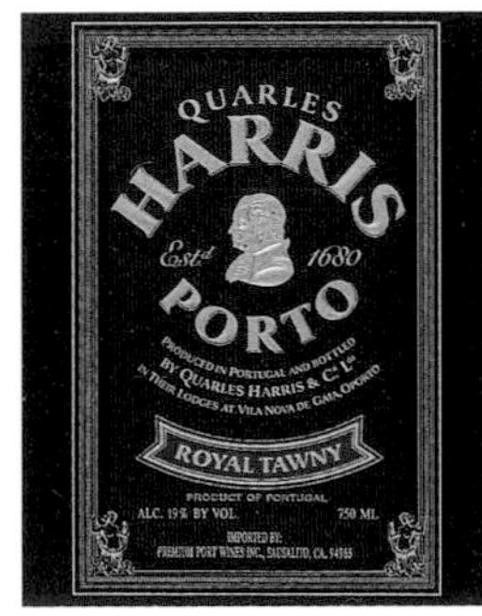

Adriano Ramos Pinto (Vinhos) S.A.

Av. Ramos Pinto, 380, Apartado 1320
4401 Vila Nova de Gaia Codex, Portugal

Ramos Pinto is one of the most innovative companies in the port industry, spearheading much of the research in the Douro. The firm has a distinguished reputation for fine aged tawnies, while their vintages, though not blockbusters, show considerable elegance and finesse.

Adriano and António Ramos Pinto founded the firm that bears their name in 1880 with the South American – specifically Brazilian – market in mind. The company soon built up a reputation both for their wines and for their well-planned marketing and promotion. Famous artists of the time were frequently utilized to produce eye-catching posters, often with hedonistic and mythological themes.

Champagne producer Louis Roederer now have a controlling interest in the firm, but it is still run by João Nicolau de Almeida, a direct descendant of the founders. João has spent many years researching the viticulture of the area. As befits a company led by a keen grower, Ramos Pinto can satisfy most of their needs with supplies from their own quintas, giving them far greater control over the ultimate quality of the wine.

> **INFORMATION**
>
> **VISITING** *Visitors are welcome to the lodge; trade visits only to the quintas. Guided tours of the lodge are offered from 10:00 to 6:00 in summer and from 9:00 to 5:00 in winter. Tel. (351–2) 3707000.*
>
> **RECOMMENDED WINES** *Quinta da Ervamoira 10 Years Old Tawny, Quinta do Bom Retiro 20 Years Old Tawny, Ramos Pinto Vintage 1991.*
>
> **OVERALL RATING** ★★★

It was João, with his uncle, Jorge Ramos-Pinto Rosas, who first identified the top grape varieties for port that are now recommended for all new planting. More recent research has concentrated on working the vineyard so that Ramos Pinto's faith in the vinha ao alto planting system verges on religious fervor. João delights in expounding his beliefs with the help of graphs and tables like an overenthusiastic science professor. The tangible example of his theories is Quinta da Ervamoira, one of the very few large vineyards to be entirely terrace-free.

Ervamoira is in the Douro Superior, in the valley of the River Côa, not far from the Spanish border. Here the grower's dream has been realized with 247 acres of prime

Douro schist planted entirely without terracing. Grapes from Ervamoira are used in vintage blends and a 10-year-old single quinta tawny.

The jewel in the company's crown is Quinta do Bom Retiro, a short but tortuous drive from Pinhão along the Rio Torto. Behind the house the winery shows the contrasts so common in the port industry: a computer-controlled winery and a well-equipped laboratory stand alongside two stone lagares still used every year for the best grapes. The sheltered position of this east-facing vineyard gives a fresh quality to an excellent 20-year-old tawny sold under the quinta name.

PRODUCTION

Bom Retiro, Bons Ares, Ervamoira, Urtiga.

Buy-in small quantities in exceptional years, but increasingly self-sufficient.

The neighboring Quinta da Urtiga features some of the oldest vineyards the company owns, with some of the terraces dating from the eighteenth century. Ramos Pinto produces a single quinta ruby from these vines in addition to using them in blends. Quinta dos Bons Ares, also in the Cima Corgo, is the fourth vineyard. Here, over 1,950 feet above sea level, it is too cool for port production, so the grapes are used to make Douro light wine. The cooler climate is, however, an advantage for vinification, so the grapes from Ervamoira are fermented here.

Ramos Pinto's strength has always been their tawnies rather than their vintages, which are unashamedly designed for relatively early consumption. The 1970 was tasted on a few occasions, most recently in Portugal in October 1996 in the presence of a company representative. The wine was already fully mature with no potential for further development. In previous tastings the wine was showing rather better; bottle variation can be a major problem for wines this old. The 1994s, in contrast, are very big wines.

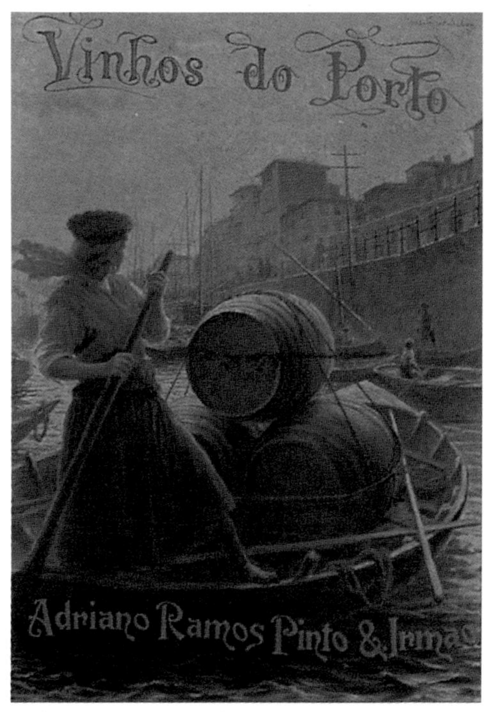

A PAINTING BY CONDEIXA WAS USED TO ADVERTISE RAMOS PINTO PORTS.

Tasting Notes

QUINTA DA URTIGA Remarkably deep, with just a hint of maturity showing on the rim of the wine. Aromatic nose of black fruits with a hint of spice and peppery alcohol. Firm tannins and reasonable concentration of peppery fruit, backed up by refreshing acidity and firm structure. Very good wine of its type, fully ready when released.

QUINTA DO BOM RETIRO 20 YEARS OLD Sheltered as the quinta is on the east-facing side of the valley, Bom Retiro is a particularly clean, fresh wine. A delicious hazelnut and fig character, quite delicate in nature, backed up by a crisp, palate-cleansing acidity.

LBV 1989 Still very deep purple red color, opaque in the center, but with a developing rich, dark fruit and dried Mediterranean fruit (figs and dates) character. Softening tannins and medium-sweetness give way to a mouthful of dark fruit flavors and a great finish. This is a traditional LBV and it should be decanted. Ready to drink now.

TASTING NOTES

RUBY

QUINTA DA URTIGA
(see page 148)

WHITE

PORTO APERITIVO Vivid golden yellow color with a fresh but rather neutral nose of candied peel and dried apricots. Off-dry with crisp acidity and medium weight. Clean and long finish. This is a traditionally-made wine, fermented in lagares and matured for some years in pipe, making it more complex than some, but still slightly lacking fruit.

AGED TAWNY

QUINTA DA ERVAMOIRA 10 YEARS OLD TAWNY A classic of its type, still retaining the slight reddish hints of youth. This is a fresh wine with a strong, nutty aroma and flavor, with balanced acids and medium weight.

QUINTA DO BOM RETIRO 20 YEARS OLD (see page 148)

RAMOS PINTO 30 YEARS OLD TAWNY Fully brown, without even the slightest hint of red remaining. A very concentrated wine, with hints of pickled walnuts and figs on the nose and a powerful palate that is sweet and full, but with perfectly balanced acidity. Inevitably at this age the wine lacks the freshness of its younger siblings, but it makes up for that in concentration and length.

LBV

LBV 1989 (see page 148)

VINTAGE

VINTAGE 1994 This wine was tasted several times, both before and since it was released. Initially it seemed light and unlikely to have a great life. However, after a few months in the bottle the tannic structure grew, closing in the fruit, normally a sign of a good, long-lived wine. It is complex, with a number of layers of flavor. It is fresh and has slightly crisp acidity, a function of having wine from the relatively shaded Bom Retiro in the blend.

VINTAGE 1991 At a 1991 tasting alongside its peers soon after release, the Ramos Pinto wine stood out as being more delicate and fragrant than most, and certainly more approachable at that stage than many of the others. Not a very long-term wine, but one to start drinking soon after the start of the new millennium.

VINTAGE 1982 Developing well, with moderately powerful, black fruit character and a pleasant, not very strong structure of acids and tannins. Drinking well now, with potential for another few years.

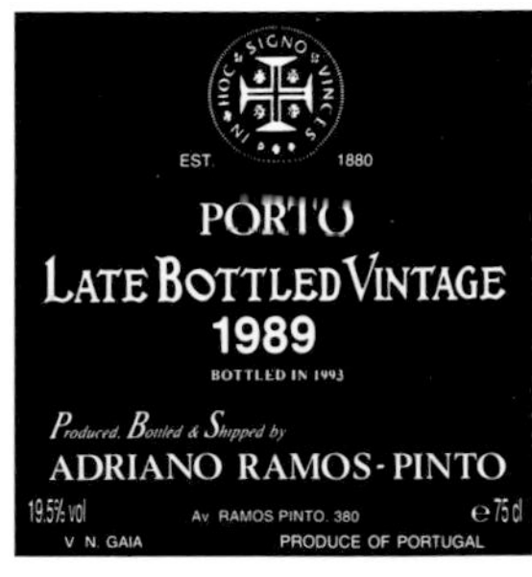

Real Companhia Velha Lda.

Rua Azevedo Magalhães, 314–
4430 Vila Nova de Gaia, Portugal

There are very few wine companies that can lay claim to having been founded as a direct result of an edict from a king. But this is exactly what happened with the Real Companhia Velha, also known as Royal Oporto. The history of Royal Oporto is closely tied with the history of the entire industry.

When the King of Portugal, José I, instructed Sebastião José de Carvalho e Melo, the Count de Oeiras and Marquis of Pombal to sort out the problems of the port industry, he did so through a company set up by royal charter, the Companhia Geral da Agricultura das Vinhas do Alto Douro. At that stage its role was regulatory – control by means of a state monopoly. One of the first, and certainly most lasting, acts of the company was to draw, for the first time in the history of viticulture, a map demarcating the region.

> **INFORMATION**
>
> **VISITING** *By appointment only to the lodge. Tel. (351–2) 303013.*
>
> **RECOMMENDED WINES** *Ruby, Aged 20 Years, Over 40 Years Old .*
>
> **OVERALL RATING** ★ *but can be* ★★

Teams of staff toured the region mapping the best vineyards and classifying their wines into three categories (see page 19). The company held a monopoly on the two top categories, and controlled prices for the entire market. These controls improved the quality of the wine and increased overall port sales so that by the 1780s port accounted for three-quarters of the English wine trade. Moreover, exports to other countries were rising all the time.

A change in the political atmosphere resulted in the temporary dissolution of the company in 1834. It returned, with all its power, in 1838, but this was to be a short-lived restoration; the company was finally disbanded in its regulatory form in 1850, when it became the trading company it is today.

Real Companhia Velha is one of the largest port firms and has been *the* largest, having only recently been overtaken by the Symington group. It is one of the most important landowners in the Douro, owning the enormous Quinta das Carvalhas, often enviously referred to by other shippers as "Royal Oporto's Mountain." Carvalhas, on the south side of the Douro opposite Pinhão, extends from Roêda downstream until the Douro curves to the left opposite Quinta da Foz. The vineyard occupies the whole of the north-facing hillside, extending over the summit and forming the upper slopes of the Rio Torto valley. It is certainly the largest quinta in the area, but not the only one in Royal Oporto's portfolio. Additionally, they own Quinta dos Aciprestes near Tua and Casal da Granja high up on the plateau at Alijó and Sidrô. These latter two are high-altitude vineyards, whose production is best suited to white port and light wine.

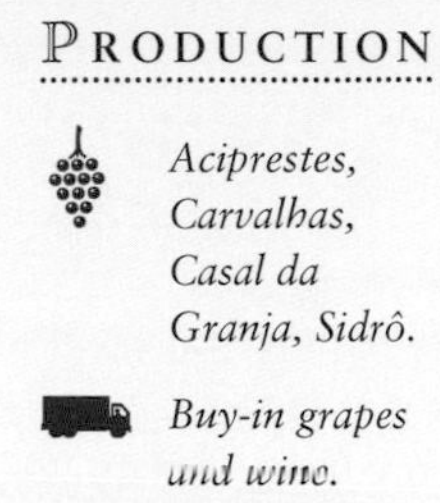

History has a strange habit of returning to the same themes. The company that was founded as a controlling body has recently become embroiled in controversy. In 1990 the Casa do Douro, then one of two regulatory bodies controlling port production, bought a significant number of shares in the Real Companhia Velha. Not surprisingly, there was strong opposition to a controlling body having a stake in owning a shipper. At the time of this writing, the Casa is set to lose most of its regulatory powers, and a new body has been established to take them over. The purchase has, however, left the Casa do Douro technically bankrupt, a predicament that has yet to be resolved.

Real Companhia Velha declares vintages very frequently, but they do not particularly have a reputation for them. Their vintages tend to be coarse and lack refinement. Their other wines, however, are sound examples of their type, and some are quite remarkable.

PORTS MATURING IN THE EARTH-FLOORED LODGE.

TASTING NOTES

REAL COMPANHIA VELHA AGED 20 YEARS Clear, pale orange-brown color with a distinctly aged and fairly intense baked fruit and nut flavor. Sweet and medium-bodied. Less aggressively spirity than the 10 year old, with a good intensity of flavor.

ROYAL OPORTO RUBY Deep ruby in color with a very full, ripe, dark fruit character, this wine showed very well against its competitors. Full weight plus some tannic background and a reasonable length would lead one to believe that this was a premium rather than a basic ruby at a totally blind tasting.

REAL COMPANHIA VELHA OVER 40 YEARS OLD Very pale orange-brown with a nose of medium intensity, very aged, as it should be, giving caramel, dried fruit, and some sweet spices, even slightly gingery. Sweet with balanced acidity and moderate body. Good fruit concentration, with enough structure to hold it.

TASTING NOTES

RUBY

ROYAL OPORTO RUBY
(see page 152)

REAL COMPANHIA VELHA QUINTA DOS ACIPRESTES RUBY The company claims this is older than the basic ruby, but it looks and tastes younger. Deep purple hue with a full flavor of plums and blackberries. Full-bodied with some backbone, and a good length.

WHITE

ROYAL OPORTO EXTRA DRY WHITE Medium gold color with a light, fresh, and fruity nose. Very crisp citric palate with just a little hint of sweetness. Light to medium weight and a moderate length. A pleasant, if basic quality, wine that is good before a meal, or mixed with tonic or lemonade.

REAL COMPANHIA VELHA QUINTA DO CASAL DA GRANJA WHITE A more premium dry white than the Royal Oporto version. Made only from grapes grown on the cool quinta, it is fruitier and has hints of apricots. Off-dry, or even medium (although it is labeled "Branco Seco"), it has more to offer than the basic wine.

ROYAL OPORTO WHITE The sweeter version of the above. Similar characteristics, but the sweetness balances the citric acidity more and appears to bring out the fruit character, making it seem fuller and more flavorful.

TAWNY

ROYAL OPORTO TAWNY Aged a little longer than the ruby, this is pale ruby in color with a light and youthful, very fruity nose. Balanced palate, medium-sweet with just balanced acidity; medium weight and just slightly spirity. A pleasant quaffing port.

REAL COMPANHIA VELHA QUINTA DAS CARVALHAS TAWNY Made from grapes from the flagship winery, and aged a little longer, this wine shows hardly any age on the appearance, just a hint of browning to the edge. The nose is of nutty and some stone fruit, still youthful. Fuller than the Royal Oporto version, but without much more structure or length.

AGED TAWNY

ROYAL OPORTO 10 YEARS OLD Full, rich appearance, red-brown hue, the perfect 10-year-old color. Fairly dumb nose initially, but eventually giving dried fruits and some nuttiness, with an earthy hint as well. Medium sweet palate with quite aggressive alcohol and a medium length.

REAL COMPANHIA VELHA AGED 20 YEARS (see page 152)

REAL COMPANHIA VELHA OVER 40 YEARS OLD (see page 152)

VINTAGE

ROYAL OPORTO 1994 VINTAGE Medium depth of color; full, plummy nose. Medium-sweet with firm, slightly aggressive tannins (not a bad thing in a wine so young), and medium weight. One of the best Royal Oporto vintages tried, but not outstanding for the vintage, which is generally very good.

ROYAL OPORTO 1987 VINTAGE Already showing some signs of maturity, this is medium ruby in color. The bouquet is already developed, with hints of sweet spice and fruit, giving raisins, grapes, and dates. Medium weight with remarkably soft tannins for a wine of this age. Mature now, with little chance of further development.

ROYAL OPORTO 1985 VINTAGE Deeper than the 1987, but that is to be expected given the better vintage. Curiously it appears equally mature, already ruby, with even the faintest hints of garnet on the rim. Rather unpleasant nose. The palate is more appealing – medium-sweet with softening tannins and medium weight, but with a short finish.

Romariz – Vinhos, S.A.

Rua de Rei Ramiro, 356, Apartado 189
4401 Vila Nova de Gaia Codex, Portugal

Romariz is one of the less well-known port shippers. Originally started in 1850 by Manoel da Rocha Romariz to trade with the Portuguese colonies, in particular Brazil, the firm now concentrates on the European market, although South American sales are still important. The last Romariz retired from the firm in 1966, when it was sold to Guimaraens & Co. (not Fonseca Guimaraens). More recently, in 1987 a British investment group bought the firm and will use their capital to develop the brand further. We are likely to see more of Romariz wines in the future.

INFORMATION

VISITING *Visitors are welcome to the lodge; call first for opening times. Tel. (351–2) 306980.*

RECOMMENDED WINES *Reserva Latina.*

OVERALL RATING ★★

Not owning a quinta, Romariz buys in wine from Douro growers who make it either in autovinifiers or by remontagem. Lagares are not a feature here. The wines are matured at the company's lodge in Vila Nova de Gaia, to which tourists are welcome.

PRODUCTION

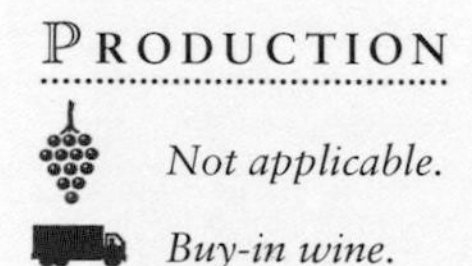

Not applicable.

Buy-in wine.

The range of wines is small and includes all the standards, but Romariz is particularly proud of their Reserva Latina, an old tawny without a specific stated age. It has been awarded a number of prizes in international wine competitions.

Tasting Notes

RESERVA LATINA An old tawny port that does not claim any particular age. Vivid red tawny in color, with an intense cinnamon spice character and some of the mature style of a very old cognac. Medium-sweet, with moderate acidity and reasonable concentration on the palate. A complex wine with an interesting mix of youthful characters and considerable age, which shows the benefits of blending.

10 YEAR OLD Fairly deep red tawny in color; a light, slightly spirity note with some almond hints, but mostly of hot spices and dried fruit. Medium-sweet with crisp acidity and medium weight. Pleasant enough, but not as complex or interesting as the Latina.

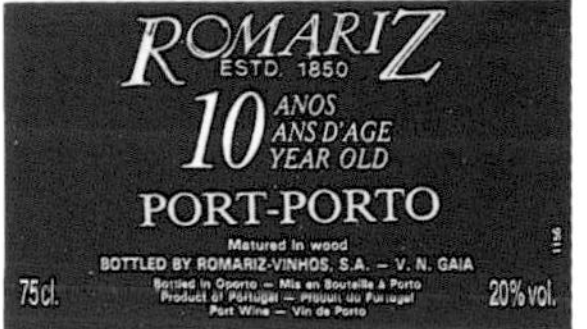

1963 COLHEITA Russet brown in color; remarkably, still showing some red after all this time. Very mature nose of old, damp wood and the wild mushroom-like character of some old spirits. Sweet, crisp, refreshing acidity and great concentration of flavor, far more powerful palate than the nose implies, with a complex nutty and mature finish.

Rozès, Limitada

Rua Cândido dos Reus, 526/532
Apartado 376, 4401 Vila Nova de Gaia
Codex, Portugal

The year 1855 was a very important one in Bordeaux. It was then that the local chamber of commerce, along with merchants of the town, classified the finest châteaux of the left bank as the Médoc and Sauternes, thus establishing a hierarchy of fine wines that still exists today. At the same time one Bordeaux merchant, Ostende Rozès, was setting up the only originally French port house, Rozès.

> **INFORMATION**
>
> **VISITING** *The lodge in Vila Nova de Gaia is open from July to September. Visits are also possible at other times of the year by appointment. Tel. (351–2) 3792607.*
>
> **RECOMMENDED WINES** *Vintage 1991.*
>
> **OVERALL RATING** ★★

A small amount, only about 1 percent, of Rozès wine comes from the Quinta do Monsul, in the Baixo Corgo, south of the Douro River just opposite Régua. This quinta has a history that dates back to the beginning of the Portuguese nation; its first recorded owner was Dom Alfonso Henriques, the first king of Portugal. Most of the grapes come from growers in the Cima Corgo from around Pinhão and São João da Pesqueira. Rozès claims that over 80 percent of their supplies come from vineyards rated A or B, and the lowest rated vineyard they use is C.

Grape quality is assessed on arrival at the winery, and only the best go to the lagares; the remainder is vinified in modern pumping-over tanks. Foot-trampled grapes go to the potential vintage lotes, and remontagem is used for the wines destined for shorter aging.

Rozès is now owned by the French luggage-to-champagne conglomerate, LVMH. Apart from Moët et Chandon, it also owns the cognac companies Hine and Hennessey, a clutch of champagne houses, and sparkling wine facilities in many countries. Perhaps it is the influence of the sparkling wine side of the business that dictates the style of Rozès port: delicate and fine, never the strapping, gutsy style produced by the British houses, nor the sweeter, more jammy, or caramel characters of many Portuguese shippers.

Tasting Notes

INFANTA ISABEL 10 YEARS OLD Very pale orange tawny with a light and fresh nose; very delicate. Clean, fresh palate of fresh figs and raisins. Medium-sweet with crisp acidity and a good length. Elegant style, but because it lacks the power of some, could be unfairly overlooked in a comparative tasting.

VINTAGE 1991 Very deep in color; still quite purple in 1996. Slightly volatile, linseed oil character at first on the nose, giving way to plums and grape characters. Very intense palate with massive concentration of fruit, moderate tannins, and a good length. A good wine for the medium-term.

RUBY

RUBY Medium depth, vivid ruby hue with a light, fruity nose, more raspberry and cherry than plums. Lively palate, a little spirity but refreshing.

WHITE

ROZÈS WHITE Deep golden yellow in color, with a mature candied peel and dried fruit nose. Sweet with balanced acidity and a moderate finish.

LBV

LATE BOTTLED VINTAGE 1991 A modern-style LBV, with six years in cask before it is filtered and bottled. Deep ruby color, giving no hint of maturity, nor of exceptional youth. Ripe plums on the nose with a hint of raisins, but moderately intense and quite elegant. Sweet palate, full-bodied, and remarkably youthful, showing very little development. Firm and balanced structure and a reasonable length. Lighter in style than some LBVs, but harmonious and elegant.

Monsul

99% of annual production.

Sandeman & Ca., S.A.

Largo de Miguel Bombarda, 3, Apartado 2
4401 Vila Nova de Gaia Codex, Portugal

The port trade is dominated by brands, but only the Sandeman Don, a silhouetted figure wearing a student's gown and a broad-rimmed hat, is universally recognized by most wine drinkers as the trademark or symbol of a port house.

Sandeman recently celebrated its bicentennial; it was founded in 1790 by the first of many George Sandemans to be involved in the business. Never an apathetic man, he reportedly set out from Perth, Scotland, to make a fortune on which he hoped to retire by the end of the century, if not sooner. At this time, he was 25.

The firm was not originally set up in Oporto, or indeed in Jerez, as sherry was the other arm of the business. It was established near Cornhill in the City of London, which was, at the time, one of the main centers of the British wine trade, being conveniently situated for the London docks. The initial capital of 300 pounds came from young Sandeman's father, also George, a cabinetmaker in Perth.

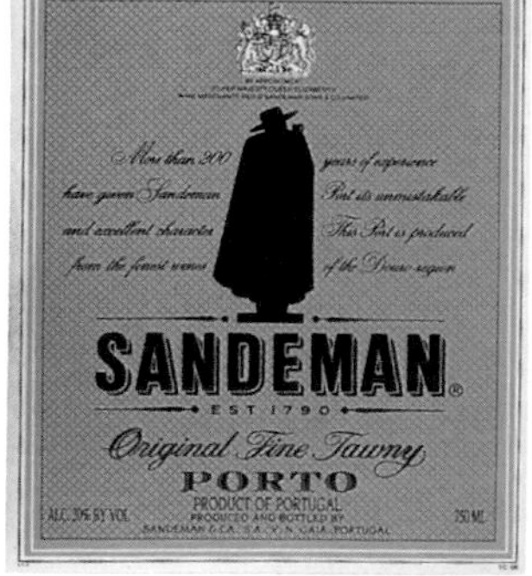

It was a good time to set up business. In the 1790s the port trade as a whole was doing very well, as was sherry. These Iberian wines had a virtual monopoly of the market, largely due to the supply of French claret having dried up, not to be restored until after Waterloo in 1815. The war had its costs, however, and prices increased dramatically in the first few years of Sandeman's trading. Success in times of high inflation is a remarkable feat.

Information

Visiting *Visitors are welcome to tour the lodge in Gaia; open daily from 10:00 to 6:00, closed for lunch. There is also a visitors' center, plus tours and a museum. Tel. (351–2) 3702293. Also check out the museum at Vale de Mendiz near Pinhão Tel. (351–54) 72333, and the Cambres wine center near Régua Tel. (351–54) 323626.*

Recommended Wines *Imperial Aged Reserve Tawny, Quinta do Vau 1988.*

Overall Rating ★★

QUINTA DO VAU.

On George Sandeman's retirement the firm was taken over by another George, his nephew George Glas Sandeman, although one of the elder George's sons continued to work in the firm. It is one of George Glas's direct descendants who now manages the firm. The remainder of the nineteenth century was, for Sandeman, dominated by the same problems that plagued the rest of the industry. Political upheavals and vineyard scourges made an impact here as elsewhere, although Sandeman fared better than many in that it had no vineyards, and so missed the direct expense of replanting.

By 1870 Sandeman was the largest exporter, accounting for 9 percent of total port exports. Indeed, for most of this century Sandeman has featured heavily in the bulk exports. This was helped in the early 1960s, when Sandeman bought Offley Forrester, another large volume shipper. Within a few years they had sold half the shares to the Italian drinks group, Martini & Rossi, who bought the rest when Sandeman was taken over by the originally Canadian, now multi-national, Seagram group.

Seagram bought Sandeman in 1980. In the early days of Seagram control, the firm continued to concentrate on its bulk sales, with only the occasional good vintage being produced. Seagram built things up

SHALLOW PICKING BASKETS.

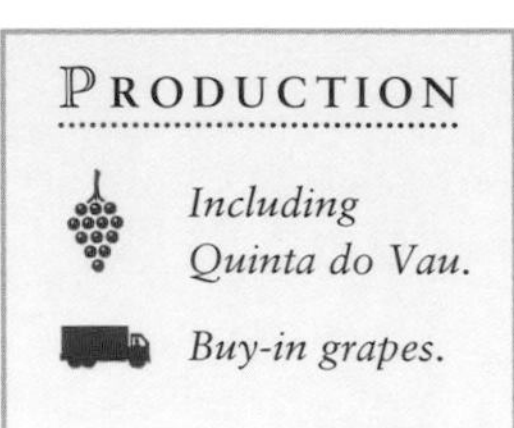

so that eventually Sandeman was the world's biggest single port brand in volume terms, but popularity was accompanied by an inevitable loss in quality. Recently, however, a different course has been charted. With George Sandeman having returned from a number of foreign postings, the move is toward quality rather than quantity. This is shown by their refusal to declare a 1991 vintage; since the wines simply were not as good as the single quinta wines from the 1988 vintage of Quinta do Vau.

Quinta do Vau supplies the top grapes, those that will go into vintage wines. This huge quinta located south of the Douro is planted almost entirely on patamares. The quinta is just a farm; there is no elegant house for receiving guests, just a workmanlike block in the middle, home to the winery and the vineyard equipment. Here, temperature-controlled stainless steel is the order of the day, whereas at many of the other wineries used by the company, autovinification stands side by side with remontagem. George Sandeman makes no apologies for this, believing that the rush to pumping over is too hasty. For him, autovinification still works so there is no need to replace it, especially since it is cheap to run and, because it uses no power, environmentally friendly, too.

Sandeman has a number of wineries in the area, though fewer than in the past, when they rented several at various strategic places. The firm also has a lodge near Régua, where ports mature more rapidly than in Oporto. The Régua lodge is used to good effect for the basic tawny, which seems older than it is.

THE SANDEMAN DON.

The main lodge is on the waterfront at Gaia, making Sandeman one of the first, and often the only, lodge most tourists visit. A professional public relations team runs regular tours throughout the year. Additionally Sandeman has opened a port museum near Régua.

As for the company's wines, the basic ruby and white ports are sound examples of their types, if unremarkable. The tawny stands out as being very mature both in appearance and flavor, a result of Douro maturation being carefully handled. Although lacking the power of an aged tawny, it is certainly an interesting wine that could easily confuse in a blind tasting.

Tasting Notes

FOUNDERS RESERVE This wine is exported to many countries around the world except the United Kingdom. A moderately mature wine; spice and fruit on the nose and palate, with medium weight and a very elegant finish.

PARTNERS' RUBY The United Kingdom version, has a more youthful, gutsy, fruity style; full-bodied and very full flavored. Produced after market research showed this style to be popular in the United Kingdom, it is blended to take on Cockburn's Special Reserve head-to-head.

IMPERIAL AGED RESERVE TAWNY Quite pale onion skin-pinkish-brown color, with a light and elegant, mature nose. Slightly smoky and herbal. Medium-sweet with crisp acidity and light to medium weight, yet full-flavored with a good length. A refreshing apéritif tawny that is aged for about eight years; easily as good as many 10 year olds, and could pass as such in a blind tasting.

TASTING NOTES

20 YEARS OLD TAWNY Pale orange-brown; full, mature nose of spice and pipe tobacco. Medium-sweet to sweet with balanced acidity and great concentration of mature dried fruit flavors, with some smokiness and a slightly caramelized finish.

QUINTA DO VAU 1988 Beginning to show some maturity on the rim, but still quite dark. Full and ripe blackcurrant and hot plum notes on the nose. Sweet with balanced acidity and still very firm tannins. Elegant, medium weight with a very long length. This wine will go on and on.

VINTAGE 1980 Deep ruby-red, with a full nose, if a little stalky, very slightly unripe and a bit green. The palate is sweet and full with a minty freshness and a good acid and tannic balance. The tannins are firm still, but softening, showing a long, fruity finish. Drinking well now, but will keep and improve for a few years yet.

C. da Silva (Vinhos) S.A.

Rua Felizardo de Lima, 247, Apartado 30
4401 Vila Nova de Gaia Codex, Portugal

INFORMATION

VISITING *No.*

RECOMMENDED WINES
Presidential 20 Years Old.

OVERALL RATING ★

Trading under the names "Presidential," "Dalava," and "da Silva," C. da Silva dates back to the middle of the nineteenth century, when Clemente da Silva formally founded the firm. But like so many port companies, members of the family were traders long before that.

Although the company does have one small vineyard, da Silva does not own a quinta as such. The firm relies on some 700 individual farmers to supply them with grapes, which da Silva turns into wine at their own winery. All of the winemaking is carried out using autovinification.

Their lodge is in Vila Nova de Gaia, rather than the Douro, to allow for slower maturation of the wines. This is illustrated by the company's current portfolio, which includes wines dating back to the 1930s. Some of the stock is older still, going back to the founding of the company, but this stock is blending wine, not commercially available and used only as a seasoning to add extra complexity to younger products.

The majority of the da Silva wines are young ruby and tawny blends destined for the French and Belgian markets. However, vintages are occasionally seen, and the old reserves (colheitas) are important on the home market. Recent growth areas for the company have been Switzerland, the United States, and the Pacific Rim countries. The somewhat limited range tried for this book, has been of light, fairly simple wines.

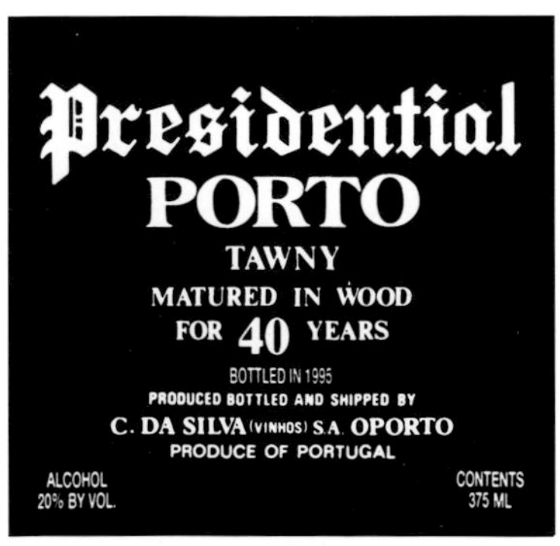

Tasting Notes

PRESIDENTIAL 10 YEARS OLD
Pale orange-brown in color, light-weight nose, quite spirity, with fully developed hazelnut character. Sweet and spirity palate; pleasant enough, but lacks depth and complexity.

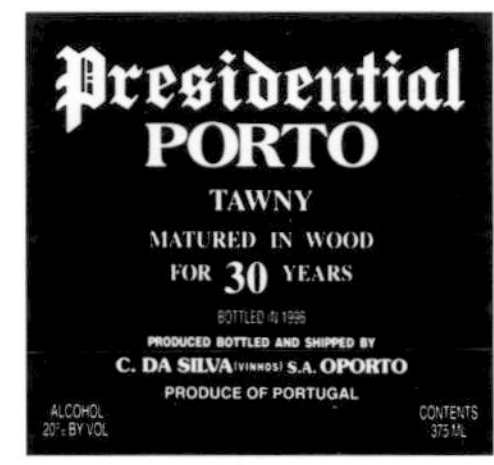

AGED TAWNY

PRESIDENTIAL 20 YEARS OLD
Clear, medium-depth tawny brown, with a medium-intense nutty and caramel bouquet, again quite spirity. Sweet with balanced acidity, noticeable spirit, and pronounced caramel notes. Medium length.

BOTTLE MATURATION IN THE DA SILVA LODGE.

Silva & Cosens Lda.

Trav. Barão de Forrester, 85, Apartado 19
4401 Vila Nova de Gaia Codex, Portugal

The famous Dow's brand applies to wines made by the far less known Silva & Cosens company, one of the half dozen shippers in the Symington group.

Initially started by a Portuguese merchant, Bruno da Silva, in 1798, the company took the name Dow after one James Dow, who became a partner of the firm in 1877. The Symington connection came about in 1882 when Andrew James Symington joined the company, he was subsequently made a partner in the early part of the twentieth century.

The quality of Dow's ports has always been based on their flagship farm, Quinta do Bomfim, which is situated next to the main street in Pinhão. Bomfim's vineyards supply about 340 pipes of port each year, but the winery has a production capacity far in excess of that. Until recently, Bomfim has been the main vinification center in the Cima Corgo for Dow's, although the Symingtons have built a large winery on the south side of the river a few miles away, which was first used for the 1996 harvest. Although the company sold Zimbro and Senhora de Ribeira, they still buy in grapes from these quintas, both of which are still used in the blend, and from other quintas in the area. Demand at vintage time is so great that the line of traffic waiting outside Bomfim has been famous for many years.

In contrast to its sister company Graham's, Dow's produces some of the driest ports. Although all ports are basically sweet, Dow's tends to be less sweet and a little more austere in character than many, perhaps not as immediately appealing as a result. That said, these wines are some of the finest. It is worth remembering that sweetness can be used to cover faults in wine, not just in port but in other wines throughout the world. Drier styles have to be good as they cannot rely on this cloak to mask flaws.

INFORMATION

VISITING *Only with an introduction through a wine merchant, and by appointment.*

RECOMMENDED WINES *Vintages, especially 1980, 1985.*

OVERALL RATING ★★★

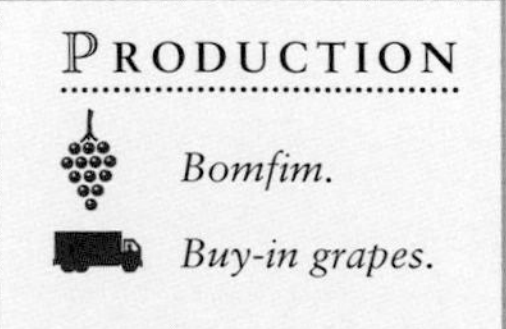

TASTING NOTES

10 YEAR OLD Very red-brown color, mature but not really expressing its age. Full dried fruit nose of raisins and candied peel, along with some mixed spice. Firm, clean palate, with the spirit giving it grip, and a very long, elegant finish.

20 YEAR OLD One of the deepest colored 20 year olds, dark walnut brown. Pungent dried fruit and herbal, leafy nose; medium dry palate with balanced acidity and rich, smooth texture, almost fat in the mouth yet at the same time retaining freshness.

1980 VINTAGE The 1980s are generally rather light; Dow's is an exception. Still very deeply colored with an intense herbal and medicinal nose. Full weight and a good length. Not the best Dow, but one of the best 1980s.

Tasting Notes

RUBY

"AJS" VINTAGE CHARACTER AJS, Andrew James Symington, was the first of the Symington clan to leave Scotland for Oporto, founding the Symington port dynasty. This is a well-made premium ruby: ruby red in appearance, with a full, fruity, quite youthful nose, and a medium-bodied palate. However, it has only a little of the character or style of a true vintage.

WHITE

DRY WHITE A modern-style dry white, fermented without skin contact and aged only for a short time. Made mostly from the Malvasia grape, this wine is pale lemon in color, with a youthful, floral nose and crisp palate. A pleasant apéritif, provided you get a fresh bottle since it does not benefit from bottle aging.

AGED TAWNY

10 YEAR OLD (see page 166)

20 YEAR OLD (see page 166)

SINGLE QUINTA VINTAGE

1984 QUINTA DO BOMFIM Developing ruby red with a full, aromatic nose of flowers and fruit. Medium to full weight and firmer tannins than the appearance leads one to expect. Drinking extremely well now, this wine will continue to improve for a few years yet.

VINTAGE

VINTAGE 1994 Very intense black core, one of the deepest of the 1994s. Hugely concentrated, yet remarkably open nose of ripe fruit and sweet spices. Rich though not sweet palate, with massive tannic structure, balanced acidity, and great weight and length. An extremely good wine, a particular favorite among the 1994s, and a wine for the very long term.

VINTAGE 1991 Deep, black color with a remarkably open nose of damson plums. Rich fruit on the palate, making it initially seem very approachable now, but with massive tannic structure coming across at the end. One of the top 1991s, needing a long time to come around, before it is ready to drink.

VINTAGE 1985 This is still one of the most backward examples of the 1985s. Deep purple ruby in color, the wine is still closed, with a light floral hint to the nose, remarkably ungenerous at first. On the palate the fruit comes out, behind a firm structure of tannin and acidity that will take a long time to weaken. A great wine in the making; start to drink it in the second decade of the twenty-first century.

VINTAGE 1980 (see page 166)

VINTAGE 1970 Still quite deep in color, although the hue is now ruby rather than purple. Very opulent and open nose. Complex flavors of dark fruits, herbs, and fruitcake spices. Full, concentrated palate that has now knitted together to form an integrated whole. This wine is now mature. Drinking very well at the moment and will continue to do so for many years.

Traditional terracing at Quinta do Bomfim.

Skeffington Vinhos, Lda.

Rua do Choupelo, 250, Apartado 1311
4401 Vila Nova de Gaia Codex, Portugal

INFORMATION

VISITING *No.*

RECOMMENDED WINES *Vintage Character.*

OVERALL RATING ★★

Skeffington is one of the least well-known port houses, although their wines are quite widely distributed since the company specializes in the Buyers' Own Brand (BOB) market. An associate company within the Taylor's group, Skeffington is thereby also related to Fonseca. Skeffington has its own sources of supply and runs as a separate brand within the group. Being a second-tier brand, the wines are not as fine as either of the more famous cousins, but this is not to denigrate the brand. Obviously the wines are made to the parent company's standards, which are exacting even for the BOB market. Moreover, blind tastings have proved that Skeffington can hold its own with some of the more famous ports.

The name dates back to the middle of the nineteenth century. Charles Neville Skeffington was a partner for the Yeatman family (of Taylor, Fladgate and Yeatman fame). Skeffington was a man of the Douro, one of his roles being to source grapes and wine from smallholders. In recognition of this, the Taylor's group named their new company after him. He built up strong links with a number of growers, and many of today's suppliers are direct descendants of the people he worked with some 150 years ago.

The company was launched in the early 1980s when Taylor's realized that the own label market was becoming more competitive, and that their main brands would be devalued if they entered the price-sensitive area of own label brands. Before it was made compulsory for all port to be bottled in Oporto, the wine was sold with both the shipper's and the importer's name on the label, since the importer would probably have bottled the wine. Subsequently the brand has become more important and has needed support.

Skeffington does not own any quintas; they buy in all their wine. The backbone of the vintage blend comes from Quinta de Vale dos Muros in the Távora valley, not far from Fonseca's Panascal.

Tasting Notes

VINTAGE CHARACTER Also sold as Shooting Port, this is a very deep color for the type, deep crimson-red and extremely youthful. Full, ripe nose, very clean and fresh; fruit dominates with plums and even a little grapy hint. Full, rich palate with greater power than many at this price level. A younger but more serious ruby than many.

1985 VINTAGE Still very deep, just turning to ruby, with a moderately open nose. Not a very complex nose yet of damson plums. Medium weight with moderate tannins and clean acidity. Very well-made wine that will be drinking remarkably well in the next few years.

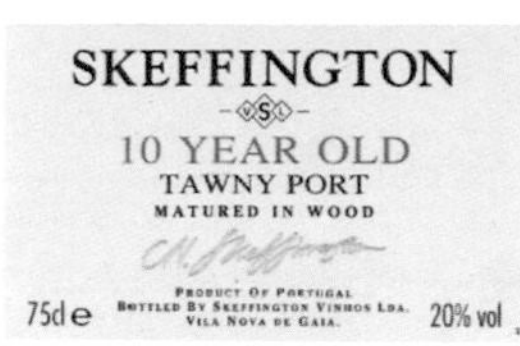

Smith Woodhouse & Ca., Lda.

Trav. Barão de Forrester, 85, Apartado 19
4401 Vila Nova de Gaia Codex, Portugal

Smith Woodhouse is one of the lesser of the Symington brands, and one that even the owners seem to underrate, both in terms of its image and its wines. Initially started in 1784 by Christopher Smith, a one-time member of the Westminster Parliament and Lord Mayor of the City of London, the firm was taken over by W. & J. Graham in the early years of the twentieth century. Thus when Graham's was bought by the Symingtons in 1970, it became part of their empire. During the Graham years Smith Woodhouse was treated as a sort of second-class port producer within the company, a practice that has continued under the Symingtons, despite the fact that some excellent Smith Woodhouse ports are made.

INFORMATION

VISITING *Only through an introduction from a wine merchant, and by appointment.*

RECOMMENDED WINES *Traditional LBV.*

OVERALL RATING ★★

A small fraction, about 8 percent, of Smith Woodhouse ports comes from the company's own vineyard, Santa Madalena in the Rio Torto valley. The rest is bought in and vinified at Bomfim or the new winery the Symingtons have just built. As with all the Symington ports, the majority is made by autovinification, a method much heralded by the wine makers here, although elsewhere its value is debated.

About a quarter of a million cases of port are produced under the Smith Woodhouse label. The company produces a range of adequate, but not stunning, ruby, tawny, and white styles sold under their own name as well as under retailers' brand names. The Smith Woodhouse name still appears on these bottles, but the blend will be different for different retail customers.

But the main focus of the brand is with the premium ports, especially the late bottled vintage, which is a fully traditional style, matured for only about four years in wood, then bottled without filtering so maturation can continue in the bottle. Unusually, the wines are not released into the retail market until they are ready to drink, between six and ten years after bottling. These wines are far more like vintage ports than most LBVs and will, of course, need decanting.

Tasting Notes

OLD OPORTO CLASSIC VINTAGE CHARACTER One level up from the basic ruby is Old Oporto. This wine has spent about five years in wood maturing, and is softer on the palate and more complex in flavor than the basic ruby. Full-bodied and full-flavored, but with low tannin and a medium length.

1994 VINTAGE Really deep color, almost black, with a very closed nose, hardly revealing anything. Unlike the palate, which is a concentrated mixture of spice and fruitcake. Sweet, with powerful and quite aggressive tannins. Full, fat fruit flavor and a long length. A long-term wine with some elegance.

SMITH WOODHOUSE

Lodge Reserve
VINTAGE CHARACTER
PORTO

PRODUCT OF PORTUGAL
IMPORTED BY:
PREMIUM PORT WINES INC., SAUSALITO CA. 94965

SMITH WOODHOUSE
FOUNDED IN 1784
Years 10 Old
PORTO
FINEST TAWNY MATURED 10 YEARS IN CASK
PRODUCT OF PORTUGAL
IMPORTED BY:
PREMIUM PORT WINES INC., SAUSALITO CA. 94965

SMITH WOODHOUSE
SWC
FOUNDED IN OPORTO 1784
1994
VINTAGE PORTO
BOTTLED 1996
Shipped and bottled by
Smith Woodhouse &Ca Lda
OPORTO
PRODUCT OF PORTUGAL
IMPORTED BY
PREMIUM PORT WINES INC., SAUSALITO, CA

Production

Santa Madalena.

92% of annual production.

TASTING NOTES

RUBY

OLD OPORTO CLASSIC VINTAGE CHARACTER (see page 171)

TAWNY

OLD LODGE TAWNY An undated wine, with no specified age; a style of wine once made by all shippers, but since largely superseded by the specified age tawnies. Still showing some red in the hue. A full, rich roasted almond and hazelnut character backed up by rather more youthful fruit, perhaps from younger components in the blend, making a refreshing tawny.

LBV

TRADITIONAL LATE BOTTLED VINTAGE The current vintage is 1982. Like a vintage port, this is very full and rich, but with the extra maturity that comes from long storage in wood. Cedar and lead pencils, a little smoky, with plums and spice on the nose. Quite complex. Sweet and full palate, with all the structure of a lesser vintage port at a lower price. Much better than many other LBVs.

VINTAGE

1994 VINTAGE (see page 171)

1991 VINTAGE Medium color only, still purple of course, with a spirity nose of medium fruit intensity, giving damson plums. The palate reveals much more intensity than the nose; full and powerful with softer tannins than some and a great length. Good concentration but not as structured as some; probably a medium-term wine, one to drink before opening the Graham and Warre vintage of the same year.

1985 VINTAGE This is still a blockbuster of a wine. Hardly showing any age on the rim, still dark and purple-red in color, it has developed rather more on the nose, giving a spice and fruit character. Full and rich on the palate, with firm tannins and showing no signs of its years. A long-term wine.

1983 VINTAGE Lighter than the 1985, but still full and rich. Beginning to show some maturity on the rim, with fruitcake and dark fruit jam hints on the nose. This still has firm structure and enough fruit to hold for another five to ten years before the tannins fade.

1980 VINTAGE Now mature, this is an elegant but not great wine. Perfumed and a little spirity on the nose; the tannins have softened to give a velvety feel to the palate and a long finish.

TRADITIONAL LBV AND CRUSTED PORT.

Taylor, Fladgate & Yeatman – Vinhos, S.A.

Rua do Choupelo, 250, Apartado 1311
4400 Vila Nova de Gaia Codex, Portugal

INFORMATION

VISITING *Yes to lodges. Invited guests only permitted to visit quintas. Tel. (351–2) 3719999.*

RECOMMENDED WINES *All vintages.*

OVERALL RATING ★★★

Better known simply as Taylor's, this firm's vintage ports are consistently higher in price than any other, except for the fabled Nacional from Quinta do Noval. In effect Taylor's wines have become the "first growth" (phrase used to describe the finest Bordeaux wines) of port, at least among vintage wines.

Initially established in 1692 by John Bearsley, the company has gone through many name changes in its day, but after the arrival of Joseph Taylor, John Fladgate, and Morgan Yeatman in the early nineteenth century, the company took its present name and has kept it. The current managing director, Alistair Robertson, is a descendant of the Yeatman family, as is Huyshe Bower, who has been with Taylor's since 1959. Alistair Robertson's daughter Natasha and son-in-law Adrian Bridge are also involved in the company's management. Viticultural matters had been looked after by the large and effusive Bruce Guimaraens of Fonseca Guimaraens, which Taylor's bought in 1948. Bruce retired in 1995, passing the mantle on to his son David.

Taylor's status has always been a result of their premium-quality ports, in particular the vintages. Since 1908 the dramatic amphitheater vineyard at Quinta de Vargellas in the Douro Superior has provided the backbone for these blends. Vargellas had an outstanding reputation as long ago as 1823, when its wines were discussed in glowing terms in letters between London and Oporto. However, when Taylor's bought the quinta in 1893, its fortunes were at a very low ebb following the destruction of the vineyards by phylloxera. Huge sums of money were invested to put the company at the forefront of viticultural innovation, a position it still holds. The vines planted by Frank Yeatman (a descendant of the co-founder John Yeatman and a very keen viticulturalist) were much the same varieties as the ones the IVP recommends today. There is even evidence that some single variety vinification was carried out, but no conclusions are recorded. Often when a full vintage is not declared, a single quinta vintage from Vargellas is. This is nearly always lighter in style than the full Taylor's vintage, but is frequently better than most other firms' full vintage wine.

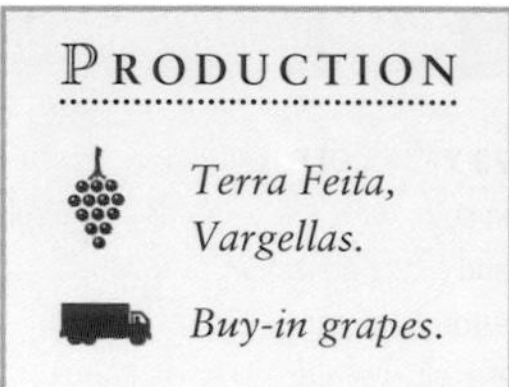

Taylor's also owns Quinta de Terra Feita in the Pinhão valley. An unusual vineyard, this is essentially one large hill that is flat on top, and a few smaller hills. Viewed from the Pinhão to Sabrosa road the setting looks very artificial, and indeed the main hill was flattened by removing the top 62 feet in 1983. Like Vargellas, all the wine from Terra Feita is made in lagares and is used in the vintage blend or for LBV. Some single quinta vintage wines have also been produced in occasional years.

As with many houses, the Taylor vintages are the wines that attract press coverage, but the more accessible LBV is also noteworthy. Although the port industry has long produced vintage wines bottled later than the required three years, Taylor's was the first company to create a successful brand from an LBV – and the first to bring the wines to prominence. Taylor's LBV is a modern style: bottled after six years in cask after stabilizing and filtering, a vintage wine without the trouble of decanting.

First Estate is the company's less widely available premium ruby. The name recalls Casa dos Alambiques, Taylor's first property in the Douro, which was the first to be owned by any British shipper. The estate still supplies Taylor's, but today First Estate does not come entirely from these vineyards. The company also produces an outstanding range of aged tawnies that tend to be rich and fruity in style rather than nutty, particularly the 10 year old. The typical characteristic of Taylor's ports is power and strength, but at the same time the wines show considerable elegance.

FRANK YEATMAN (RIGHT).

Taylor's is the oldest British port house that still retains its independence, having avoided the impersonal world of company acquisitions and takeovers. Indeed, the shoe has been on the other foot with the purchase of Fonseca in the 1940s and, more recently, the company has bought shares in its overseas agents and distributors in order to establish better control over its brands.

Tasting Notes

20 YEARS OLD Quite dark brown in color with a very intense caramel and fudge nose. Spirit showing through but not as overtly as with the 10 year old. Fairly sweet but balanced and elegant, not at all cloying, a fault sometimes found in other tawnies.

QUINTA DE VARGELLAS VINTAGE 1991 Still very closed on the nose; a complex wine with aromatic, tropical fruit hints. Extremely high tannin levels, along with a very full, rich body, should allow this wine to age for a remarkably long time.

1985 VINTAGE Fuller and more open than the 1983, bursting with ripe, hot, dark fruit and black pepper nose. Very firm tannins and full body. The richness of the vintage makes this attractive now, but the wine needs a good few years to reach its peak.

Tasting Notes

RUBY

FIRST ESTATE It is a pity that this wine does not enjoy a wider following, since it is one of the fullest and richest of the premium rubies. Like Fonseca Bin No. 27, it has enough structure and weight to be interesting.

AGED TAWNY

10 YEARS OLD Reddish-orange in color, aromatic dried fruit nose. Medium-sweet with balancing acids and a medium to full, concentrated flavor. Great length.

20 YEARS OLD (see page 175)

LBV

LATE BOTTLED VINTAGE 1990
One of the most remarkable things about Taylor's LBV is the consistency of the style of the brand, year in and year out. Dark ruby in color with a rich, black fruit character, this is still quite a youthful style, despite its six years of aging. Full-bodied, concentrated style; one of the best of its type.

SINGLE QUINTA VINTAGE

QUINTA DE VARGELLAS VINTAGE 1991 (see page 175)

QUINTA DE VARGELLAS VINTAGE 1984 This is a better wine than the 1982. Relatively deep ruby color with an intense nose and a full, fruity, floral palate. Very firm tannins and balanced acidity, both of which will help this wine mature for a number of years yet, although it is drinking well now.

QUINTA DE VARGELLAS VINTAGE 1982 Moderately deep color, still ruby. Light floral hints on the nose with a medium body. Not as intense as most Taylor's, but with good fruit and some firm tannins remaining. Ready to drink now, but will hold for a few years.

VINTAGE

1994 VINTAGE A very deep wine, almost black. Closed but fruity nose. Huge, powerful palate with massive tannic grip and complex flavors of blackberries and dark chocolate, and even strong coffee.

1992 VINTAGE Inky-black color, one of the deepest of the vintage. Soft fig and date nose, surprisingly open for a wine of this age. Medium-sweet, very firm tannic grip covering up myriad layers of flavor.

1980 VINTAGE Tasted against other Taylor's, this was slightly disappointing. Tasted against other 1980s, it was outstanding. Lighter than most Taylor's; aromatic, dark fruit character, only medium-bodied but one of the best of the vintage.

1977 VINTAGE Still opaque, almost black in the core with only the narrowest of ruby rims. Complex nose of both red and black fruit and dark chocolate, even spice, but still closed; not nearly ready. Full-bodied, classic Taylor's strength and elegance. A great port that should not be opened until the beginning of the next century.

1970 VINTAGE Still deep ruby in the core, showing garnet hints only right toward the rim; remarkably youthful for a wine of this age. Powerful, dark berry fruit character with some spice and leather from aging, giving a small hint of the wine's maturity. Highly intense. Medium-sweet; huge power and concentration of developed fruit balanced by very full body and robust tannin and acid structure, which holds it all together. Enormous length.

1985 VINTAGE (see page 175)

1983 VINTAGE Very deep color; again, quite closed on the nose but with a full, ripe palate of fruitcake and spice. Firm tannins and a great length. Still not at its peak, despite early indications that this would be an early-maturing vintage.

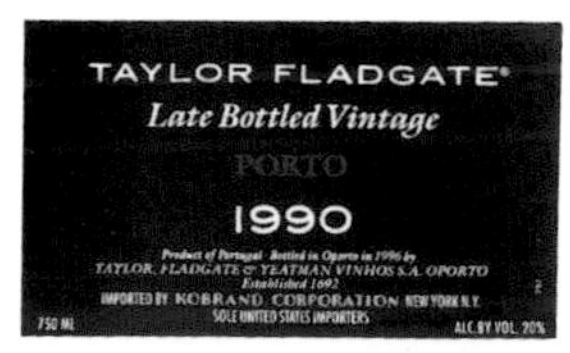

Vinoquel – Vinhos Oscar Quevedo, Lda.

Av. Marques Soveral,
5130 S. João da Pesqueira, Portugal

INFORMATION

VISITING *Yes. Tel. (351-54) 44328.*

RECOMMENDED WINES *LBV.*

OVERALL RATING ★★

Vinoquel defies the standard port wine trade categories. The company is family owned and Douro-based, yet it is more than a single quinta. On the other hand, Vinoquel does not export, preferring local sales, so to call them a shipper is to stretch the truth a little.

Based in São João da Pesqueira, the firm was originally established by Óscar Quevedo but is now run by Cláudia Quevedo, who is not only a managing partner in the company, but also devotes time to her studies at the local university at Vila Real.

About 60 percent of the company's production comes from their own vineyards, Quinta Vale d'Agodinho and Quinta da Senhora do Rosário, a total of about 99 acres of prime Cima Corgo land. The vineyards are typical of the region, with some traditional terraces, a little vinha ao alto where feasible, and patamares where money has allowed.

The balance of the wine comes from neighboring class A vineyards, but it is all vinified by Vinoquel at their São João da Pesqueira winery. Here, modern wine making is the order of the day. All of the wine is made by pumping over, remontagem, in temperature controlled vats to maintain as much of the aromatic flavor of the grapes as possible.

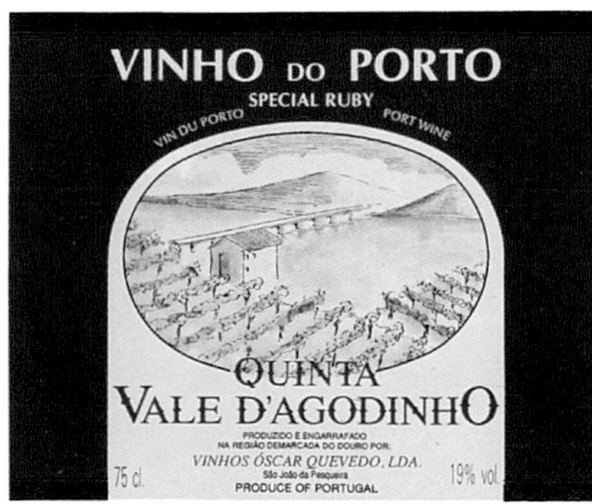

The ports are sold under two labels. If all the wine comes from the quinta then the Quinta Vale d'Agodinho label is used, but if the wine is sourced from other vineyards it is labeled Porto Quevedo. Currently the wine is only sold in Portugal, at the winery itself and through a limited number of retail outlets. Vinoquel is one of those unusual producers who value domestic sales above exports.

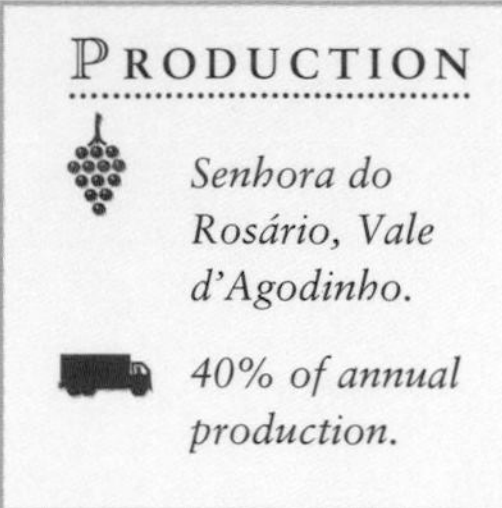

PRODUCTION

Senhora do Rosário, Vale d'Agodinho.

40% of annual production.

This has resulted in a loyal following for the wines which no amount of advertising could buy. Of course this means that the winery is open to the public, with the usual tours and tastings.

Although the range includes ruby, vintage, and tawny wines, only the LBV has been tasted for this book. It is impossible to genuinely assess the quality of a wine maker on one tasting, but if all the wines are of the same standard as the LBV, then this is a company that deserves greater recognition.

TASTING NOTES

QUINTA VALE D'AGODINHO LATE BOTTLED VINTAGE 1992 Deep but very mature garnet wine with a rich ripe nose of smoke and cooked fruit, again showing some maturity which many LBVs seem to lack. Medium-sweet with crisp acidity and only the faintest touch of the baked character so many Douro-matured wines have. Medium weight with a long, clean finish.

Warre & Ca., S.A.

Trav. Barão de Forrester, 85, Apartado 26
4401 Vila Nova de Gaia Codex, Portugal

Three years after the Great Fire of London, and over a century before the American Declaration of Independence, Warre, the oldest of the British port shippers, was established. Now part of the Symington group, Warre offers an opulent style that fits comfortably between that of W. & J. Graham's and Silva & Cosens. Warre's ports do not have the rich, sweet style of Graham's ports, yet neither do they have the tight, austere character of some of the Dow wines.

Information

Visiting *Only through an introduction by a wine merchant.*

Recommended Wines *Traditional LBV, Vintages: 1994, 1991, 1983, 1970.*

Overall Rating ★★★

The company started out in Viana do Castelo, trading English woolens and cod for wines from the Minho. Soon the business developed and the richer, fuller wines from Régua replaced the local wine, now called vinho verde. By 1729 the company was based in Oporto and the first Warre, William, joined the firm.

The Warres were intimately involved in Oporto life and the history of the wine. William married Elizabeth Whitehead, sister of John Whitehead, who was later British Consul to Oporto, and instrumental in designing and building the Factory House (see page 25). Their eldest son, William, was also to become Consul. Warre was the first British firm to invest in land on which to build a lodge on the south side of the Douro, at Vila Nova de Gaia.

Like Croft, the history of the firm is closely tied to the Peninsular War. A third William Warre, born in 1784, became Lieutenant General Sir William Warre, who served throughout the war with the 52nd light infantry. It seems Lord Wellington was very fond of his port since both Croft and Warre were regular suppliers during his campaigns.

The mighty Symington empire started with Warre when Andrew James Symington, the first of the port Symingtons, joined the firm. "A.J." had arrived from Scotland in 1882 and started work for a certain John Graham, a textile merchant. However, he soon took to the wine trade and, by 1905, had become a partner in Warre. The two families ran the company until the 1960s, when the remaining Warre family members sold their shares to the Symingtons. Despite no longer having equity in the company, the present William Warre, a Master of Wine, is still involved in sales and marketing for the firm from his base in London. Subsequent share swaps and purchases have resulted in the Symington group becoming one of the most powerful in the port industry, and have made the family into one of the great wine dynasties, despite the fact that they originated from a country better known for producing whiskey.

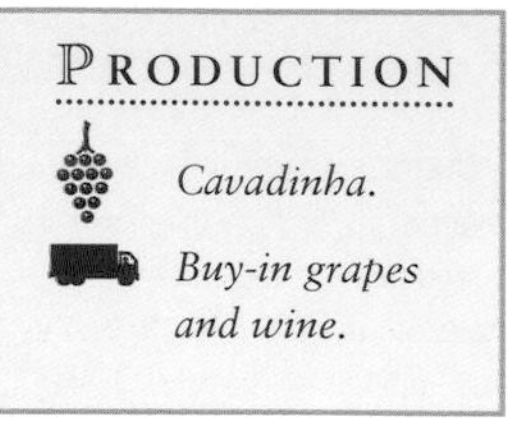

Warre has always been classed as one of the top port houses. Grapes come from the company's quinta, Cavadinha in the Pinhão valley, as well as the surrounding area, and from the Rio Torto on the south side of the Douro. Like so many port producers, the company has been buying grapes and wine from the same farmers for generations.

Wine making takes place mostly at Cavadinha, which is one of the best equipped wineries in the valley, or at Bomfim. However, a new wine making center, conveniently close to the Régua-Pinhão road, is likely to become more important. Fifteen percent of the wine is trodden by foot; the remainder is made by autovinification. Although autovinification is less popular today than it once was, the quality of Warre's ports shows that it can produce excellent wines. Over 57 percent of Warre's ports are premium categories, compared with an industry average of less than 9 percent. If there is one notable characteristic about Warre's ports, it is their power. The wines' strength is their structure and concentration of fruit, particularly in their vintages, which are among the best available.

QUINTA DA CAVADINHA IN THE PINHÃO VALLEY.

Tasting Notes

WARRIOR FINEST RESERVE Warrior is reputedly the oldest brand name in the port business, in constant use since the 1850s. Deep ruby red in color, hardly showing any age, this is a rich and very fruity wine. Full-bodied and full-flavored, it seems to be the sweetest of the company's range.

SIR WILLIAM 10 YEARS OF AGE A fruity tawny, with concentrated, ripe, plummy fruit backed up with the more mature flavors of hazelnuts and almonds. A full-flavored and full-bodied tawny.

1983 VINTAGE Still very young, and therefore quite dumb on the nose, has masses of ripe, dark fruit undertones and huge structure. Firm tannins and enough acidity to balance the sweetness, and a very long finish. A wine for the very long term.

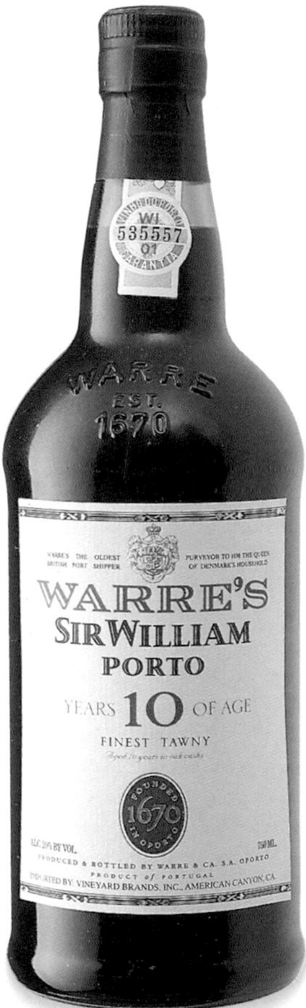

Tasting Notes

RUBY

WARRIOR FINEST RESERVE
(see page 181)

AGED TAWNY

SIR WILLIAM 10 YEARS OF AGE
(see page 181)

NIMROD This is Warre's older tawny. Longer cask aging has increased complexity and maturity, so that the wine is more nutty and spicy, with hints of cinnamon on the nose. It still retains fruitiness, although less so than Sir William, and is medium- rather than full-bodied.

LBV

TRADITIONAL LBV LBV is a growth area in the port industry. Today every firm seems to be making one, so competition is fierce – it is a brave company who will sell theirs at a premium price. Warre's LBV is unusual, even among traditional LBVs, in that it is bottled after four years, without filtration, and then kept for a further six to eight years before it is sold. The result is a fully mature wine, full-bodied and with enough structure to make it seem like a real vintage port, which is as the LBV should be. The LBV currently available from Warre is the 1982. Pale garnet red in color with a mature nose of red fruit and spice, with some woody characters. Medium weight and complex palate, leading to a lingering finish.

SINGLE QUINTA VINTAGE

QUINTA DA CAVADINHA VINTAGES In less-than-good years, the firm produces a single quinta wine from Cavadinha. The 1979 is currently drinking well, and has an almost fennel-like perfume to it. The 1982 has also come around and is drinking well, but this one has enough structure to last a few years yet. Warre's declared the 1991, so the 1992 was made as a single quinta. This is a very light wine for Warre's, with very attractive red fruit and cherry characters. A wine to drink in the medium term, perhaps a millennium wine?

VINTAGE

1991 AND 1994 VINTAGES Both 1991 and 1994 are still very closed with the spirit, tannins, and blackberry-black currant fruit pulling in different directions at once. Both will be good; the 1991 in another 10 to 15 years, and the 1994 even further down the line. The latter has massive concentration with spicy plums and chocolate fruit; a wine with a complex character.

1985 VINTAGE The jury is still out about where Warre's 1985 is likely to go. It has so much fruit, and is so very open and opulent now – it is difficult to believe it can possibly last. At the same time, it has a powerful structure with ripe but firm tannins. To hedge all bets though, it is probably wise to have a few bottles tucked away to see.

1983 VINTAGE (see page 181)

1980 VINTAGE Warre's 1980 is a good wine for the vintage, but is now quite forward and developed. Garnet rather than ruby-colored, very open, with a developed leather and spice nose. Medium-sweet with softened tannins and a pleasantly long finish. Currently drinking well, but with enough structure to hold for some time. This is unlikely to improve dramatically.

1970 VINTAGE This has now finally reached the peak of its maturity. However, it still has fairly firm tannins and enough fruit to live for a long time.

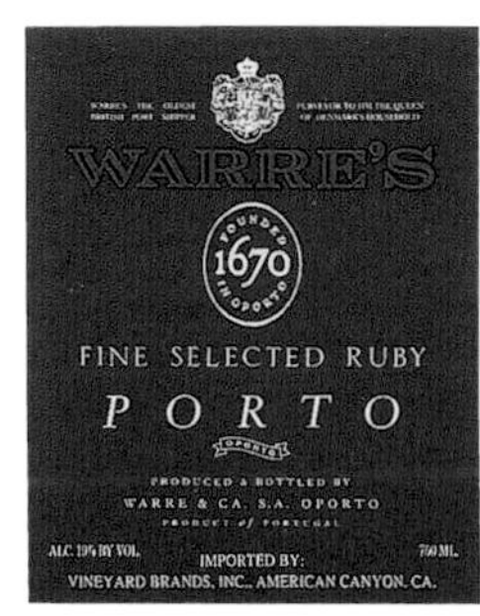

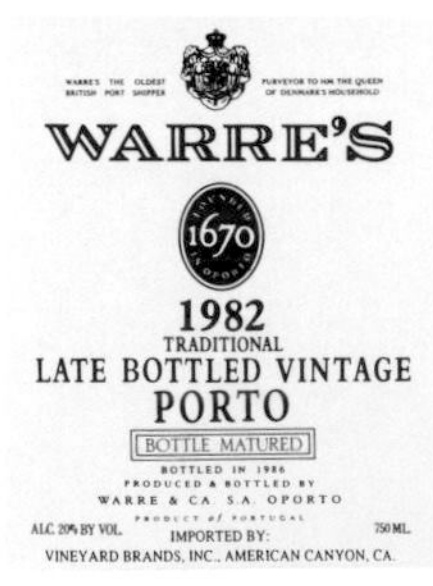

Wiese & Krohn, Sucrs., Lda.

Rua de Serpa Pinto, 149, Apartado 1
4401 Vila Nova de Gaia Codex, Portugal

INFORMATION

VISITING *No.*

RECOMMENDED WINES
20 Years Old.

OVERALL RATING ★★

Most people divide port shippers into two major groups: British and Portuguese. It may come as a surprise to learn there are Spanish (Osborne), German (Burmester), and Dutch (Niepoort) companies in town, not to mention Norwegian. Wiese & Krohn, usually sold under the name of Porto Krohn, is just such a rarity.

The Portuguese national dish is *bacalhau*, dried salt cod that it is said, is prepared and eaten in a thousand different ways. However, cod is not a local fish, and must be imported from the cold waters of the North Sea. Theodor Wiese and Dankert Krohn were in the business of supplying fish to the Portuguese and, understandably, shipped port wine on the return leg of the journey, setting up the port shipping business in 1865. In 1910 a Portuguese man called Edmundo Carneiro started working for the firm. Twelve years later he became a partner, eventually buying a controlling interest. The Norwegian company thus became Portuguese, but it has retained the original name.

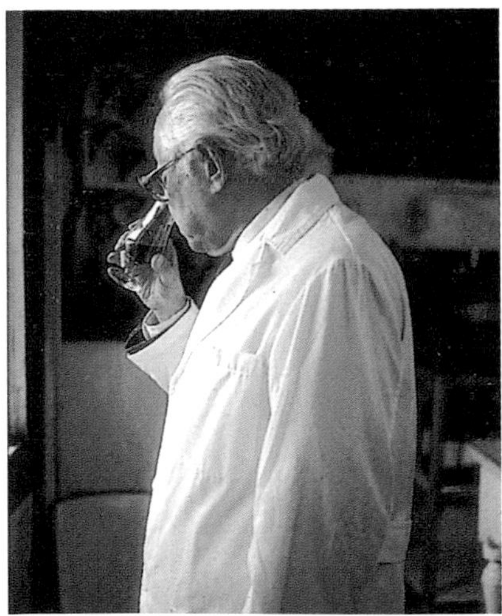

THE BLENDER'S JOB IS TO ENSURE A CONSISTENT PRODUCT IS PRODUCED, YEAR IN AND YEAR OUT.

Working in the port industry clearly facilitates one's longevity: Edmundo's son, Fernando, took over the reins in 1936 and only retired, or rather semi-retired, in 1986. Fernando's son, José, and daughter, Iolanda, are in charge of the company today. Unusually for a port house, most of the vinification is overseen by two women, Iolanda Carneiro and Maria José Aguiar.

Wiese & Krohn has only recently started to grow their own grapes, having bought the class A Quinta do Retiro Novo in 1989. Just up the road from Bom Retiro, this is a small vineyard whose winery is clearly visible from the road up the Torto valley. Confusingly, this quinta is not connected in any way to the more famous neighbor down the valley. Retiro Novo supplies 90 pipes of port each year, or about 5 percent of the company's needs. The rest comes from traditional suppliers, many of whom have been selling their grapes or wines to Krohn for decades. Some of the grapes are vinified at Retiro Novo; the rest is bought as wine made by the small growers. In total, a little more than half is produced by autovinification, but remontagem is becoming more important. The wines are aged at Vila Nova de Gaia rather than in the Douro, but the house style is very caramelly, similar to Douro-matured wines.

Krohn has always specialized in aged tawnies, which have an excellent reputation. A few samples of their vintage wines have proved to be light and early-maturing but elegant. The tawnies, whether colheitas or stated age, have a singular, rich unctuousness about them, smooth and quite viscous. Generally, Krohn wines are very distinctive and in some ways rather un-port-like, so they may surprise some people.

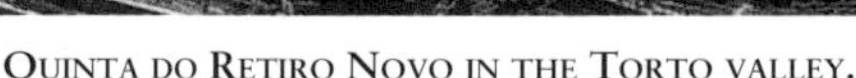
QUINTA DO RETIRO NOVO IN THE TORTO VALLEY.

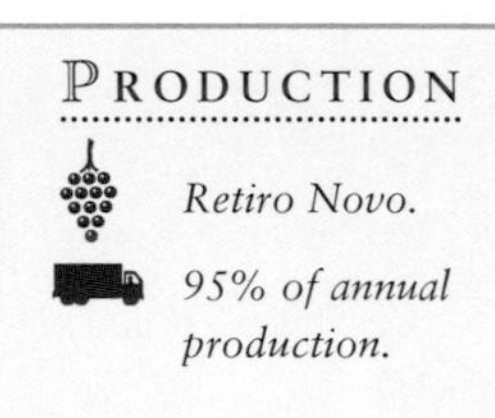
PRODUCTION

Retiro Novo.

95% of annual production.

Tasting Notes

20 YEARS OLD Tawny amber, not as deep as the 1965, with a very developed nose showing considerable complexity. Dried fruit, nut, and medicinal herb character; sweet with low acidity and a long, if slightly spirity, finish.

COLHEITA 1985 Deep tawny brown in color; full and mature nose that still retains a little dried fruit but is mostly hazelnut. Sweet, with balanced acids and an amazingly viscous texture in the mouth. Long, nutty finish.

COLHEITA 1965 Slight haze in wine, but not anything to worry about. A deep walnut brown color; clean, spirity, and mature nose. Maturity is the dominant feature. Sweet with relatively low acid and the viscous texture of a younger wine with a fudge and toffee character. Exceptionally long finish.

SECTION TWO

Cooperatives and Single Quintas

A small grower with only a few vines to cultivate cannot afford the investment needed to run a full-scale winery. Equipment is expensive, and is only used for a few weeks of the year. For thousands of growers in the Douro the investment is too high, so they have to sell their grapes at the end of the season. Many sell them to the shipping firms, but others rely on the cooperative movement, which has always been strong in Portugal.

Cooperatives are wineries which are jointly owned by member farmers whose production individually would be too small to justify the establishment of a full working winery. Many growers sell directly to the shipping firms; indeed many shippers have been dealing with the same vineyards for generations. But for those who do not have the security of a long-term arrangement there are co-ops called *adegas cooperativas* in most towns. Owned by the growers, the role of the co-op is to make wine for its members and to sell it, either in bulk to the shipping firms or, increasingly, under the cooperative's own label. The first two entries in this section are cooperatives.

There is no exact definition of a quinta, but for the purposes of this book the term has been understood to mean a "wine farm." Some port has been sold under a quinta name for many years, Quinta do Noval (see page 202) perhaps most famously, but for a long time the main emphasis has been on the shipper's name, rather than the vineyard. Indeed, until the advent of the European Community (EC) in 1986, the rules discriminated against single quintas, who were not allowed to export their wines directly, and had to sell them through the shipping firms.

A new law, enacted on May 8, 1986, allowed vines to be exported directly from the Douro region, without going through the lodges of Vila Nova de Gaia. Since then, after a slow start, a whole host of farms has taken advantage of the change in the rules to offer their wines directly to the public. The advantage of single quinta wines is that they offer individuality. The disadvantage is that there can be a lack of consistency.

Adega Cooperativa de Alijó

Av. 25 de Abril
5070 Alijó, Portugal

High above the Douro River, acting as a turning point on the convoluted road from Pinhão to Tua, sits the town of Alijó. With a population of 3,000, this is a large place by Douro standards and an appropriate home to one of the more important cooperatives. Adega Cooperativa de Alijó boasts an annual wine production of about 130,000 U.S. gallons, mostly light wines with some sparkling and some port.

Originally set up in 1960 with only 130 members, Adega Cooperativa de Alijó now has over 1,100 associates. All have small- to medium-sized vineyard holdings, mostly old, walled terraces with the mixed planting that was once the norm in Portugal. The disadvantages of the planting systems are, to some extent, made up for by the fact that the vines are also old, which increases the flavor concentration of the wine.

Information

Visiting *Visitors are welcome.*
Tel. (351–59) 959101.

Recommended Wines
Pedra Lascada White.

Overall Rating ★

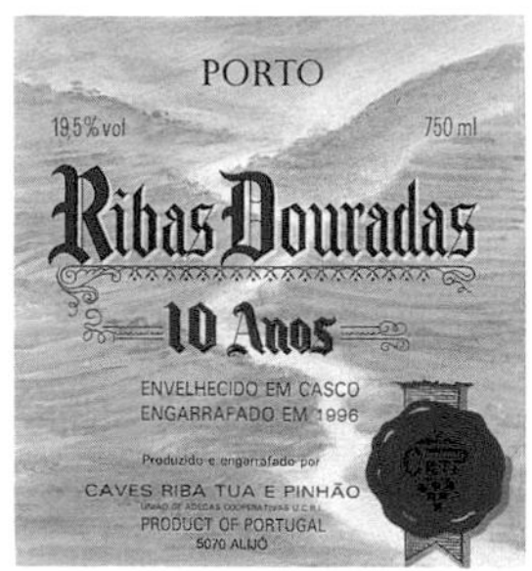

Tasting Notes

PEDRA LASCADA WHITE This long wood-aged white is the medium amber color of a 20-year-old tawny, and indeed has a similar aged bouquet: mature and spirity, yet still with some dried fruit. Medium-dry with fairly low acidity; medium weight and length. An interesting wine.

TAWNY Medium red-brown with a lighter nose than Xisto Velho; mature and nutty, but quite caramel-like and spirity. It is also marginally sweeter with a little less acidity but relatively full on the palate, with a boiled candy character and medium length.

LOVELY CHARM TAWNY Clear red-brown in color with a full, open, caramel nose, rather like boiled candy. Medium-sweet with balanced acidity; fairly full flavor and body. The boiled candy, confected character comes through on the palate, giving the wine a slightly cloying finish. Pleasant if lacking elegance.

Adega Cooperativa de Vila Flor

Estrada Nacional, 5360
Vila Flor, Portugal

Vila Flor is one of the most charming towns in the Douro, right up in the Douro Superior. Most of the houses are the traditional, simple whitewashed buildings so common in the area, but there are also garish and vivid colors more typical of Africa than Portugal, the trappings of a colonial past. The grand church bears witness to the town's aristocratic past. But as with many Douro towns, Vila Flor is not wealthy now, the economy relying as it does on agriculture, in particular vines, olives, and almonds.

The average vineyard holding here in the Douro Superior seems, on paper, to be quite high. However, with a few very large quintas, like Cockburn's in the Vilariça Valley, and Ramos Pinto's Ervamoira, the figures are distorted. Most farmers here, as is true elsewhere, have very small vineyards, hence the need for the co-op.

From a small beginning in 1962, the co-op now has 1,000 members, each supplying an average of just under seven pipes of wine a year. For most of the co-op's history the wine has been sold to the major shipping firms; it was not until 1996 that the first bottled wines began to appear under the co-op's own brand name. At the moment only one wine is available, but there is every indication that the wines will be well received as the range increases.

Information

Visiting *By appointment. Tel. (351–78) 52421.*

Overall Rating ★

Tasting Notes

TORGO TAWNY Although a relatively basic tawny, this is a very good value wine. Genuinely tawny in color, with a rich hazelnut bouquet, still youthful enough to have some dried fruit to it. Medium-sweet, very well-balanced acid, alcohol, and fruit, with a remarkably long length. Retains a freshness that makes it very attractive.

Sociedade Agrícola E Comercial da Quinta do Bucheiro, Lda.

Rua de S. Caetano, Celeirós do Douro, 5060 Sabrosa, Portugal

Quinta do Bucheiro at Celeirós do Douro, on the Pinhão to Sabrosa road, has been in the same family since it was founded in 1717 by Joaquim Pinheiro. The quinta produces port as well as light wines, the latter made from grapes that are both grown on the quinta and bought in from farmers who enjoy the luxury of 10-year contracts with Bucheiro.

The quinta vineyard was totally replanted during the time of the World Bank scheme (1970s–1980s), so patamares dominate, enabling "total" mechanization according to the owners, but all things are relative, and even here not every function can be carried out by tractor.

Wine making and maturation are carried out on the premises. Thus the quinta has significant storage and bottling facilities, capable of handling the production of nearly one and a half million bottles per year.

Originally selling their wines in bulk, the quinta began planning for direct sales in 1977. Now they offer a full range of ports up to a 20 year old. Only one sample was tasted for this book, a 1989 late bottled vintage.

Information

Visiting *Quinta do Bucheiro is on the* Rota do Vinho do Porto, *visits by appointment only. Tel. (351–59) 939225.*

Overall Rating ★

Tasting Notes

LATE BOTTLED VINTAGE 1989
Age further in the bottle before consuming, so decanting is recommended. Medium garnet in color, with a fully mature rim. Pronounced earthy nose, vegetal and definitely mature now. Sweet with crisp acidity and a little tannin, but somewhat dried-out fruit and a short finish.

Quinta da Casa Amarela

Riobom – Cambres, 5100 Lamego
Portugal

The quinta with the yellow house, Casa Amarela stands on the south side of the Douro between Régua, the regional capital, and Lamego, the town that, according to legend, is the original home of fortified port wine.

The quinta's vineyard is comprised entirely of walled terraces, and the vines average 45 years of age. At this age the quality of the grapes is very high, and the concentration of flavors is massive. However, the yield is low, making each bunch expensive to produce. Total production is about 100,000 pipes, half of which is white port. Most is sold in bulk to major shipping firms, with only a small percentage sold as a quinta wine.

INFORMATION

VISITING *By appointment. Visits include tours of the vineyards and winery as well as lunch. Quinta da Casa Amarela is part of the* Rota do Vinho do Porto *itinerary. Tel. (351–54) 66200.*

OVERALL RATING ★★

THE YELLOW HOUSE THAT GIVES THE QUINTA ITS NAME.

The family of the present owner, Dona Laura Maria Valente Regueiro, has owned the property since 1885. In 1979 the family started to lay down a stock of wine for eventual sale as a single quinta wine. Such transactions were forbidden at the time due to the shippers' monopoly on sales, but with the coming of the European Community the rules would inevitably be relaxed. In May 1986 individual quintas were permitted to sell their own wines.

At the moment the only wine available is the 10-year-old tawny. There are plans to produce a 20-year-old tawny as well when stocks have reached the required maturity. The quinta does not intend to enter the standard port market with inexpensive rubies and the like. Dona Laura is quite happy to leave that to the major shipping firms while she concentrates on the premium end.

TASTING NOTES

10 YEARS OLD Deep mahogany brown in color, deeper than most 10 year olds, with hardly a hint of red. Intense and almost cognac-like maturity on the nose, slightly cooked and a hint vegetal, with a pickled walnut character. Medium-sweet, with a mouth-filling palate; very intense flavor backed up by the spirit and tannin.

Quinta do Castelinho (Vinhos), Lda.

Quinta de S. Domingos, Apartado 140
5050 Peso da Régua, Portugal

Right on the border between the Cima Corgo and the Douro Superior, on the river, just downstream from the Valeira dam and near the small but important town of S. João da Pesqueira, is the medium-sized quinta of Castelinho.

The quinta has been in the Saraiva family for decades. For many years the family maintained a stock of old wines which, until the rules governing the sale of single quinta wines changed in 1986, they were not allowed to export, but could sell to shippers, or keep for personal use. In 1990 after the rules had been relaxed the family created a sales company to market their wines both locally and abroad.

INFORMATION

VISITING *The property at Quinta de São Domingos in Régua welcomes tourists; groups with reservations can eat here as well. Tel. (351–54) 320100.*

RECOMMENDED WINES *Colheita 1982, 1962.*

OVERALL RATING ★★

In this steep part of the region all the vineyards are terraced, and both traditional terracing and patamares are evident in the 99 acres of vineyards. All the grapes are trodden by foot in the quinta's lagares and, as a single quinta wine, only grapes from here may go into the blends.

Many single quinta wines, especially those from this hot part of the Douro, take on the characteristic "Douro bake," a cooked taste that comes from the heat of the summers, which cannot be blended out because of the restrictions on what makes up a single quinta wine. Through careful grape handling and vinification, and by keeping the lodges as cool as possible, Castelinho has managed to keep this in check. The wines all exhibit a lovely freshness and cleanness that few Douro-aged wines have.

Recently the family has bought Quinta de São Domingos in Régua, formerly owned by Ramos Pinto. The expanding town has overtaken the quinta; once surrounded by vineyards, it finds itself in an isolated plot of vines in the middle of suburban sprawl. Here there is a lodge and a small winery, in addition to a well-equipped tourist center where audiovisual presentations and tastings are held to promote the wine.

TASTING NOTES

WHITE Particularly pleasant if it is consumed young – fresh fruit salad character, medium-sweet, and good fresh fruit flavors.

10 YEARS OF AGE Brilliantly clear, topaz brown with an orange rim. Cooked citric character, rather like marmalade in the making, hardly spirity at all. Clean, fresh palate, medium-sweet, but with refreshing citric-like acid that cleans the palate and gives a long, refreshing finish.

COLHEITA 1962 Pale orange-brown in color with a very pronounced, and obviously mature, bouquet of spice and nuts. Like the younger wine, fruit is still present in abundance, with raisins and figs showing through. Medium-sweet with balanced acidity and slightly cooked. A very good fresh wine.

Tasting Notes

WHITE

WHITE (see page 194)

AGED TAWNY

10 YEARS OF AGE (see page 194)

20 YEARS OF AGE Paler color than the 10 year old with a delicate, fresh nose of nuts and peel. Perhaps a little sweeter on the palate, but still balanced. Medium-bodied with fresh acidity and an elegant finish.

COLHEITA

COLHEITA 1982 Clear, medium depth orange tawny. Very pronounced, perfumed nose of vanilla spice, dried fruit, and candied peel. Not overtly spirity. Medium-sweet with moderate acidity, spirit a little more obvious here. Mulled wine spices on the palate, with dried fruit. Good intensity of flavor and a good long finish.

COLHEITA 1962 (see page 194)

VINTAGE

VINTAGE 1994 Deep purple-ruby in color, it is a full-flavored wine with some of the freshness of the other wines, but also with a slightly jammy sweetness that overpowers the structure.

Tasting in the lodge.

Large oak tonels in the Douro lodge.

Quinta do Côtto (Montez Champalimaud, Lda.)

Cidadelhe, 5040 Mesão Frio, Portugal

> ## Information
>
> **Visiting** *Quinta do Côtto is on the Port Wine Route and is open all year round. Tel. (351–54) 899269.*
>
> **Recommended Wines** *1989 Vintage.*
>
> **Overall Rating** ★★

There are very few really large or famous quintas in the Baixo Corgo. Most of the top farms, those rated A and B in the Cadastro grading are in the Cima Corgo, with a number further upriver in the Douro Superior. Conventional wisdom has it that the Baixo Corgo is good only for light (unfortified) wines and the cheaper ports, and that quality comes from further upstream. Miguel Champalimaud disagrees. One of the greatest critics of the port wine establishment, Miguel Champalimaud, owner of Quinta do Côtto, has set out to prove the conventional wisdom wrong through the quality of his wines. This was the first quinta to take advantage of the new (1986) rules permitting the direct exportation of port wine from the valley, and the wines have been well received at most trade tastings.

The quinta has a very long history. It seems the quinta was originally a sanctuary for Araújo Cabral Montez against the troops of King Alfonso III in the thirteenth century and it has stayed in the same family ever since – Miguel Champalimaud is a direct descendant. The Champalimaud name is of French origin. General Champalimaud, a Field Marshal in the Peninsular Wars, originated from Limoges, in southwest France. His daughter Dona Carlota Casimira married into the Montez family. (Such are the complicated convolutions of Portuguese names, as the family name Montez has become Champalimaud.) At the time of the original Companhia Geral da Agricultura das Vinhos do Alto Douro during the "reign" of the Marquis of Pombal, members of the family were executives with the company, ironic given the present owner's views on the establishment.

The relatively gentle slopes of this part of the Baixo Corgo enable most of Quinta do Côtto to be planted without terraces. Where there are steeper plots, patamares have been installed, but the trend will be to vinha ao alto as and when the older vineyards need replanting. At present they are in rows across the hillside, making mechanization difficult.

Where Miguel Champalimaud really disagrees with the rest of the port wine industry is in his wine making. Not only does he dismiss lagares as being good only for folklore and journalists, he dismisses the very existence of tawny port. For him this oxidized style is an anathema, since oxidation is avoidable. Today, he believes, fruit is all-important, and can and therefore should be preserved.

Most of the production has been, and still is, sold to other shippers, but in exceptional cases a small amount of Quinta do Côtto port is bottled and sold under the quinta label. A vintage was declared in 1982 and has achieved notable success in blind tastings. The current wine is the 1989 vintage and there are high hopes for the 1995. At the time of this writing it is too early to say if this wine will be available as it has yet to be approved by the Instituto do Vinho do Porto.

Tasting Notes

1989 VINTAGE Very deep ruby red. Fully ripe, but elegant, nose of dark fruits, coffee, and continental chocolate. Medium-sweet with balanced acidity and high but very ripe tannins. Great concentration although only medium to full bodied. Long, fruit-dominant finish that almost covers up the spirit. A wine that will repay longer aging.

Sociedade Agricola da Quinta do Crasto

Rua de Gondarém, 834 R/CDt°
4150 Porto, Portugal

INFORMATION

VISITING *While Quinta do Crasto is not currently open to the public, this is likely to change in the future.*

RECOMMENDED WINES *LBVs.*

OVERALL RATING ★★

Standing on the north bank of the Douro, with commanding views both upriver and down the river, Quinta do Crasto has, to the observant visitor, a familiar feel: it appears on the famous blue tiles at Pinhão station.

The quinta belonged to Ferreira 150 years ago, who sold it to the grandfather of the present owners, Jorge Roquette and his family, in 1910. The vineyard occupies about one-third of the quinta's 321 acres. Much of it is on bulldozed terraces, but the vineyard also has a little vinha ao alto and some traditional terraces, which will probably remain as is for the sake of appearance.

Equally traditional is the wine making. The best grapes are trodden by foot, although mechanical means of extraction are also utilized. Crasto produces both port and light (table) wines, and although the lagares are generally meant for port, it is not unknown for the wine maker, David Baverstock, to allow a lagar to ferment to dryness in order to produce his acclaimed Douro red wine. David is an Australian who has worked in Portugal for a number of years and has made ports for the Symingtons and light wines both in the Douro and in the south of the country. He brings Australian expertise and technical skills to the myriad grape varieties that grow in Portugal. Another famous name in the port trade, Christiano van Zeller, the former head of Quinta do Noval, joined Jorge Roquette as a wine and marketing consultant in 1994.

Quinta do Crasto appears only as a vintage or LBV; lesser wines are sold to shipping firms. Of a total of about 35,100 gallons produced, only between 4,000 and 6,000 cases are sold as Quinta do Crasto. There are examples of older vintages in the private cellar, but the commercial vintages are a recent innovation that began with the 1978s.

The vintage wines are very full, while the LBVs are of the traditional style needing decanting even at a fairly early stage in their lives. These wines do not have the consistent taste of a mass-market blend, and generally reflect the vagaries of the vintage.

Tasting Notes

1990 LATE BOTTLED VINTAGE Opaque black core with a narrow rim, looks very young. Intense and very open damson plum nose; a little jammy. Sweet and very concentrated palate, with firm tannins and a great length. This needs another two or three years before it reaches its peak.

1991 LATE BOTTLED VINTAGE Compared to the 1990, this is equally deep in color, and with a similar damson plum nose, but without the slightly cooked character. Sweet and full-bodied with very firm tannins and a very long, elegant finish. Again, this needs a few years of bottle age before it is fully mature.

1994 VINTAGE This is quite a blockbuster. Very dark core with a purple rim, though not as deep as one or two of the others in the tasting. Full fruit and pepper nose, with slight hints of the green pepper smell you sometimes get with cabernet sauvignon; minty hints as well. Full-flavored with firm but not too aggressive tannins; a long finish.

Quinta do Infantado – Vinhos do Produtor, Lda.

Rua Paulo da Gama, 550–8 E,
4150 Porto, Portugal

Quinta do Infantado, literally the "Quinta of the Prince," was established in 1816. It has a fitting name since in its early days the quinta was owned by Prince Dom Pedro IV, son of King João VI of Portugal, emperor of Brazil. At the end of the eighteenth century, the quinta was sold to João Lopes Roseira. Unfortunately he died soon afterward, leaving his wife, Dona Margarida and three sons. Dona Margarida died in 1984 and her grandson João is now in charge.

> **INFORMATION**
>
> **VISITING** *Yes. Tel. (351-2) 6100865.*
>
> **RECOMMENDED WINES** *Vintage 1985.*
>
> **OVERALL RATING** ★

The grapes from the quinta have been, and occasionally still are, sold to Taylor's and Sandeman, but since the late 1970s, before it was normal practice, Infantado had been aiming to supply an estate bottled wine. Initially the wines were available only on the domestic market, which was legal, as the restriction forbade only export sales. Before long the movement had grown and Infantado became one of the first members of AVEPOD, the "Association of Wines from Single Quintas." AVEPOD is now a major promotional body within the industry.

About half the total vineyard comprises old, walled terraces, and the rest is modern patamares. Unlike many other quintas, Infantado uses very little herbicide. One of the problems with patamar terraces is keeping the weeds off the supporting earth bank. Although not yet totally organic, Quinta do Infantado does make particular efforts to protect the environment.

The vineyard is split into two sections: Barreiro, which is fully organic and is used to make a vintage character wine, and Serra, which is entirely planted with Touriga Nacional grapes, used for vintage ports. All Infantado wines, from the basic rubies through to the vintages and colheitas, are bottled on the estate, making possible that all-important "estate bottled" claim on the label.

Tasting Notes

LBV 1991 A traditional LBV, bottled after four years in cask. Deep, vibrant ruby color with just a hint of maturity on the rim. Light and delicate nose, a little leafy but reminiscent of red fruits, without excessive spirit. Very sweet and a touch cooked on the palate, but with balanced acids and firm structure.

VINTAGE 1985 Medium to deep color with a broad ruby, garnet rim. Overtly spirity on the nose, unusual for this vintage, with a hint of cloves along with ripe damson fruit. Rich full palate with firm tannins but developed fruit which makes this ideal for current drinking.

TOURIGA NACIONAL VINTAGE 1991 The nose has green capsicum and black fruit flavors, currently fairly subdued. Black currant and dark cherry-like on the palate, with balanced sweetness and acidity, and with firm but ripe tannins. A good wine for the medium term, but currently rather one dimensional.

Quinta do Noval – Vinhos, S.A.

Avenida Diogo Leite, 256, Apartado 57
4401 Vila Nova de Gaia Codex, Portugal

If any producer has put the word "quinta" into the English language, it is Noval. Certainly the most famous quinta in the port industry, Quinta do Noval has been both a quinta and a shipper since the wines came to prominence with its legendary 1931 vintage.

The quinta, with its whitewashed walls and immaculate terraces, occupies a commanding position above the Pinhão valley. Looking out from the Sabrosa to Pinhão road, one gazes over the flat-topped hill of Taylor's Terra Feita and the eyes are drawn to Noval, not by the grandeur of the house but by the sections of white wall in the vineyard. The walled terraces are unusually prominent in this vineyard, as the areas on either side of the stone staircases leading from one terrace to another have been whitewashed in the traditional way to improve visibility. So visible is the quinta that it becomes a navigational tool for visitors, even if they are going to other houses. Directions are often given with reference to the house.

Information

Visiting *Noval maintains a small tasting room and shop at Vila Nova de Gaia. Tel. (351–2) 302020. The quinta is not open to visitors.*

Recommended Wines *LB, 20 Year Old Tawny, 1963 Vintage Nacional, 1994 Vintage Nacional.*

Overall Rating ★★★

The earliest recorded history of the quinta dates back to 1715, but it came to be recognized for the quality of its wines when they were sold through the shipper Rebello Valente, who eventually bought the vineyard. After spending vast sums of money replanting, phylloxera hit, and the family had to sell the quinta. It was bought by António José da Silva, who was responsible for replanting onto grafted vines, and who first built the precise and geometric stone walls that are so famous today.

António's daughter married Luis de Vasconcellos Porto, who was brought into the firm. It was he who invented the broad terraces that can still be seen both at Noval and throughout the Douro, in an effort not only to reduce costs but also to aid ripening. He had noticed that on the traditional flat-topped terrace only the front row was exposed to the sun, so angled the terrace top better to expose the other vines.

Vasconcellos Porto was responsible for promoting the quinta on the export markets, a task continued by his descendants, the van Zellers. Christiano van Zeller sold the quinta to the wine investment arm of a French insurance group, AXA Millésimes in 1993, since which time an Englishman, Christian Seely, became managing director.

A distinction should be drawn between wines labeled "Noval" and those called "Quinta do Noval." While it may or may not always have been true, in recent years only those wines from the vineyard itself have carried the quinta designation. About one-third of the company's production is sourced here; the rest is bought in as grapes and made into wine on the premises. About half is trodden by foot and, for the last two vintages, Noval has been experimenting with a robot in the lagar. This stainless steel mechanized treader punches down the grape skins with hydraulic rams up to 24 hours a day, never once asking for another cigarette or glass of brandy.

In another innovative move, Noval has closed their Gaia lodge, preferring to mature all the wines in a largely air-conditioned lodge at the quinta. Not only is this cheaper to run, with lower accommodation costs, but additionally, with traffic a constant nightmare for exporters trying to maneuver trucks around the narrow streets of Gaia, it is easier to export from here. Roads to the valley are improving all the time.

As a moderate-sized shipper, selling more than one million bottles per year, Noval produces a full range of wines. It is their vintages and colheitas for which they are particularly famed, especially Nacional, a rare vintage wine made from ungrafted vines from the oldest part of the vineyard, which has never been attacked by phylloxera. The name comes from the vines being planted on their own roots, "into the nation" as it were and not, as has been suggested, from the grape variety. Indeed, Nacional, far from being pure Touriga Nacional, is made from an unusually high percentage of Sousão. Under the old regime, Nacional was never officially sold, but small allocations were given to wine merchants if they ordered enough Noval vintage wines. It soon became widely traded on the auction market, with no benefit to the producer. Under the new management, future vintages will be available in very small quantities to the trade.

Most of the following wines were tasted at Noval in October 1996, courtesy of Christian Seely and Dirk Niepoort.

Quinta do Noval, high above the Rio Pinhão.

TASTING NOTES

NOVAL LB A very high-quality ruby, deep ruby in color, with a powerful, fruity nose of dark fruits with damson plums. Medium-sweet with refreshing acidity and quite full tannins. Full-bodied and fresh in a way few Portuguese house or Douro-aged rubies are. An excellent and inexpensive wine.

20 YEAR OLD TAWNY Fully brown now, with a very full, marzipan-almond nuttiness. Medium weight but great power and spirity grip in the mouth; a long finish.

1994 VINTAGE NACIONAL Appearance and texture very similar to the Noval vintage, but with an added layer of sweet spiciness.

TASTING NOTES

RUBY

NOVAL LB (see page 204)

OLD CORONATION RUBY For a basic ruby, this wine has remarkable depth and structure. Deep in color; very young, fruity nose. Medium body and quite good concentration.

AGED TAWNY

10 YEAR OLD TAWNY Medium-depth tawny brown, a light nose of flowers and fruit, only the vaguest hint of nuttiness. Medium-sweet, medium to full flavor with that freshness coming through again. A very good example of the genre.

20 YEAR OLD TAWNY
(see page 204)

OVER 40 YEARS OLD TAWNY
Fully brown; no hint of red left now. Mature "rancio" nose, like a very old cognac. Wild mushroom hints, with spicy dried fruit. Medium-sweet and medium-bodied with good grip, but a slightly short finish.

COLHEITA

COLHEITA 1984 Similar in appearance to the 10 year old, with which it is inevitably compared, but lighter and more delicate. Firm, nutty character with full flavor and a very good length.

COLHEITA 1982 Fuller and richer than the 1984; very powerful fruit and nut character, with strength and concentration. At a tasting, opinion was split on the relative merits of the '82 and '84 wines. The 1982 was held to be more powerful, (but Noval preferred the finesse and delicacy of the 1984.)

COLHEITA 1976 Sharper and high-toned volatile nose (perhaps some acetone?). Still quite fruity, albeit dried, fruit palate. Dried figs, dates, and raisins with massive concentration and a huge length. A slightly off-putting nose, but excellent palate.

COLHEITA 1971 Earthy and rustic nose with an aggressive palate that is still sweet, with some tannic-like grip and noticeable spirit. Good concentration, but maturity dominates in a way it does not in the 1974.

COLHEITA 1937 Neither the 1968 nor the 1964 is impressive, but the 1937 is still very good. Deep mahogany brown; obviously fully mature, with a fine, dry, oloroso sherry-like dried fruit richness and concentration. Roasted almonds, toffee, and fruit characters, with a silky palate and long length.

LBV

LBV 1990 Like so many, Noval claims to be the originator of LBV, but there is no doubt that for a long time they dropped out of the race. Recently, with LBVs becoming so popular, they have returned with their own version. Light to medium depth, not as deep as many, but with a full palate, powerful fruit, and firm tannins. This wine varies from year to year, depending on the weather conditions, whereas the LB is more consistent. There have been years when the LB has been preferable to the LBV; for the 1990, it is the other way around.

VINTAGE

1994 VINTAGE Black core with a narrow rim, closed but concentrated damson plum fruit flavors; full, rich, and tannic. Will last a long time.

1994 VINTAGE NACIONAL
(see page 204)

1991 VINTAGE One of the deepest of the 1991s; very closed nose, hardly giving anything away, yet not spirity. Massive and almost aggressive palate, very intense, sweet concentrated flavors of prunes, figs, and chocolate. A very big wine, and one of the highlights of the vintage.

1970 VINTAGE NACIONAL
Medium depth only, rich and now mature, but with firm tannins as well as good acidity, which will maintain the wine for many years.

1963 VINTAGE NACIONAL This is still very young. Just about ruby red with a massive fig nose, huge tannins, and great power. Not even approaching its peak yet. (Apparently the Quinta do Noval of the same vintage is already totally mature, and will not develop further.)

Quinta de la Rosa – Vinhos Porto, Lda.

Quinta de la Rosa
5085 Pinhão, Portugal

No one traveling from Régua to Pinhão, whether by road, rail, or river, could possibly miss Quinta de la Rosa. The huge collection of quinta buildings, with the name emblazoned in elegant script on the winery wall, is one of the most visible of all port wine quintas.

It became Quinta de la Rosa at the beginning of this century when it was bought for Claire Feuerheerd, of the port company Feuerheerd, now part of Barros, Almeida & Ca. It is now owned by Sophia and Tim Bergqvist, descendants of the Feuerheerds who held on to the property when they sold the brand to the Barros, Almeida group during the Depression of the 1930s.

Since then the wine has been sold to Croft and Delaforce and, most recently, to Sandeman. Sandeman also used the winery to produce about 600 pipes of wine from other vineyards. The change in the law allowing single estates to sell their wine coincided with a change in attitude at Sandeman when they reduced their production and no longer needed the additional facilities. At that point the Bergqvists decided to get back into the port shipping market and sell a single quinta wine.

There has been a considerable amount of investment recently, especially in replanting the old, walled terraces with patamares. Important research has involved mechanizing the old terraces to reduce the cost of cultivating old vines, which tend to produce the best wine. The Bergqvists also believe that the traditional haphazard planting, where vines are mixed in the vineyards, adds complexity to the port wine.

From just under 200,000 vines, about 200 pipes of port are produced each year, along with light wine and a single estate olive oil. The wine is matured at the quinta, which explains the vast size of the quinta buildings. At this time the range is all red, with vintage and LBV being the most interesting.

INFORMATION

VISITING *The Bergqvists have wholeheartedly welcomed the increase in tourism in the Douro and Quinta de la Rosa is very much open to visitors. Not only are the usual tours available, but bed and breakfast or self-catering accommodation is also on offer. Tel. (351–54) 72254.*

RECOMMENDED WINES *LBV 1991, vintages.*

OVERALL RATING ★★

Tasting Notes

FINEST RESERVE Whilst this wine is not unpleasant, this is a less than impressive wine. Medium ruby in color with a rather hot, jammy nose; medium-sweet and medium-bodied but with a slightly cloying, finish. The dated wines are much better.

LATE BOTTLED VINTAGE 1991 Currently very deep garnet red, just beginning to show a little maturity on the rim. Full ripe nose, with plums and prunes as well as a floral hint coming through. Very full and concentrated mouthful, full-bodied with quite firm tannins. Drinking very well now, but will not suffer from a few years of bottle age.

VINTAGE 1994 Black at the core with only the narrowest of purple ruby rims; closed yet concentrated nose of very ripe, dark fruit and plain chocolate. Full-bodied with massive fruit; very firm, almost aggressive tannins that are now overpowering, but will soften with age to give an outstanding rich port.

Quinta do Sagrado Comércio de Vinhos, Lda.

Rua da Reboleira, 7–1°
4000 Porto, Portugal

Quinta do Sagrado adjoins Quinta da Foz, the flagship vineyard of the A. A. Cálem & Filho port house. Owned by the same company, it is usually considered as part of Quinta da Foz, but recently the company has released a limited range of wines under the Quinta do Sagrado brand.

Right in the heart of the Cima Corgo, Quinta do Sagrado occupies a hilltop position overlooking the Douro just west of Pinhão, down the river from Quinta da Foz. This is a small quinta, only some 30 acres, of which only three-quarters are planted in blocks of only the recommended grapes. Unlike its larger neighbor, all of the vines here are planted on modern patamar terraces. In contrast, Foz still has a large area of old vineyard supported by walls, which Cálem would like to convert in the long term.

Quinta do Sagrado wines are generally of sound rather than exciting quality, as befits a second label.

INFORMATION

VISITING *No, but see* *entry for A.A. Cálem & Filho, Lda. on page 79.*

RECOMMENDED WINES *Vintage Character.*

OVERALL RATING ★

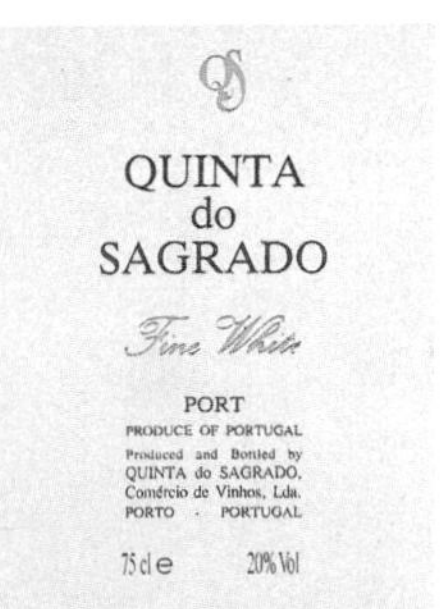

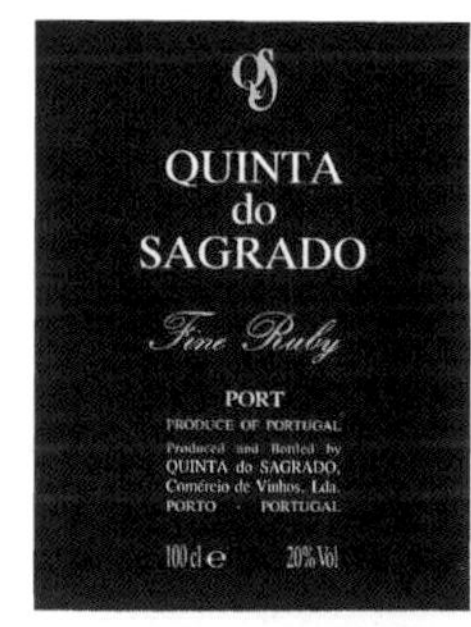

TASTING NOTES

VINTAGE CHARACTER Deep ruby red with just a hint of maturity on the rim. Full, rich nose of spiced fruits, and preserves. Medium-sweet palate with a little grip. Quite full-bodied with a good length for its type. A good example of a vintage character wine.

10 YEARS OLD Hazelnut brown in color; reasonable depth. Moderately spirity nose with a hint of pickled walnuts. Medium-sweet and very clean palate that lacks the power of some, yet does not have the elegance of others. Somewhat short finish. Pleasant to drink, but lacks interest.

1990 VINTAGE Medium depth; ruby rather than purple. Full and very open nose, fruity and beginning to show a little development. Medium weight on the palate with soft but noticeable tannins. This is already drinking fairly well, but it does not have long-term staying power. This is one to drink in the next five to ten years.

Sociedade Vitivinicola da Quinta de Santa Eufêmia, Lda.

5100 Parada do Bispo, Portugal

Close to the town of Régua, on the south bank of the Douro is Quinta de Santa Eufêmia. This quinta is one of the newest players in the port trade, having only started bottling and exporting their wines in 1994. The quinta, though, has a history dating back 100 years before this.

Established by Bernardo Rodrigues de Carvalho in 1894, the quinta spent its first century supplying wines to the shippers at Vila Nova de Gaia. Over the years the purchase of neighboring plots has expanded the vineyard, but it still occupies only 86 acres, 100 times the size of an average vineyard in the Douro. Nevertheless, it is small compared to many single quinta producers. From this about 28,600 U.S. gallons are produced, of which a little over one-quarter is white wine. At this size it is worth installing vinification equipment other than just lagares, so the wine maker makes 40 percent of the production in autovinificators, and the balance by foot.

The family has always maintained a small stock of wine for their own and quinta consumption, and this has formed the base of the commercial wines. Consequently they have been able to release some quite mature wines, including a remarkable white port that has been aged in barrel for 25 years.

The range is small but increasing. The wines currently available, the 10- and 20-year-old tawnies, as well as the basic tawny and reserve (vintage character) are to be joined by ruby, dry white, and colheita, all planned for imminent release. This will further help the company's export drive, the success of which has been remarkable. Over half the production is now exported; about one-fifth to the United States, the rest to the Benelux countries and northern Europe.

Information

Visiting *As part of the* Rota do Vinho do Porto, *Eufêmia is open to visitors for tours and tastings, and has accommodation and refreshment facilities. Tel. (351–54) 331752/ (351–2) 9426306.*

Recommended Wines *Very Old Reserve White.*

Overall Rating ★

TASTING NOTES

VERY OLD RESERVE WHITE This is a remarkable wine. Few white ports have an interesting character; this one does. Deep golden hue with a light, slightly spirity and definitely aged nose of candied peel and lemon marmalade. Sweet and full-bodied for a white, but with wonderfully refreshing citric-like acidity that leaves the palate clean.

20 YEARS OF AGE TAWNY Very pale amber in color with a delicate, if alcoholic, nose of dried fruit and caramel. Sweet with medium body; palate rather dominated by the spirit. A light style of tawny that is refreshing if well chilled, but lacks the concentration of a number of other brands.

GIGOS AWAITING THE HARVEST.

Quinta de Val da Figueira

**Rua do Ribeirinho, 472, Foz do Douro,
4150 Porto, Portugal**

Just west of Pinhão, beyond Ferreira's Quinta do Porto, is Quinta de Val da Figueira. This vineyard's recorded history goes back to the middle of the eighteenth century. Although it was not mentioned when the Douro region was first demarcated, it was certainly producing port soon after this time.

Perhaps the quinta's greatest claim to fame took place in 1878, when the then owner, Dr. Joaquim Pinheiro de Azevedo Leite Pereira, planted the first vines grafted onto American rootstocks, thus making them resistant to phylloxera. A plaque commemorating this event is displayed in the *casa das lagares* (treading house).

Being a fairly small producer, vinifying grapes only from the quinta, all the wine is trodden by foot. There is little financial advantage in buying equipment when the volume is so small, and most producers still believe that the foot is the best means of extracting the grape juice.

The quinta is owned by Alfredo Cálem Holzer, related by marriage to the A.A. Cálem family. Understandably, the wine has historically been sold to Cálem, but since the 1986 change to the rules on single quintas selling their own port, the wine has been offered as a single quinta wine.

Val da Figueira is a small quinta, with only 47 acres under vine; production has been raised to about 100 pipes per year, through replanting and careful husbandry. Having been on the market under its own name for only a little over a decade, the company currently offers just two wines: a 10-year-old tawny and a vintage port. Quinta de Val da Figueira declared 1987, 1989, 1991, and 1994 vintages, all of which are available at remarkable prices. The 10 Years Old tawny and the 1991 Vintage are the only wines that have been tasted for this book.

INFORMATION

VISITING *By appointment only. Tel (351-54) 72159.*

RECOMMENDED WINES *10 Years Old.*

OVERALL RATING ★

Tasting Notes

10 YEARS OLD Pale orange-red in color; very bright. Light and very mature nose, spirity but not at all baked. Floral and mineral, slight petroleum hints, with vanilla spiciness. Medium-sweet with balanced acidity and low tannin. Perhaps a little light on the palate, but complex and balanced with a long finish.

1991 VINTAGE Medium deep ruby color; not as dark or purple as some. Full and open fruitcake and plum nose, youthful and fresh. Medium-sweet with only moderate tannin. Medium weight with noticeable alcohol. Given time this wine will develop, but it is one to drink in the medium term rather than one to keep for decades.

QUINTA
de
VAL DA FIGUEIRA
PORT
10 YEARS
OLD
AGED IN OAK CASKS
BOTTLED AT THE PROPERTY
ALFREDO E. CÁLEM HOLZER
5085 PINHÃO
PRODUCE OF PORTUGAL
75cl e
20% vol.

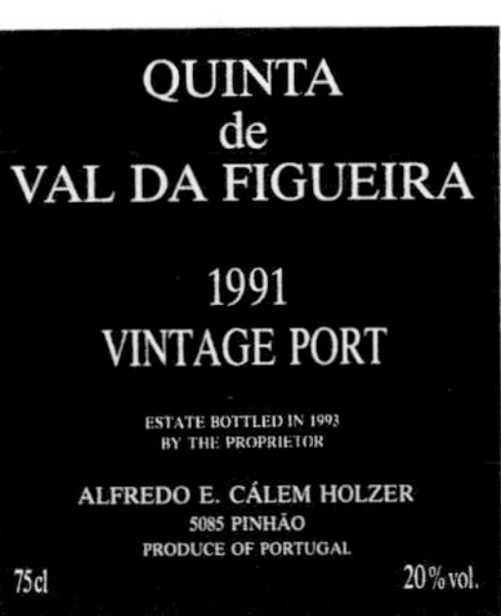

Quinta de Ventozello – Sociedade Agricola E Comercial, S.A.

Praceta Engº. António de Almeida, 70-9º
Sala 419, 4100 Porto, Portugal

Quinta de Ventozello sits on the south bank of the Douro River, upstream from Pinhão and just opposite Croft's Quinta da Roêda, right in the heart of the Cima Corgo. Spanning 1,729 acres, it is an ample site with an astonishingly long history. References to the quinta have been found in medieval manuscripts dating back to 1288.

Its present borders were established in 1826, at which time it was owned by the royal monastery of S. Pedro das Aguias. Since 1958 it has belonged to a company called Edmundo Alves Ferreira, which now trades using the quinta name.

A few old stone walled terraces still exist, but large areas of the quinta have been replanted with patamares and vinha ao alto, simplifying the maintenance of the half a million or so vines that are planted here. The quinta house itself stands some way back from the river, separated from it by an olive grove. The stone-walled terraces surround the building complex while the view upriver shows the newer patamares like a scar across the lower half of the hills. Above the line of the vineyard the scrub has been left untouched.

Although growing methods are not totally organic, Ventozello avoids chemical fertilizers, preferring natural techniques. All the wine is made in lagares; there are no mechanical methods here. As a single quinta selling only its own wine, the lodge is at the quinta, so the wines have the distinct Douro bake. This particular character of Douro-aged ports is not unpleasant, but it does make the wines very different from their Vila Nova de Gaia counterparts.

The quinta encourages tourist visits, offering a range of facilities: tours, and guest house accommodation, even providing tennis courts and a swimming pool, unusual in this part of the world.

Information

Visiting *Yes. Tel. (351–2) 6093691.*

Recommended Wines *10 Years Old.*

Overall Rating ★★

TASTING NOTES

10 YEARS OLD Pale yet very vivid orange amber with an intensely smoky and very spirity nose; distinct burnt caramel touches. Sweet with an intense wood smoke palate, some dried fig notes as well. Slightly spirity but with good concentration and flavor.

20 YEARS OLD Very pale tawny amber, only a little more brown than the 10 year old, with a perfumed and nutty aroma. Again very spirity. Medium-sweet and medium-bodied with that burnt caramel flavor and a long, but alcoholic, finish.

Sociedade Agricola da Quinta do Vesuvio

Trav. Barão de Forrester, Apartado 26
4401 Vila Nova de Gaia Codex, Portugal

Information

Visiting *Only through introduction by a wine merchant.*

Recommended Wines *1990, 1991, 1994 Vintage.*

Overall Rating ★★★

On the south side of the Douro, farther upriver from Canais and Vargellas and well within the Douro Superior, lies one of the world's great vineyards, Quinta do Vesuvio, stretching across 988 acres of prime, class A vineyard land. Vesuvio is said to comprise seven hills and 30 valleys, which may be an exaggeration but does give some impression of its size.

Originally a corn farm, Vesuvio had its first commercial vines planted by the Ferreiras, who took the quinta over in 1823. Dona Antónia Ferreira's hospitality at the quinta was legendary, and it was after a lunch here that Baron Forrester was to have his fatal accident (see Forrester & Ca., S.A., page 111). During Dona Ferreira's reign the vineyards were well tended and subjected to experimental work, but phylloxera would have a devastating effect, reducing the yield to almost nothing. At this point, probably out of desperation, the Ferreiras attempted to cultivate silkworms.

Because of the Portuguese inheritance rules, by 1989 Vesuvio was owned by 18 members of the Ferreira family. They decided to sell it to the Symington group, who has since been able to make the investments necessary to bring the vineyard back to its former glory.

Taking advantage of the new rules passed in 1986 (see page 186), the Symingtons decided to introduce a new concept into the port industry: a single quinta that produces only vintage port. Thus Quinta do Vesuvio is released only as a vintage; if the wine is not good enough for that, it is sold to other companies.

The property produces the equivalent of about 23,000 cases of wine, all in lagares, but lagares with a difference. They are fitted with removable cooling or heating pipes, which gives the wine maker the best of both worlds, allowing good extraction from the human foot as well as temperature control to vary the rate of fermentation as required.

TASTING NOTES

1994 VINTAGE Only medium depth of color with a broad ruby rim, but with a very closed nose. Still very young, almost yeasty character from fermentation, with dark chocolate and fruitcake hints. Medium-sweet and medium weight with firm tannins and acids. Suitable for medium- to long-term drinking.

1989 VINTAGE Although still youthful and very immature, this is already an attractive wine. The tannins are soft and the wine is medium- to full-bodied, very fruity. It is drinkable now, but needs time to show its best.

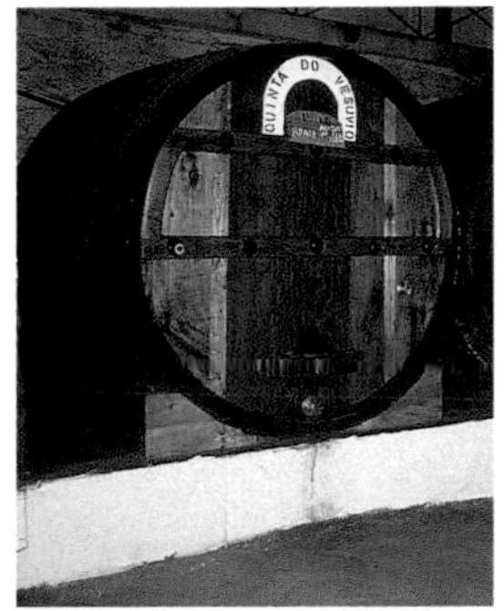

TONELS IN THE VESUVIO LODGE.

Tasting Notes

SINGLE QUINTA VINTAGE

1994 VINTAGE (see page 217)

1992 VINTAGE A rather spirity nose, more so than some of the others, with a youthful red fruit character. Not as intense or complex as some of the other 1992s or other vintages from this quinta. Fresh, if rather delicate, fruit on the palate, with firm tannins and a medium to full body, showing more than the nose suggested. Not a great Vesuvio, but one to drink while you are waiting for your stocks of 1991 to come around.

1991 VINTAGE One of the blackest and deepest of all the 1991s. A closed nose eventually reveals a character of plums and coffee. A medium to sweet palate, which is still partially obscured by a wall of ripe tannin that will help preserve this wine for a very long time. Quinta do Vesuvio 1991 is one of the best wines of a good vintage. It will not be ready to drink until well into the first decade of the twenty-first century.

1990 VINTAGE This has always been a massive wine. Opaque when released, it has hardly changed and is still closed – it is almost as inaccessible as the quinta itself. Hot dark fruit, some vanilla spice with even a little cinnamon on the nose. Sweet, full, but fresh palate with massive, and preserving, tannic structure; very full-bodied. Some of the other wines from the 1990 vintage have a cooked character that this, fortunately, has missed, making it a splendid wine for the long term.

1989 VINTAGE (see page 217)

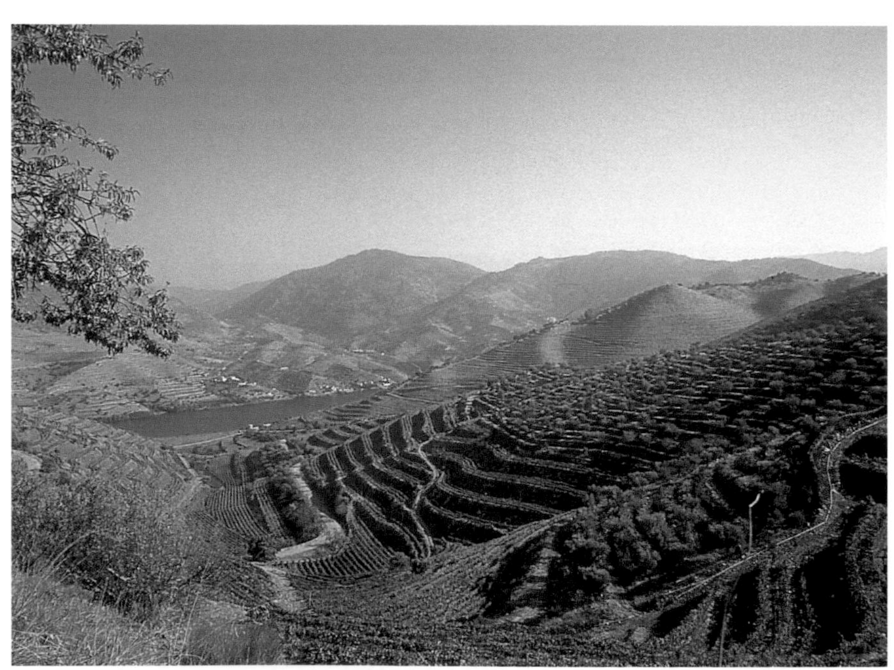

Old and new terraces at Quinta do Vesuvio.

Glossary

Adega A winery where the grapes are processed and made into wine. Particularly relevant with regard to the cooperatives, Adegas Cooperativas.

Autovinifier A self-circulating vat that uses the carbon dioxide pressure produced by fermentation to circulate the must, thereby extracting color and tannin

Bagaçeira Raw spirit distilled from grape skins and stalks, traditionally consumed by the treaders late into the night.

Block Planting Cultivating only one grape variety in a particular area of the vineyard, in contrast to the historical method of mixed planting, in which the vines on a row are of different varieties.

Cadastro System A method of rating vineyards. Each vineyard in the Douro region is rated on a scale from A to F. The rating, or Cadastro grading, takes into account a number of factors both natural (altitude, soil composition, and so on) and manmade (the age of the vines). The best wines come from grades A and B, so these deliver a higher price to the grower. More important, the higher the grade, the greater the proportion of grapes that can be made into port.

Casa do Douro With the IVP, this has long been one of the controlling bodies in the industry, representing the interests of the growers. At the time of this writing, its future is in doubt due to financial problems.

Casco Portuguese for "cask." Used on labels for the Portuguese market; specifies tawnies and colheitas that have been matured in wood.

Colheita Literally, the Portuguese word for "harvest," and therefore, vintage. However, in the case of port, colheita denotes a tawny port with a date of harvest, not to be confused with vintage port.

Douro Bake A term sometimes applied to wines matured in the heat of the Douro valley, rather than at Vila Nova de Gaia. Such wines can develop a "cooked" character, resulting in a caramel taste in the wine.

Fortification The act of adding a high-strength spirit to the fermentation must in order to kill the active yeasts, both to improve the alcohol content and to retain a considerable amount of residual sugar.

Garrafeira A Portuguese term used for wines, indicating long aging before release. The process is more important for unfortified wines, but one or two producers still make garrafeira ports.

Gigo The traditional basket used by grape pickers. Weighing between 100 and 150 pounds when full, it is carried shoulder-high from the vineyard to the quinta or to a waiting truck.

IVP Instituto do Vinho do Porto (Port Wine Institute), one of the controlling bodies of the port industry. It is responsible for public relations, testing and tasting wines, and issuing the control seal, the Selo Garantia, attached to every bottle.

LBV Late Bottled Vintage. Technically it is deep red port, matured in cask for between four and six years.

Lagar A granite or, sometimes, concrete, treading tank, where all the best ports are trodden by foot.

Lodge Maturation warehouse used for port wines. Most firms store their wine at Vila

Nova de Gaia, on the south bank of the Douro opposite Oporto. However, one or two have moved the maturation upriver into the vineyard region, and single quinta wines are mostly matured at the quinta.

Must Fermenting grape juice destined to become wine.

Patamar A modern type of vineyard terrace cut by bulldozer, incorporating tracks that can be used by tractors and other equipment to permit a limited amount of mechanization when harvesting.

Pipe The traditional maturation cask for port; also a measure of bulk port. Although the actual size of a maturation pipe varies from 145 to about 172 gallons, officially the size is 145 gallons for a production pipe, and 141 gallons (or 712 bottles) for a pipe that is to be sold. Growers typically talk in terms of the number of pipes of wine they get from the vineyard, rather than hectoliters, as in most parts of Europe.

Quinta Wine farm or estate. It may or may not have a house, which may or may not be grand. There is no clear distinction between a quinta and a vineyard, except that in the Douro the larger vineyards are called quintas. In wine terms, the word is roughly equivalent to the French "château."

Remontagem A "pumping over" process in red wine making, in which the fermenting grape juice must is taken from the bottom of the vat and sprayed over the cap of skins that naturally floats to the top, in order to extract color and tannin.

Ruby Young red port, matured for about three years before release.

Schist Hard but crumbly, slate-like rock that overlays the granite bedrock in the Douro region.

Seco "Dry." In the case of dry white port, however, the term usually means off-dry which is somewhere in between dry and medium dry.

Single Quinta Port Port made from grapes grown at the quinta that is named on the label. Single quinta vintage ports have been available for some time, but now the market is expanding to include rubies and tawnies.

Tartrates Harmless crystals that can form in wine as it matures. Since they cause unnecessary concern to consumers they are usually removed from wines meant for early consumption, by chilling and filtering the wine before it is bottled. Vintage and traditional LBV ports are not stabilized in this way since sediment is expected.

Tawny A wood-aged port that has lost its initial red color to become brown or tawny. Range from basic wines, to fine aged tawnies.

Terrace The terrain in the Douro region is one of steep hillsides, which in the past have required terraces for the vineyards: reworking the land so that vines are planted on step-like areas of flat or gently sloped land, which are supported by walls or earth banks. The original terraces are called *socalcos*, and newer ones are called patamares.

Varietal Port A wine made from only one grape variety, usually used as part of a blend but sometimes sold as a wine in its own right.

Vila Nova de Gaia The transpontine suburb of the city of Oporto, Portugal's second biggest city. Here most of the Port shippers' lodges can be found, in an area as demarcated as the vineyard region itself.

Vinha ao alto Vineyard plantings without terraces, the rows of vines being perpendicular up and down the hillside. Not feasible for very steep slopes but where used, they enable a degree of mechanization.

Addresses

ORGANIZATIONS

Gabinete da Rota do Vinho do Porto
Rua dos Camilos, 90-5050 Peso da Regua
PORTUGAL
TEL: 00351 54 320145
FAX: 00351 54 320149

Instituto do Vinho do Porto
Rua Ferreira Borges, 4050 Porto
PORTUGAL
TEL: 00351 2 2071600
FAX: 00351 2 2080465

Região Turismo Douro Sul
Rua dos Bancos, 5100 Lamego
PORTUGAL
TEL: 00351 54 65770
FAX: 00351 54 64014

Port Wine Institute
Unit 3, Imperial Studios, Imperial Road
London SW6 3AG, ENGLAND
TEL: 020 7751 9170

Wine and Spirit Education Trust
Five Kings House, 1 Queen Street Place
London EC4R 1QS, ENGLAND
TEL: 020 7236 3551
FAX: 020 7329 8712
WEBSITE: www.wset.co.uk

Wine Appreciation Guild
155 Connecticut Street
San Francisco, CA 94107, U.S.A.
TEL: 00351 54 320145
WEBSITE: www.wineappreciation.com

MAGAZINES

Decanter
1st Floor, Broadway House
2-6 Fulham Broadway
London SW6 1AA, ENGLAND
TEL: 020 7610 3929
FAX: 020 7381 5282
WEBSITE: www.decanter.com

The Vine
76 Woodstock Road, London W4 1EQ
ENGLAND
TEL: 020 8995 8962
FAX: 020 8995 8943

Wine Magazine
Wilmington Publishers
6-14 Underwood Street, London N1 7JQ
ENGLAND
TEL: 020 7549 2548
FAX: 020 7549 2550

Wine & Spirits
Winestate Publications, Inc.
818 Brannan Street
San Francisco, CA 94103, U.S.A.
TEL: 001 415 255 7736
FAX: 001 415 255 9659

Wine Enthusiast
103 Fairview Park Drive, Elmford
NY 10523, U.S.A.
TEL: 001 415 345 8463
FAX: 001 914 592 0105
WEBSITE: www.winemag.com

Wine Spectator
M. Shanken Communications, Inc.
387 Park Avenue South, 8th Floor
New York, NY 10016, U.S.A.
TEL: 001 212 684 4224
FAX: 001 212 481 1540
WEBSITE: www.winespectator.com

Bibliography

Bradford, Sarah. *The Story of Port.* London: Christie's, 1983.

Caravalho, Manuel. *A Guide to the Douro and to Port Wine.* Porto: Edições Afrontamento, 1995.

Fonseca, A. Moreira et al. *Port Wine.* Porto: Instituto do Vinho do Porto, 1981.

Howkins, Ben. *Rich, Rare and Red.* London: Heinemann, 1982.

Hönsch, Helmut. *Caracterizaçao dos Factores Ecológicos e da Susceptibilidade de Erosao dos Novos Tipos de Implantaçao da Vinha na Regiao Demarcada do Douro.* Vila Real, undated.

Johnson, Hugh. *World Atlas of Wine.* London: Mitchell Beazley, 1985.

Liddell, Alex and Price, Janet. *Port Wine Quintas.* London: Sotheby's, 1992.

Mayson, Richard. *An Analysis of the Effects and Implications of Varying Types of Cultivation on Port Viti/Viniculture.* Sheffield, 1983.

Mayson, Richard. *Portugal's Wines & Winemakers.* London: Ebury Press, 1992.

Oliveira, Manuel. *Run-Off and Soil Erosion in Vineyard Soil of Douro Region (Cima Corgo) Portugal.* Vila Real, 1995.

Robertson, George. *Port.* London: Faber & Faber, 1978.

Robinson, Jancis. *The Oxford Companion to Wine.* Oxford: Oxford University Press, 1994.

Symington, Paul. *Port Wine.* (A Symington company publication used for publicity purposes.)

Vizetelly, Henry. *Facts about Port and Madeira.* London: Ward Lock, 1880.

Warner Allen, H. *The Wines of Portugal.* London: George Rainbird, 1963.

Index

Page numbers in *italics* refer to picture captions.

Author's Acknowledgments

Particular thanks are due to an enormous number of people who have helped with the research for this book. Many in the marketing and public relations departments will, unfortunately, have to remain anonymous. It would however, be wrong not to mention some people by name. The following have all helped with my general research into port, or specifically with the research for this book: Dr. Bianchi de Agiuar of the IVP, Carlos de Almeida and George Sandeman of Sandeman, Fernando Alves of ADVID, Adrian Bridge of Taylor, Fladgate and Yeatman, Jeremy Bull formerly of A. A. Cálem and Filho, Dr. John Burnett of Croft, Peter Cobb and Vasco Maghlães of Cockburn Smithes, Bruce Guimaraens of Fonseca Guimaraens Limited, Dirk Niepoort of Niepoort Ports, João Nicolau de Almeida and Jorge Rosas of Ramos Pinto, and Christian Seely of Quinta do Noval.

My thanks are also due to an understanding family, who had to put up with an invasion of bottles and a disturbed domestic routine; to Clare Hubbard, for all her efforts as an efficient go-between and whose chivvying kept the project moving; and to Gareth, John, and the others who selflessly helped with the tastings.

Thanks to Berry Bros. & Rudd of London for supplying the decanting funnel and port tongs.

Picture Credits

Forrester & Ca., S.A: pp2, 21(t), 30(b); Instituto do Vinho do Porto: pp18, 20(t), 22(t), 60; Manoel D. Poças Junior-vinhos S.A: p30(t); Adriano Ramos Pinto (Vinhos) S.A: p21(b); Sandeman & Ca., S.A: pp20(b), 24, 27; Sociedade Agricola da Quinta do Crasto: p29(b); Godfrey Spence: pp7, 10(t), 14(b), 15, 26, 29(t), 31(t), 34, 49; Symington Port Shippers: pp10(b), 16, 17, 48; Taylor, Fladgate & Yeatman-Vinhos S.A: pp11, 14(t), 31(b), 35, 42.